MW01257853

Fund your cause with
Direct Mail

Fund your cause with
Direct Mail
Secrets of Successful
Direct Mail Fundraising

Benjamin Hart

JAMESON BOOKS, INC.
OTTAWA, ILLINOIS

Titles from Jameson Books are available at special discounts for bulk purchases, for sales promotions, premiums, fund raising or educational use. Special condensed or excerpted paperback editions can also be created to customer specifications.

For information or other requests please write: Jameson Books, Inc., 722 Columbus Street, Ottawa, Illinois 61350

Mail Orders: 800-426-1357
Telephone: 815-434-7905
Facsimile: 815-434-7907

www.jamesonbooks.com

Printed in the United States of America

Jameson Books titles are distributed to the book trade by MidPoint Trade Books, 27 West 20th Street, Suite 1102, New York, NY 10011. Bookstores please call 212-727-0190 to place orders.

Bookstore returns should be addressed to MidPoint Trade Books, 1263 Southwest Boulevard, Kansas City, KS 66103

ISBN 0-915463-96-2

6 5 4 3 2 1 / 09 08 07 06 05

Table of Contents

CHAPTER 1

The Amazing Power of Mail

This book is for everyone who cares deeply about a cause. And this book is for anyone who must raise funds to advance their cause.

Many people want their lives to count for something. If you've picked up a copy of this book, it's probably because you want to make a difference. You want your life to be meaningful. You want to be part of a cause that's bigger than you are. You want to leave the world a better place than when you entered it.

This book is for anyone who wants to accomplish some good in the world.

Specifically, this book is about how to write and mail letters that will persuade people to join your cause and send back contributions so that you can achieve the things you want to achieve.

This book is for anyone trying to raise money for:
- ▶ a charity
- ▶ a school
- ▶ a college
- ▶ a church, synagogue, or other religious institution
- ▶ a hospital
- ▶ a research institute
- ▶ a library

- ▶ a museum
- ▶ a sports team
- ▶ a political campaign
- ▶ an issue-advocacy crusade
- ▶ emergency disaster relief
- ▶ a legal defense fund
- ▶ a family in need
- ▶ hungry children
- ▶ food and shelter for refugees
- ▶ religious missionaries
- ▶ or just about any cause, club, or special project where voluntary contributions are needed.

If you follow the principles outlined in this book, you will be able to use direct mail successfully to raise money for any cause or need that has stirred your heart and moved you to take action.

More importantly, direct mail allows you to reach out to other people—hundreds, thousands, perhaps even millions of people—and rally them to take unified, coordinated action with you.

I am a professional direct mail fundraiser. Direct mail fundraising allows me to do two things I love: writing and politics. I love the "war of ideas."

Direct mail allows me to reach people on issues of concern to me and that I hope will be of concern to others. My direct mail letters have made a significant difference in the political landscape over the years.

My letters reach tens of millions of people each year, mostly aimed at advancing conservative political causes. But the principles in this book will work just as well to raise money for liberal causes as well as nonpolitical charitable causes.

My letters have raised hundreds of millions of dollars for candidates and causes I care about. Many of my letters have a larger circulation than the *New York Times*.

Every morning I actually look forward to jumping out of bed at precisely 6:00 a.m. so I can get to my computer and write a direct mail letter on a political or public policy issue that I feel strongly about—a letter that will likely be mailed to a million or more people, a letter capable of mobilizing a vast army of voters and activists to take some unified, coordinated political action.

Usually this action involves passing or stopping legislation in Congress, or electing or defeating a candidate for public office. This is what gets me up and writing in the morning.

What makes my work in direct mail fundraising especially satisfying to me is the impact my letters have, not just in the political and public policy arena, but also in helping to address all kinds of serious problems and needs, such as helping disadvantaged children, repairing the Vietnam War Memorial, helping hospitalized veterans, or raising money to cure cancer, Alzheimer's disease or leukemia.

If you don't care who gets the credit, you can accomplish great things with direct mail. Almost all fundraising letters I write are signed by others. I have no desire to be famous. What I like to do is help others acquire contributions and supporters to fund and carry out their nonprofit mission—assuming I agree with the mission. I have found direct mail fundraising incredibly exciting and psychologically rewarding. I believe I'm doing a lot of good with direct mail.

With my letters, I am empowering individuals to make a difference in the world by giving people a way to band together for a shared goal.

My direct mail letters give realistic hope that the average person can make a difference. Organizations built with direct mail empower average people to actually help shape the course of events and to achieve great things.

Direct mail allows the average person to influence events by tapping into an organized effort involving the mobilization of thousands, hundreds of thousands, or even millions of like-minded individuals: average people who share a common goal.

Direct mail is about building communities and constituencies united by a shared mission.

The $15 contributor certainly understands that a $15 donation will not have much impact by itself. But thousands of $10, $15, $20, $30, and $50 contributions from people, all united behind some great cause, can achieve something worthwhile and can sometimes even shift the tide of history.

How Direct Mail Helped Organize the American Revolution

Alexis de Tocqueville, the great 19th century student of American democracy, observed that Americans are joiners.

Americans have always loved to join associations and band together to achieve a common cause. Tocqueville believed that this characteristic had the effect of greatly strengthening America's democratic system of government. Tocqueville saw this urge to join with others for a shared purpose as something of a distinctly American impulse.

It's interesting to note that the American Revolution was organized largely through the circulation of pamphlets, circulars, and fliers (an early form of direct mail) that catalogued the latest outrages by the British government. These pamphlets, circulars, and fliers were distributed in churches, in public meeting places, and door to door—many by Samuel Adams through his Sons of Liberty organization.

Samuel Adams and the Sons of Liberty formed local Committees of Correspondence in towns across the land to facilitate the widespread distribution of these pamphlets, circulars, and fliers. The Boston Tea Party was organized this way. An announcement circulated by Adams' Committees of Correspondence declared the time and location of the momentous event that triggered the start of the American Revolution.

America's founding fathers thought mail to be so important to the nation's strength and prosperity that the Continental

Congress created a postal service in 1775 and appointed Benjamin Franklin the first Postmaster General. Congress passed the first postal act in 1789. This ensured a national communications system and served to unify the country, thus strengthening the idea that America would truly become "one nation indivisible."

Benjamin Franklin may have been the first American to use direct mail as a marketing vehicle for his business. He published a book catalogue and mailed it to solicit orders. Franklin reassured his prospective buyers with a money-back guarantee, promising this: "Those persons who live remote, by sending their orders to said B. Franklin, may depend on the same justice as if present" (*Catalogue Success,* January 2001, p. 25).

Of course, modern advertisers know that the money-back guarantee is essential to any commercial direct mail product offer.

Though we did not have scientific polling at the time of the American Revolution, historians agree that most Americans did not, in fact, support a war with Britain. About a third were for it, about a third were against it, about a third were not sure or had no strong feelings either way—much like political debates on important matters today.

But Samuel Adams and the leaders of the American Revolution, along with their Committees of Correspondence, were very well organized. They were able to quickly mobilize their supporters to resist the British authorities by sending a letter through their Committees of Correspondence network. Paul Revere was a prominent member of this network, galloping his horse from town to town, distributing fliers and urging the colonists, especially members of the Sons of Liberty, to get their muskets and fire on approaching British soldiers.

Great events in America's history have always been organized this way. The abolitionist movement also used pamphlets, circulars, and fliers to great effect to argue the evil and injustice of slavery and to mobilize people to act in unified, coordinated fashion. The end result was the abolition of slavery.

So you can see that this method of educating and mobilizing the public for great causes and great actions goes back a very long way in America's history; is, in fact, part of the fabric of America's character and political system, as Tocqueville observed.

Modern cause-driven, direct mail fundraising follows this long tradition in America.

How Direct Mail Strengthens Democracy

It is my strong belief that cause-driven, direct mail fundraising continues to reinforce democracy in America.

Here's why.

You have often heard that in America "everyone has one vote, and just one vote," or "everyone's vote is equal."

But that's not really true.

Congress and elected officials will listen much more closely to you if you have a large mailing list and hundreds of thousands of like-minded followers.

If you are the head of a major cause-driven organization, and if your organization has 100,000 supporters who think like you do, your opinion actually represents 100,000 votes. The head of the NRA, Wayne LaPierre, represents more than two million voters. In effect, this makes Wayne LaPierre "one man, two million votes."

When LaPierre walks into a congressional office, he is able to get the riveted attention of the elected official. It's not so much that the congressman is afraid of LaPierre the person, who is a very pleasant man. But the politician is very concerned about the NRA's mailing list, especially if the NRA is in any way unhappy with the politician's voting record in Congress.

The same can be said of the Sierra Club, Green Peace, the American Association of Retired Persons, Mothers Against Drunk Driving, or the American Cancer Society. The heads of these large organizations certainly have far more influence in Washington than just one voter.

But rank-and-file members of these organizations also magnify the power of their vote exponentially simply by choosing to become members—that is, by becoming part of a large organized constituency, united for a Common Cause (which, by the way, is the name of yet another very influential nonprofit organization in Washington, D.C.).

All these organizations have enormous multimillion dollar direct mail marketing operations. They are powerful, not just because of the huge amount of money they raise through the mail, but even more so because of the large constituencies they have gathered and organized with direct mail programs.

These organizations are often derided as special interest groups and even as harmful to America's political system. I argue the opposite.

Though I certainly do not personally agree with what some of these organizations are promoting, I believe that the existence of all of these organizations together serves to strengthen democracy by allowing average people to become more deeply and intensely involved in issues and causes they care passionately about.

Isn't that what we want in a democracy: people actively involved and engaged in the issues of the day, momentous issues that could decide the future of the nation and even the world?

One person, standing alone, really cannot have much say at all in the public debate. One person's lone voice is just not loud enough to be heard.

But one person's voice can be heard loudly and clearly in the public debate if joined with others, many others, who believe as she does, and who are organized.

We really would not have much of a democracy or public debate if people could not join together to form large organizations to make their voices heard on matters of importance to the nation. Without these organizations, the public debate would only take place between government officials and elites. The big billion-dollar media organizations would have a lot of say. So would large banks, financial institutions, and multinational conglomerates. But the average citizen would be left out of all important public policy discussions.

There would be no way for the average citizen to be heard, except perhaps every two years on Election Day. But there would be no other way for the average citizen's voice to be heard by politicians on a near daily basis concerning issues that are debated every day in the corridors of power. This would not be much of a democracy at all.

Voluntary associations are only found in democracies. And they are the first casualties of tyranny. When the communists took over Czechslovakia, for example, the first move they made against voluntary associations was to abolish the Boy Scouts. Independent churches and religious institutions were also crushed, as were all other voluntary associations. The proliferation of voluntary associations is indeed the surest barometer in a society of the health of democracy and freedom.

In America today there are more than 500,000 nonprofit organizations, other than religious organizations. When we include the approximately 330,000 religious organizations, this brings the total to more than 830,000 nonprofit organizations currently conducting fundraising campaigns in America.

More than in any other nation in human history, the proliferation of voluntary associations has been the lifeblood of the American republic.

America's founding fathers understood the importance of voluntary associations for sustaining freedom, which is why they enshrined in the U.S. Constitution's First Amendment the "right of the people to peaceably assemble." This principle, more commonly called the principle of freedom of association, is a fundamental right in America—a bedrock of liberty and essential to a fully functioning democracy.

One important way issue-advocacy organizations strengthen democracy, in particular, is that they give more weight in the political process to the opinions of informed, actively engaged voters—and appropriately so.

After all, why should the vote of an informed citizen who

cares deeply about an issue be completely canceled out by the vote of an uninformed person who doesn't care much at all about any issue, but just happened to vote because it was convenient that day?

The impact of my vote can be magnified exponentially simply by joining an organization whose entire mission is to solve a problem or promote an issue I care about. My membership in such an organization also allows me to vote as often as I want, not once every two years or so in an election, but every month or every week by signing a petition or sending back a contribution that will then be used to advance my cause.

Joining such an organization also gives me a bigger megaphone to shout my views across the land and more clout in the halls of government, where decisions affecting my life and my family's life are made every day.

My vote and my voice can be magnified many times more still if I take the initiative to form my own organization.

Isn't that exactly what Samuel Adams did when he formed the Sons of Liberty and set up his Committees of Correspondence to get the American Revolution rolling?

Direct Mail Works for Small Organizations and Local Causes

Direct mail is not just for large national crusades involving hundreds of thousands or even millions of people.

Small organizations and local causes often have far more loyal supporters than large impersonal national charities and organizations, so they can often have productive direct mail fundraising programs.

Direct mail is essential for just about any successful fundraising campaign, even if it only involves a few hundred or a few thousand potential supporters for the cause or project.

For example, perhaps your church or synagogue desires a new building, one that's bigger than the one you're in now, one that will accommodate three times the number of people.

Attendance by members at religious services is never 100 percent every week. So not everyone will hear the vision for the proposed new building directly from the pastor or rabbi. You'll need to use the mail to send to your members and likely supporters the budgets, blueprints, and an inspirational letter that paints a vivid picture of all that can be accomplished with this new facility. Even those who attend religious services faithfully every week must be encouraged regularly to consider increasing their financial commitment so that you can turn this dream into a reality, quickly and on schedule. And you will want to use the mail to send regular updates and progress reports to maintain enthusiasm and support for this grand new project.

Or maybe your town needs a new recreation facility, but your town council hasn't put it in the budget, because the town council doesn't want to raise taxes again. A direct mail fundraising program targeted at residents of the town could be an ideal way to raise all the funds you need for such a project.

The first mail piece might include a blueprint of what is envisioned, a budget, and a letter explaining to town residents all the benefits of this new recreation center. Such a center could provide a place for their kids to play, along with sports programs. Perhaps it would include a swimming pool, tennis courts, basketball court, skateboard park, baseball diamond, soccer field, and exercise rooms. Such a facility could be a great place for townsfolk to gather, meet, and strengthen the sense of community.

If a new recreation facility is truly needed, a well-executed direct mail fundraising program to residents of this town should be helpful to raise the funds for such a worthwhile project.

Or perhaps you want to raise money for your school, college or university, fraternity, local Lions Club, Cub Scout pack, book club, local library, Parent-Teachers Association, the campaign to save Trout Brook, a crusade to stop developers from tearing down the historic Evans Farm Inn, or to raise the travel budget for a children's sports team.

The correct and appropriate use of direct mail will enable you to raise funds for whatever cause you care about or whatever nonprofit organization you're involved in. As importantly, you can use the mail to rally a powerful constituency, sometimes a very large contingent, to achieve great things.

Direct mail has been used successfully to raise money to refurbish the Statue of Liberty, build and maintain war memorials, libraries, museums, memorials to fallen police officers, and to preserve Civil War battlefields and other historic landmarks.

Most of the time, we really don't need to raise taxes to carry out these kinds of worthy tasks. A well-run fundraising campaign will be enough, if the need is genuine. America is the most generous nation on earth. Every year Americans donate tens of billions of dollars of their hard-earned money to all kinds of charities, religious institutions, schools, universities, and nonprofit organizations of all kinds. Americans are ready, even eager, to contribute to a worthy cause or to help someone truly in need.

The Number One Secret to Successful Direct Mail Fundraising

This book is jam-packed with rules, laws, maxims, principles, concepts, precepts, commandments, and case studies on how to create successful fundraising letters.

But here is the most important point in this entire book:

A successful direct mail fundraising letter must look, feel, and read like a personal communication from one person to another.

That's the number one secret of successful direct mail fundraising.

If your friend were to come to your home in person and ask you to pitch in $20 to help pay the heating bill for a neighbor who had just lost his job, would you contribute? You would contribute, because your friend had made this request in person, and there was clearly a need.

You would probably contribute even if you did not fully understand the need, just because it was your friend, standing in your kitchen, asking for your help.

As much as possible, your letter must strive to capture this sense of one person standing in someone's kitchen making a one-on-one personal appeal for help.

This book will show you how to achieve this effect with your letters when writing to thousands, hundreds of thousands, or even millions of people you don't know about your cause.

The Big Difference Between Direct Mail Fundraising and Advertising

The main difference between direct mail advertising and fundraising is this: direct mail advertising aims to sell a tangible product. People get something specific in return for the money they send back in response to a direct mail offer.

A direct mail advertising copywriter will examine the product to be sold, extract the benefits to the reader, describe the features, explain why this product is different and better than competing products, offer a money-back guarantee, and then go ahead and write spell-binding copy the reader can't put down. The commercial direct mail offers highlights on how the product will make the reader richer, healthier, younger looking, more beautiful, sexier, or more admired, or will make the reader's life easier, more comfortable, and more convenient.

Direct mail advertisers appeal almost entirely to the reader's self-interest. *Free* is one of the most powerful words in direct mail advertising.

There are certainly many similarities between direct mail advertising and fundraising. But there are some important differences. The biggest difference is that in direct mail fundraising, we are asking the reader to do something that, at least at first glance, seems completely unnatural. We are asking the reader to give money away.

In direct mail fundraising, all we really have to offer is a cause. We are asking the reader to stop using the commercial or self-interest side of the brain and instead to use the charity side of the brain. The direct mail fundraising copywriter's job is to write a letter so persuasive that our reader (whom we've never met) will send a contribution back in the mail . . . and receive *nothing* specific in return, except a promise that some good will be accomplished with the donation.

Instead of appealing to self-interest, as you do when writing commercial direct mail advertising, you must appeal to the heart. Fortunately, almost everyone has a part of them that wants to do good for others, make the world a better place, or be part of a cause that's bigger and more important than they are. People give out of their gratitude for the blessings they have, or because of religious faith or patriotism, or just because there is a little voice inside (their conscience) that tells them to be generous.

People also give because they want to be part of a community, or they want to be respected, or they want to be on the right side of an issue, or they want to be recognized for their good deeds, or they like the free gift you sent them, or they feel guilty about something, or they want their taxes cut or Social Security benefits protected, or they want to fight back, or be heard, or see social change, or they want to elect or defeat some politician. So there can be, and often is, a self-interest element to inspiring people to send a contribution.

Still, my point stands. While describing ways the reader can benefit by contributing can certainly strengthen many fundraising letters, the direct mail fundraiser must primarily appeal to the side of the reader's brain that wants to be generous, that wants to do good for others. This is no easy feat. But it can be done, consistently and with near ironclad predictability, if you learn the principles outlined in this book.

Why Direct Mail Continues to Grow

In the age of the Internet, email, a cell phone for every person, and instant communication, many predict the demise of direct mail marketing.

Direct mail as an advertising medium has been around longer than radio, television, and even the telephone. As we've now seen, Samuel Adams used a primitive form of direct mail to organize the American Revolution. And Benjamin Franklin launched a mail-order catalogue business.

Some of the creative giants of modern direct mail advertising, like the great Claude Hopkins, were at the peak of their careers at the turn of the century—the last century.

Direct mail (now called "snail mail") sounds so archaic.

But surprise, surprise!

Direct mail is getting stronger, not weaker.

Direct mail marketing continues to increase every year. The Direct Marketing Association reports that more than $50 *billion* a year is now being spent in the U.S. on direct mail marketing—nearly that which is spent on television advertising. And money spent on direct mail marketing continues to increase about 6 percent every year.

At the peak of the Internet mania, I heard two Internet marketing "experts" predict the end of magazines, newspapers, retail stores, and even the U.S. Postal Service. Today, Internet (also called "interactive") marketing still accounts for a pittance compared to what companies and charities are spending on good old-fashioned direct mail marketing.

It's also worth noting that my direct mail returns did not suffer much at all during the last recession and stock market downturn. While Internet companies were falling like dominos, my direct mail returns stayed steady and even increased. I am mailing more letters now than ever, and profitably.

As organizations scale back their Internet and other new media operations, good old-fashioned direct mail has come back into favor. Businesses and charities are going back to marketing basics. Direct mail is like Wal-Mart. It's not new fangled or sexy, but it's reliable. Like the Energizer Bunny, direct mail just keeps going and going and continues to increase in strength as the new media competition falls off the pace.

Just because direct mail has been around for a long time, does not mean it's technologically backward. Movies and TV have been around a long time, too. But a movie made today will look very different from a movie made in 1930 or even 1980. The same is true with direct mail. New technology, ever-improving computers, more refined list and database management, and increasingly sophisticated regression analysis and demographic modeling allow direct mail marketers to target likely customers with more laser-like precision than ever.

Not long ago, Fortune 500 companies scoffed at direct mail as junk mail. But now more than half of the Fortune 500 corporations have opened up large direct mail marketing operations.

General Foods, Procter & Gamble, IBM, Dell, Compaq, Apple, AOL, Nieman Marcus, Nordstrom, Bloomingdale's, Visa, MasterCard, American Express, America's biggest banks and financial institutions, jewelers, realtors, airlines, hotels, and automobile companies are all now marketing heavily to consumers through the mail. Why? Because they know they must use the mail to win the battle for market share; and because these huge companies now see how well direct mail works. The results are measurable and predictable. They can see a return on investment.

There was a day when many marketing experts, including large advertising agencies, believed that direct mail was only suitable for selling $10, $20, and $50 consumer items. Direct mail, they thought, was useful for magazine subscriptions, book clubs, kitchen gadgets, and to solicit small $10 and $15 donations for charities, not much more.

Today I buy Omaha steaks, gourmet Gevalia coffee, and clothes through the mail. Recently I even bought my car through the mail, a shiny black Audi A-6. I needed a new car.

A sophisticated direct marketer knew that the lease on my current car was about to expire, and knew that I would soon need a new car. A direct mail piece arrived at my home offering me a brand new Audi for much less than my local Audi dealer. The mailing promised I would pay the exact amount for the car offered in the mail piece—not a penny more. This promise got my attention. When is the price of a car ever actually the price advertised? I got on the phone, asked some questions to make sure I would be getting the exact car advertised in the mailing. And, sure enough, that was the price. Within 24 hours, the car was delivered to my home, like a pizza!

I signed the papers. If I wasn't satisfied, I could return the car within 10 days and owe nothing. No long waits at the dealer. No being held hostage for hours by an aggressive salesman trying to sell me the undercoating or extra service warranty I didn't need or want. No hassles. Instead, I had been offered and I had purchased an Audi via direct mail, a $48,000 item. What a pleasant experience! What a great way to sell cars! I will buy all my cars this way from now on.

A similar trend is happening in direct mail fundraising.

I use direct mail not just to persuade my readers to send $10, $15, and $20 contributions, but also carefully targeted, highly personal mailings to bring in $1,000, $10,000, $25,000, and $50,000 donations.

Not only is direct mail by far the most powerful and cost-effective medium for building your customer and donor base, direct mail is absolutely essential for maintaining the customer and donor bases created by all the new media.

One reason direct mail continues to grow is that it's not limited to 60 seconds or less as on radio and TV, one- or two-page presentations as in magazine ads, a computer screen as on the Web, a boring format readers can delete with one key stroke as in email, or one color as for a fax. Direct mail cannot be blocked with caller ID or other screening devices for telemarketing.

With direct mail you can have any number of inserts. You can use all the colors you want. And there are an almost unlimited number of formats you can deploy to grab and hold the attention of your reader. You can use foldouts, pop-ups, and even enclose computer disks, books, and CDs. I often send direct mail marketing letters in boxes, tubes, plastic bags, and even between two pieces of cardboard stapled together to get the attention of my readers. In direct mail you are limited only by your imagination and budget.

Of course, each advertising medium has its place. But I use the Internet, radio, TV, telephone, and fax principally to *support* the direct marketer's workhorse. And that remains direct mail.

Seven Reasons Why You Need Direct Mail for Your Cause

1. Building your organization

Direct mail is still the most effective way to build a broad base of supporters for your cause or charity.

There is not one significant charity or cause-oriented organization that you have heard of that does not have a major direct mail fundraising and marketing program. Think about it: The Red Cross, Easter Seals, The American Cancer Society, NRA, AARP, Sierra Club, Greenpeace, Common Cause, ACLU, MADD, all these organizations have mammoth, multimillion dollar direct mail fundraising, membership recruitment, and marketing programs.

If you are interested in building a significant nonprofit organization, you'll need direct mail.

2. Educating the public about your cause or issue

With direct mail, you can go into a lot more detail about your issue, cause or product than you can with a 60-second TV ad. In fact, it's a mistake to think of direct mail fundraising purely as fundraising.

About 90 percent of a direct mail package is education and getting people involved in what you're trying to accomplish.

Direct mail can legitimately be a large part of what your organization does, which is educating the public about your cause.

Often I say in the letter that I am trying to raise funds so I can send out more letters like this one and reach more people on this issue. I often send out entire books, special reports, videos, DVDs, CDs, and tapes. Part of my appeal is often to say, "Your contribution will help me reach more people with this video" or "this book."

3. Mobilizing the public for action

Direct mail is a tremendous vehicle for mobilizing large numbers of people to take unified action. Direct mail is ideal for political and issue-driven causes. For example, a staple of my issue-driven direct mail campaigns is to ask readers to sign and return a petition, which we then promise to deliver to Congress along with hundreds of thousands of other petitions we're collecting on an issue.

As part of the appeal, I ask the reader also to send a donation so we can collect more petitions, which will demonstrate to Congress that the public is demanding action on a particular issue.

In addition, I might ask readers to call and write their representatives and senators to urge that they vote a particular way. An avalanche of petitions, letters, telegrams, phone calls, emails, and faxes, all demanding action on one specific issue, gets Congress's attention.

4. Cost-effectiveness

Direct mail marketing is the opposite of broadcasting. It's narrow-casting.

Unlike television, radio, and newspaper ads, which hit everyone in a geographic region with your message, direct mail can target those most likely to buy your product or donate to your organization. Direct mail does this by allowing you to mail specifically to those who have bought similar products or donated to similar organizations in the past.

TV ads are akin to carpet bombing. TV hits everyone, including those who have no chance of ever buying your product. Direct mail allows you to strike your likely buyers and supporters with laser-like precision. TV ads work well for products that everyone buys, such as toothpaste, soda, hamburger, and laundry detergent.

Direct mail works well for magazine subscriptions, newsletter subscriptions, financial services, credit card offers, specialized products, and high-end products, as well as for charities and political causes.

For example, if you want to sell subscriptions to *Guitar* magazine, you should mail a subscription offer to people who have recently bought a guitar, not launch a major television ad campaign. The National Rifle Association looks for new members by mailing membership invitations to recent purchasers of hunting licenses and to subscribers to gun and various outdoor sportsman magazines. The Sierra Club recruits members by sending letters to buyers of camping and hiking gear and supporters of other environmental groups.

The Christian Coalition recruits members by mailing letters to buyers of evangelical Christian books, subscribers to Christian magazines, members of conservative protestant churches, and contributors to conservative political candidates and Christian causes. The AARP recruits members by sending letters and membership invitations to people who turn 55. AARP would be wasting its money by advertising on MTV.

5. Self-paid advertising

Direct mail, if done properly, is advertising that can pay for itself almost immediately. Even with *donor acquisition* (also called *prospect*) mailings, you can sometimes break even on your cost. But even if you return a more usual 75 cents in donations for every one dollar spent on the standard mass-market prospecting mail program, you're doing far better than any TV, radio, or newspaper ad campaign you're likely to launch, with far less risk.

Your big return on investment then comes from repeat mailing to your donors or customers. This is called your housefile.

Your housefile, which you'll mail at least once a month, will then generate from 50 cents to one dollar net income per letter mailed for your standard national charity. So if you build your housefile to 100,000 donors, you should be able to generate $50,000 to $100,000 per month in net income (after mail expense) for your organization. No other form of advertising brings back a higher percentage return on your investment right out of the gate.

By contrast, it's far more difficult to measure the effectiveness of TV, radio, or newspaper ads. For example, when McDonald's launches a TV ad campaign, they can't know with precision which customers are coming to their restaurants because of that particular ad campaign or which customers are coming in because of some other reason. They know they need to run ads, but they can't know exactly what their return on investment is with any particular ad campaign. So they can't precisely measure the effectiveness of their ads.

Not so with direct mail. With each mailing you know exactly what your return on investment is, because the donations or orders come back in reply envelopes in response to a particular mailing.

Even with TV, radio, and newspaper ads that are direct-response ads, it's difficult to measure the value of customers. The problem here is how do you reach your customers again for repeat business? How do you build the equivalent of a housefile with direct response from TV, radio, or print ads?

Well, really the only way to reach your direct-response TV, radio, and newspaper ad buyers again is with the mail. You have no choice but to change advertising media on your customers. You have no choice but to ask your TV responders to suddenly change their buying habits and become direct mail responders.

But the problem here is that these customers are not necessarily direct mail responsive. You know that any customer you find by mail is direct mail responsive. You don't know that with a customer you find with a TV, radio, or newspaper ad. So a customer or donor you find with a TV, radio, or newspaper ad campaign will not be as valuable as a customer you find with a direct mail campaign.

6. Freedom and independence

Without direct mail, your organization will be hostage to the whims of a few major donors. If you have three donors who are each giving your organization a million dollars, and if this accounts for your entire budget, you'll have no choice but to do whatever these donors want you to do. If they want you to stand on your head in the corner, you'll have to say, "For how long?" If they want you to jump around the room on one foot, wear a funny hat, and bark like a dog, you'll have to say, "Okay." Or, you'll need to find another line of work.

But if your $3 million annual budget comes from 100,000 supporters who contribute an average of $22 per donation, you won't need to worry about any single donor pulling the plug on your organization. In fact, if your eccentric $100,000 donor, who happens to be your largest single contributor, insists that you stand on your head in the corner, you'll be able to tell the eccentric old coot to jump in the lake, and you'll feel good about it.

7. Power and influence

Why is the NRA politically powerful? Why is the Sierra Club politically powerful? Why are elected officials so afraid of the AARP? Why is MADD able to get tougher and tougher drunk-driving laws passed all the time?

Because these organizations have millions of members who can be mobilized instantly for organized political action. These organizations have millions of members because they all have enormous direct mail marketing and fundraising programs.

Perhaps you're frustrated that the political debate in America seems to be dominated by various powerful, well-funded organizations. These organizations go by all kinds of acronyms, such as NRA, NOW, ACLU, NARAL, MADD, NAACP, ACU, CDF, and AARP. Perhaps you're frustrated that your voice isn't being heard on an issue or cause you care about.

Don't be frustrated. Instead, take action right now, today.

Use direct mail to launch and build your own organization and to increase the size of your megaphone in the public debate. Instead of being ignored, make sure that politicians, decisionmakers, the media, major corporations, and the powerful listen to your concerns and address your issue.

This book will show you how.

Or perhaps your goals are more modest. Perhaps you just want to accomplish something good in your local community. The principles of direct mail fundraising outlined in these pages will help you steer clear of rocks that will sink your ship, and chart your course to success.

CHAPTER 2

How I Got Into Direct Mail Fundraising

Before I report to you the essential secrets of effective direct mail fundraising I've learned over the years, let me tell you a little about how I got into direct mail. Ever since childhood, I wanted to be a writer. I hoped someday to write novels. But I thought I would try my hand first at nonfiction.

After I graduated from Dartmouth College in 1982, I sat down to write my first book, *Poisoned Ivy*. This was the first book that identified the "political correctness" problem that infects academia. *Poisoned Ivy* chronicled the founding of the *Dartmouth Review*, the first and most famous of the independent conservative student newspapers that were springing up at the time on campuses across America. I was one of the founders of the *Dartmouth Review*.

Poisoned Ivy did very well and received excellent reviews, even from liberals. The book generated a front-page feature article on me in the *Washington Post* "Style" section. The book received favorable reviews from The *New York Times*, the *Washington Post,* even the *Harvard Crimson*. It received negative reviews from the *Los Angeles Times,* the *New Republic* and the *Nation*. Actually, the *New York Times* reviewed the book twice, once positive and then once negative. I guess the

New York Times wanted to correct the positive review it gave the book, evidently by mistake.

So I suppose it's more accurate to say *Poisoned Ivy* received mixed reviews from the establishment media—which is great for a conservative book. Most books written by conservatives on conservative themes are completely ignored by the establishment media. So I considered any review at all, even a negative one, a victory.

I went on to write a second book, *Faith & Freedom: The Christian Roots of American Liberty.* This was a history book, which makes the case that America's political institutions and traditions have their origin in Puritan theology.

The purpose of this book was to counter the American Civil Liberties Union's argument that religious faith threatens civil liberty. The book argues, contrary to what the ACLU claims, that the Judeo-Christian tradition not only supports civil liberty, but is the source of our civil liberties.

I also did a stint at the Heritage Foundation in the 1980s as Director of Lectures and Seminars. In addition, I earned a living by writing speeches. I did some work for Ronald Reagan's 1984 presidential campaign and then for George Bush's successful 1988 Presidential campaign. I wrote speeches for many well-known political figures throughout the 1980s.

While a student at Dartmouth, I became very interested in politics and the war of ideas between liberals and conservatives, and between those who believe in God and those who don't. This, in part, was the subject of my two books, *Poisoned Ivy* and *Faith & Freedom.* My father, Jeffrey Hart, was a professor of English literature at Dartmouth College, a senior editor of *National Review* magazine, a nationally syndicated columnist, and a former speechwriter for both Richard Nixon and in 1968 for Ronald Reagan when he was Governor of California. So I was raised on a diet of politics, literature, philosophy, history, and ideas.

I still haven't gotten around to writing any novels. Someday

I will. Instead, I fell into direct mail fundraising completely by accident.

Here, in brief, is how it happened.

In 1989 I met famed Iran-Contra scandal figure Lieutenant Colonel Oliver North. He was in a lot of legal trouble at the time, being prosecuted by an Independent Counsel, and was facing potentially a long time in prison.

Colonel North was also a conservative icon because of his scheme to funnel Iranian leader Ayatollah Khomeni's money to the rebels fighting the Communist government in Nicaragua. The scheme was illegal. You can't have a White House staffer running his own independent foreign policy out of the White House without the knowledge of the President or Congress.

Oh well, a small detail.

Still, I liked Colonel North a great deal. He has a very engaging personality. He was a highly decorated Vietnam War hero. While on President Reagan's White House National Security staff, he played an instrumental role in planning the invasion of Grenada and capturing the Islamic terrorist hijackers of the *Achille Lauro* cruise ship. He achieved fame and icon status for his highly articulate and dramatic testimony before a joint committee of Congress, where he made the liberal members of Congress who were attacking him look like fools.

Not that we, as conservatives, should condone North's illegal actions on behalf of the anti-Communist rebels in Nicaragua. But his money-laundering scheme (ripping off Iran's Ayatollah Khomeni) did keep the anti-Communist rebels alive after the Democrat-controlled Congress had cut off funds. And his testimony before Congress convinced about 70 percent of America that he was right and congressional liberals were wrong to end support for the anti-Communist guerrillas in Nicaragua.

Still, the law is the law, and no doubt Colonel North should have been prosecuted for breaking the law.

I also liked Oliver North a great deal on a personal level. He believed, as I did, that the Cold War between the Soviet

Empire and the United States was a battle for America's survival. Would communist totalitarianism or freedom and democracy ultimately triumph?

The jury was out on this question at that time. In fact, it looked very much to me like the Soviets were winning and that the future could be communist totalitarianism.

North certainly thought so, which is why he took the actions he did.

I agreed with his goals, if not his illegal methods. I do think we get into dangerous slippery slope territory if you believe that worthy goals justify illegal or immoral means. The fact is we live in a constitutional democracy. And there are constitutional means for achieving worthy goals. In our system, you do that with persuasion, argument, and elections. In our system, when you lose a vote in Congress (as Reagan did regarding continued U.S. support for the anti-Communist rebels in Nicaragua), the answer is not for a White House staffer to ignore the vote in Congress and just move forward on his own with what he wants to do.

Nevertheless, I wanted to do what I could to help Colonel North avoid a long prison term. I agreed to help North raise money for his legal defense fund and launch an organization called Freedom Alliance, the mission of which was to educate the public, especially young people, about the principles of freedom and the threat of Communism.

It was very easy to raise money through the mail for Oliver North. Just send out a letter to conservatives under Oliver North's signature and contributions would pour in. We raised well over $20 million for his legal defense and for his Freedom Alliance organization.

I became fascinated by direct mail.

I would visit the caging facility. That's where they open the mail, organize the checks for deposit, and record in a computer database the names and addresses of donors along with the contributed amounts.

I would watch as trucks arrived from the post office—

trucks full of reply envelopes with checks in them for Oliver North's legal defense and for his foundation. I'm talking about thousands of reply envelopes and checks for $10, $15, $20, $25, $50, and $100 that would arrive every day.

Every so often a reply envelope contained a check for $1,000, $5,000, or even $10,000. I discovered that I really liked this direct mail fundraising business.

I spent a lot of time reading the comment mail that was often included with the donation checks, heart-felt letters written in people's handwriting to Oliver North. I made sure these letters were answered.

I wanted to learn more about direct mail fundraising.

In 1990 I was having a conversation with conservative direct mail fundraising guru Richard Viguerie at a Fourth of July barbecue at his farm. I had known Richard for many years through our conservative political activities.

Direct mail marketing had been around for a very long time. But Richard pioneered direct mail fundraising in the 1960s for conservative political causes. He got his start raising money through the mail for Barry Goldwater, who ended up winning the Republican nomination, only to be decimated in 1964 by Lyndon Johnson in one of the most lopsided landslides in presidential election history.

But Richard Viguerie emerged from this election with the largest mailing list of conservative political contributors ever assembled. Viguerie's mailing lists and direct mail fundraising system generated hundreds of millions of dollars in contributions for conservative political campaigns in the future and contributed significantly to the emergence of Ronald Reagan.

Back to the July Fourth barbecue at Richard's farm in 1990: Richard was very interested to hear about my direct mail fundraising efforts for Oliver North.

No doubt he was amused as I presented myself as some kind of expert on direct mail. The truth is, almost anyone could have raised millions of dollars for Oliver North through the mail at that time.

So Richard asked if I would be interested in trying my hand at writing fundraising letters for his clients.

I said, "Sure."

Well, the first fundraising letter Richard had me write for a conservative political action committee was an abysmal failure. Hardly any contributions came in at all. I was humiliated.

As Richard and I studied the returns, I apologized profusely. He smiled back at me. I'm sure he knew this would happen. The small mailing probably cost him $10,000. This was Richard's way to teach me that I really knew nothing about direct mail fundraising, despite my success writing fundraising letters for Oliver North, which was a special situation.

Richard asked me, "Are you interested in learning about direct mail?"

"Yes, I am!" I answered with enthusiasm. "Did you know my direct mail letter would fail before you mailed it?"

"Yes, I did," he answered. "I was 100 percent certain it would fail."

"So then, why did you mail it?" I asked.

"Because you wouldn't believe me if I told you that your letter would not work," Richard answered. "You had to see it fail for yourself."

"But this cost you a lot of money," I said. "I feel awful about this."

"It's not that much really, if the end result of this is that you learn to write successful fundraising letters for my agency and my clients," Richard said. "Are you willing to learn how?"

"Absolutely!" I said. "This is not as easy as it looks."

Richard said, "You're a good writer. But you know almost nothing about direct mail fundraising. If you learn this business, you can achieve a lot of good for the causes you care about and make a great living along the way. But you'll need to study direct mail. You'll need to read the great books on direct mail marketing. You'll need to study the masters who came before us. And, when I critique your letters and ask for changes, you'll need to do exactly what I say."

"Okay," I said.

Richard gave me three books to read, which I quickly devoured.

One was *Scientific Advertising* by Claude Hopkins.

Richard told me no one should be allowed to have anything to do with advertising, marketing, or direct mail without having read Hopkins' classic little book at least five times.

He's right.

Upon Richard's recommendation, I also read *Secrets of Successful Direct Mail* by Dick Benson and *Confessions of An Advertising Man* by David Ogilvy.

For the next 18 months or so I consumed books on direct mail marketing. And I worked for Richard Viguerie as a freelance direct mail copywriter. Richard paid me a flat rate for each direct mail package I wrote. Plus he would pay me a small royalty, I think half a penny for each letter of mine he would mail for a client.

With Richard's guidance, my direct mail packages started performing reasonably well. They would not have worked without Richard's oversight and often harsh criticism.

On many occasions, Richard said I needed to tear up the letter and start over.

I began to learn what worked and what didn't work.

What definitely does not work is eloquent and stylish writing. Save that for writing articles for the *New Yorker*.

Direct mail letters must be written at a sixth grade level.

Letters must be conversational. Don't worry so much about the formal rules of grammar. You must write as people actually speak. My background as the son of an English Literature professor and graduate of an elite Ivy League college was probably more of a hindrance than a help to my becoming an effective direct mail copywriter.

I had to unlearn much of what I knew when writing articles for *National Review* and op-eds for the *Wall Street Journal*. Direct mail copywriting is not about dazzling your readers with blinding insights and subtle points.

Unlike a magazine article, the primary purpose of a direct mail letter is not to convey information to the reader. It's not to educate the reader. It's primary objective is to cause the reader to take some specific and immediate action.

You want the reader to send a contribution. You may want the reader to take a series of other actions as well, such as complete and return a survey or sign and return a petition.

Direct mail letter writing is a lot like starting a conversation in a bar with a construction worker or over a kitchen table with a mom. Your points must be clear, simple, and to the point. Sentences longer than a dozen words or so will start to lose your audience. Eyes will glaze over.

And when I say letters must be written at a sixth grade level or lower, I am not suggesting that readers of my letters are stupid. Far from it. They're just busy. They don't have time to figure out what I'm trying to say. They'll give me a few seconds of their time to grab their interest. After that, it's time to find out why water is dripping out of the ceiling, or why all those sirens are blaring across the street, or what ballgame is on the tube.

Getting and then holding a reader's attention is job number one for a direct mail copywriter. Once that's achieved, job number two is to present arguments so compelling and so persuasive that your reader stops whatever else she's doing and sends a contribution check to a stranger.

Direct mail copywriting looks so easy to the casual observer: Short staccato sentences written at a sixth grade level. Direct mail letter writing looks like something almost anyone can do. Of course, swinging a golf club at a stationary ball looks easy, too. Only someone who's tried hitting that little ball straight and consistently knows how truly difficult it is.

Successful direct mail copywriting is very difficult. It requires years of study and practice. And you can only learn it by actually doing it and seeing for yourself through trial and error what works and what doesn't work.

I became a direct mail junky.

I couldn't wait for the trucks of reply envelopes to arrive at the cager each day. I wanted reply envelope counts as quickly as possible so I could get an early sense of whether the mailing was working or crashing. I tracked the returns from my packages carefully. I got on just about every mailing list I could find. I read scores of books on direct mail marketing.

I concluded that this is a great profession for me.

Direct mail allows me to write about the issues and causes I care about. I also found I couldn't beat the quality of life.

Instead of fighting traffic to make it to some office by 9:00 a.m. and then fighting traffic again to make it home by 7:00 p.m. or so, I found I could spend much of my day in my boxer shorts and a tee-shirt at my computer at home, unshaven, writing direct mail letters.

I also love the objectivity of direct mail.

No one ever questions my work habits, my messy office, my compensation, or performance level because my direct mail packages work. My results are measurable.

Don't get me wrong.

The objective, measurable quality of direct mail is a double-edged sword. And that can create tremendous pressure, especially when the organization I'm raising money for is depending on the success of my next letter to make payroll.

So there is quite a lot of pressure on us direct mail copywriters.

I remember I had to go to the dentist because I was grinding my teeth at night. My back molars had been ground flat. The dentist asked me if I was a Wall Street stock or commodities trader because, he told me, these professions tend to produce a lot of people who grind their teeth at night.

I said, "No, I'm a direct mail fundraiser."

"That explains it," he replied. "It seems the only people under more day-to-day pressure than stock and commodities traders are mass-market direct mail copywriters. I've seen a lot of direct mail writers who grind their teeth at night."

Nevertheless, I love the objectivity of direct mail, maybe

because I love competition. I love sports for the same reason: it's objective, measurable quality. There's a clear winner and clear loser. And there are benchmarks for success and failure.

Any writer who does not want his or her work tested objectively against someone else's work—as in a head-to-head direct mail package test—should not be a direct mail copywriter.

I've known direct mail copywriters who would rather pour gasoline on themselves, light themselves on fire, and jump down an elevator shaft than have their work tested against another copywriter's package.

I always look forward to an objective test of my work against the work of another copywriter. I certainly have not won all the competitions either. But I learned from my losses. I studied the winning package carefully, knowing with each loss that I had learned something new, and would write a better package next time. I learned not to make the same mistakes in my copy again.

I don't lose many head-to-head tests anymore.

In addition to being raised on politics and ideas under my father's influence, I also had a background in serious athletics. I was a world-ranked ski racer and one of the top junior ski racers in the country as a teenager. Even though I look more like an accountant than an athlete, I love sports and competition.

I mention this because I think it helps explain why I like direct mail so much. As in athletic competition, you succeed or fail based on results. There are no excuses. The results of your efforts are there on the scoreboard for all to see.

Direct mail for me was just another form of competition, like ski racing. It's a game I try to win. My goal is to be the Tiger Woods or Joe Montana of direct mail fundraising.

In ski racing, I would train and work all year to shave half a second off my time on a 60-second slalom run. I would ski and train all summer in the South American Andes, where it's winter in July and August. In direct mail fundraising, I feel I've had a great week if I find a way to increase returns on my control prospecting package by another couple of pennies per letter mailed, or cut the cost of my package by a few pennies without sacrificing performance.

I think the most successful people in life treat their profession like a sport or a game they try to win. They go to work, not because they must to earn a living, but because they love their work. They see their work as a competition, as recreation and fun. They see their work as a game they try to be the best in the world at.

I'm sure Bill Gates sees his work this way. He's not driven by money and never was. He's driven by a desire to build the greatest software company in the history of the world.

And now that he's on top, he wants to stay there and, like Secretariat in the Belmont Stakes, extend his lead over his rivals. Secretariat was not satisfied to win the final leg of the Triple Crown by two or three or five lengths. The more Secretariat built his lead, the harder Secretariat pushed, winning the Belmont by 33 lengths and going away. Secretariat ran because Secretariat loved running. Bill Gates does what he does, not for money, but because that's what he loves doing. Tiger Woods strives to be the best, not for money, but because he's a ferocious competitor, and because the golf course is the canvas upon which he creates his art. He loves what he does. He lives and breathes golf. That's why he does it, like a fish in water.

I believe the only way to do something really well is to treat what you're doing like a game. If you're going to spend all that time at work, why not try to be the very best at what you do? Why not have fun at it?

People are obsessed with their hobbies. Why not have your obsession be something people will pay you to do?

How you approach your job is an attitude of mind. You can either work out of necessity and see work as a chore—an attitude that will relegate you to mediocrity. Or you can look at your job as a game, a sport, as fun, as something you strive to be the best at. I think that's how Bill Gates and Tiger Woods approach their jobs. I think that's why they are the best at what they do.

I have this attitude about direct mail.

I don't know if I'll be the best. We'll know in another 20 years or so. But I'll be very good. I'm certainly going to try to be the best.

When I wrote books, magazine articles, and newspaper op-eds, it was very difficult to measure the impact I was having.

People may have been buying my books, but were people reading them? And who could tell if anyone was reading my articles? My writings just seemed to be going out there into the void somewhere, with very little feedback.

Not so with direct mail fundraising.

With direct mail you never have to wonder if your message is getting through to people. You know if your message is getting through, or not, depending on the number of donations that come back in return envelopes at the post office.

I love the scientific quality of direct mail. I love what it teaches me about human nature.

Direct mail proves that human nature is fixed and constant, like the laws of gravity and physics. The entire science of direct mail is based on this truth. The laws of marketing say that human beings will respond in a certain way to certain offers, arguments, and incentives, and that people have mostly the same basic aspirations, dreams, motivations, fears, and concerns. People behave in predictable patterns. If your mailing to 5,000 people randomly selected from a list of 100,000 prospects works, it will work if you roll out that package to the entire list.

When writing my letters, I must always put myself in the place of the reader. I like that about direct mail. It forces me to go outside myself and to walk in the shoes of others. I must be a psychologist to be a successful direct-mail copywriter. I must understand what it is that causes people to act. I must get into the psyche of my readers and give my readers arguments so compelling that they will find their checkbook, write out a check, and take the trouble to mail it to someone they don't even know and may have never heard of.

That's a tough task.

But it's doable, and doable on a regular basis, if you learn the laws of marketing.

These laws are fixed and constant. They are the same today as they were yesterday. And they will be the same tomorrow, because human nature never changes. By this I mean that the basic dreams, aspirations, fears, and motivations of human beings will never change. They were the same in the time of Caesar. And they will be the same 100 years from now. Technology changes over time, but basic human nature stays the same. The direct mail copywriter's job is to learn what it is that causes your reader to act by learning the laws of human nature, which have become the laws of all successful marketing.

Like golf, direct mail is very humbling. In golf I can occasionally hit as great a shot as Tiger Woods. And just when I think I'm starting to master the game, suddenly, and seemingly inexplicably, I find I can't hit the ball anymore at all. I'm back to playing my usual game. I'm then forced to go back to the pro for another lesson to find out what the problem is.

Even Tiger Woods needs a teacher to keep his swing on track, to make sure he's not veering off course in some subtle way, to make sure his fundamentals are sound.

The same is true for the direct mail copywriter.

You can write a blockbuster letter that breaks the bank with donations one day. And then, just when you think you've figured it out and can't fail, your next letter crashes. And it's not always apparent exactly why it crashed. I mean, I wouldn't have written the letter and spent all that money to mail it if I thought it was a bad idea. Usually the answer for a letter crashing is something like, "I care passionately about this issue, but I guess not enough other people care."

Usually the reason for failure is my own ego. I was writing about what I was interested in, not what my readers are interested in. I was writing about my desires, goals, and needs instead of writing about my reader's desires, goals, and needs.

Direct mail is indeed a humbling profession.

If one of my packages flops, I'll give a copy to my copy-writing peers and ask for their assessment of what went wrong with my package. We'll do an autopsy. We'll analyze every aspect of the package. We'll look at what lists we mailed. We'll see if there were mistakes in the way the package was assembled and produced. We'll usually come up with an answer, or at least a theory for why the package did not do as well as we had expected.

Almost always the reason for a package performing poorly is that the copywriter has made some fundamental mistake, violated some basic marketing principle tied to the iron laws of human nature.

Direct mail marketing and fundraising are sciences developed largely through trial and error. We know what we know mostly because of our past successes and failures. In direct mail we don't need to blaze entirely new trails in an uncharted wilderness. We can stand on vast databases of results of all of our past combined letter writing efforts.

We will make refinements along the way. We will discover new products and new causes to market. We will come up with a new technique here and there. But we now know the basic laws that motivate people to act, and specifically to act by sending money through the mail.

Direct mail is a great teacher. We have learned with precision through direct mail what people like and don't like. We have learned what people care about. We have learned about people's dreams and aspirations. We have learned all this over the years and decades by the responses we have received to our direct mail letters.

CHAPTER 3

How to Create a Mass Political Movement and Change History With Direct Mail

I love creating mass political movements, seemingly out of thin air, with my direct mail packages.

One of the most powerful features of direct mail is that it's mostly a communications medium that is "under the radar."

That is, the news media doesn't cover it much.

Reporters and journalists are not on direct mail donor lists because they don't contribute to political causes and probably don't contribute much at all to any cause.

As a result, the media is unable to track the early development of emerging political movements, especially movements centered around conservative issues. Entire political movements involving millions of people can be built by direct mail almost in secret, at least as far as media coverage is concerned.

Political reporters should get on every political direct mail contributor list. They could do this by sending contributions every now and then. If they did this, their jobs would be so much easier. They wouldn't need to scramble around to try to find out where these one million people came from, all organized around a single issue. But political reporters don't get themselves on political issue contributor lists. And so the media is mostly in the dark on emerging issues and developing political movements.

This allows political cause-oriented direct mailers like me to build entire political movements, involving millions of people, without being detected by the mainstream news media. This gives me a terrific advantage in designing political strategies and building mammoth grassroots populist movements around a single issue or theme.

A great example of how this can work was the emergence of the Christian Coalition in the 1990s.

To the news media, the Christian Coalition seemed to come out of nowhere. "Where did this million-member organization suddenly come from?" the media kept asking.

The Christian Coalition was built and financed entirely with under-the-radar direct mail, invisible to the news media during the organization's early development.

Ralph Reed, the Christian Coalition's Executive Director, hired me to try a direct mail prospecting test in February 1992.

Ralph and I had been long-time friends. We had met in 1983 in Washington, D.C., probably through some political function. He was Executive Director of the College Republicans at the time. I had recently graduated from Dartmouth College, was putting the finishing touches on my book, *Poisoned Ivy,* and was shopping it around for a publisher.

Ralph and I hit it off, and we maintained a close friendship when he left politics in the 1980s to get his Ph.D. in American history from Emory University. His plan, I suppose, was to become a college professor.

Meanwhile, Pat Robertson, the Christian broadcaster, ran a surprisingly successful campaign for president in 1988. He defeated then-Vice President George Bush in the Iowa caucus, which nearly finished off George Bush the elder's presidential campaign. Robertson also won several caucuses and built a substantial mailing list of conservative Christian direct mail contributors.

After the 1988 presidential election, I bumped into Robertson at a meeting of the Council for National Policy, a group of influential conservatives who meet four times a year to discuss political strategies to advance the conservative cause. He knew me because I had appeared on his "700 Club" TV program to promote my new book, *Faith & Freedom.* He liked the book. He knew about my role in co-founding the *Dartmouth Review,* and I guess he had a favorable impression of me.

He told me he wanted to start a new political organization that would be dedicated to moving pro-family, pro-traditional values legislation through Congress. He asked me if I might consider heading up this new organization, or if I knew other talented young Christian conservative political activists I could recommend. I told Pat I was writing another book and couldn't do it, but that I thought he ought to talk to Ralph Reed who was finishing up his Ph.D. at Emory.

I knew the academic life moved at too slow a pace for Ralph. I knew Ralph missed the political battle and was itching to find a way back to the front lines of the war of ideas. So Pat talked to Ralph. In fact, I believe Ralph may have been at that same meeting. And they may have talked that very day.

Soon Ralph was the Executive Director of the new Christian Coalition—an organization that, in late 1989, had no office, no money, and zero members. But Ralph did have access to Pat Robertson's presidential campaign mailing list.

He sent out a fundraising letter under Pat Robertson's signature to the list announcing the launch of the Christian Coalition. The letter performed well, as it should because the Robertson for President list consisted entirely of die-hard Pat Robertson supporters.

Ralph also hired a telemarketing firm to call the Robertson for President list asking for support. Soon the Christian Coalition had a base of supporters that could fund office space and a small staff.

But in early 1992, Ralph told me that the direct mail fundraising agencies he had used could not make fundraising letters work to lists other than the Robertson for President list.

He told me that Christian Coalition's growth had stymied

because he had not been able to make the prospecting (or donor-acquisition) mailings work to outside rental lists.

Ralph is a brilliant political strategist.

He is highly articulate and is a master at dealing with the media. He lives and breathes politics and is a tireless worker. But he needed a lot of help with his direct mail program.

"Not only have our prospecting letters failed to recover their cost," an exasperated Ralph told me. "Most of these prospecting letters haven't even managed to pay for the postage. The prospecting program is a complete disaster."

"Why don't you let me try a prospect letter for you?" I suggested.

I had never proposed the idea to Ralph before. I'm generally reluctant to enter into business relationships with close friends, fearing that if the business relationship sours for any reason this could affect the friendship. Still, Ralph clearly needed help to make his donor-acquisition program work.

I described to him the work I had been doing with Americans to Limit Congressional Terms, helping to build a donor file of 300,000 names in about 18 months with a prospect package I had written through Richard Viguerie's agency. And I described a large very successful prospecting program I was doing on my own at that time for Campus Crusade for Christ (out of the basement office in my home), adding some 10,000 new donors per month to their housefile.

"Do you think you could do that for us?" Ralph asked.

"I think so," I said. "I'll write a prospect letter for you, and then let's get a test out in the next few weeks. We'll see what happens."

"Great!" Ralph said. "Get to work on it."

Within about a week I had a complete prospect package on Ralph's desk for approval. It included a six-page fundraising letter signed by Pat Robertson, a survey, and a Congressional Scorecard.

The letter asked for donations to help print and distribute 40 million Congressional Scorecards and Voter Guides in time for the 1992 presidential and congressional elections.

The idea behind the project was to ensure an *informed* Christian vote on Election Day.

The Congressional Scorecard I included with the fundraising letter showed the voting records of every member of the House and Senate on key issues of concern to Christian conservatives.

The letter made the case that politicians mostly ignore the concerns of Christians because Christians are not well organized politically. And most Christians, or people in general for that matter, have little idea how their elected representatives are actually voting in Washington.

The letter told the reader that the enclosed Congressional Scorecard is designed to show millions of Christians whether their elected representatives in Congress have been voting in Washington on the side of traditional moral values or against traditional moral values. And the letter encouraged readers to use the information in the Congressional Scorecard to take informed action on Election Day.

This is an important point concerning prospect or donor-acquisition mailings.

Since prospect mailings are doing very well if they break even on cost, it's important that the mailing be the program you're raising money for in order to keep faith with the donors.

I say explicitly in the letter that the reason we need donations is to distribute more copies of the enclosed Congressional Scorecard—in other words, send out more of these direct mail packages.

In effect, we're saying the more donations that come in, the more of these Congressional Scorecards we can mail to ensure an informed Christian vote on Election Day.

The letter further went on to outline Christian Coalition's broader mission, which was to transform America's 40 million or so evangelical conservative Christians into an organized political force that would make sure issues of concern to Christians are not ignored by politicians in Washington.

We tested 15 lists that we rented, selecting 5,000 names from each list (an "Nth" name select in direct mail jargon) for a total test mailing of 75,000 letters, at a cost of about $35,000.

Ralph complained a little about the cost, and said this was a very large test for Christian Coalition. I explained that the election was coming up in a few months, and we would probably only have time for one big rollout mailing if the package is as successful as I expect it will be.

"All right," Ralph said nervously. "Move forward."

The mailing was an astonishing success. The prospect test actually netted money.

The results showed we could mail 3 million prospect letters if we wanted to. I recommended we mail 1.8 million letters, which would cost about $650,000. I recommended mailing only lists that netted significant money in the test.

Ralph was very nervous.

He warned: "If this mailing doesn't work, not only will this be the end of the Christian Coalition, it will be the end of our friendship."

"I really think it's the thing to do," I said. "It's time to put the Christian Coalition on the political map, and this mailing will do it. The test results show you will likely net $400,000 from this mailing and gain about 70,000 new donors for Christian Coalition, which in turn will generate millions of net dollars for Christian Coalition in the future. You'll also be the new 800-pound gorilla in the political arena. You have to do this. I'll basically camp out at the printer and mailshop to make sure the mailing is done right, no glitches."

We ordered the lists. And the huge mailing, the 1.8 million-letter rollout, went out in early September.

I was nervous. Confident, but still nervous.

After all, I was still just working as a direct mail consultant, doing mostly copywriting from the basement office of my townhouse in Alexandria, Virginia.

I had a pretty good handle on copywriting. But I was not entirely confident of my expertise in other areas of the direct mail business. Did I order lists correctly? How do I know that I was getting exactly the same kind of names I had tested? I went over and over the list orders to make sure they had been done correctly. I got confirmation in writing as to exactly the kinds of names that were being delivered. For the most part, I wanted donors who had made at least one contribution of at least $10 to an organization in the last 18 months.

But what if the mailshop people (those who assemble, insert, and mail the packages) forget to include the reply envelope? Oh my gosh, what a catastrophe that would be!

I'd better run over to the mailshop to make sure everything looks the way it's supposed to look.

At any rate, the mailing went out. All I could do now was wait and pray that I had done everything right.

Eight days after the mail date, the first responses came in.

By day 12, the initial trickle of reply envelopes had turned into a Noah's Ark-style flood. Ralph wanted the donations to come back to the Christian Coalition offices in Chesapeake, Virginia.

I warned him that there was no way his small staff could handle the flood of reply envelopes that would suddenly arrive in tidal wave fashion. The reply envelopes would swamp his offices.

Until this time, Ralph had a couple of elderly ladies opening reply envelopes and depositing the donation checks.

About 14 days after my mailing went out, 40 trays of reply envelopes showed up at the Christian Coalition's office on one day. One of the elderly ladies tasked with opening the envelopes had to be hospitalized for stress caused by the event.

For these two elderly ladies, the 40 trays of reply envelopes and donation checks that had arrived one Monday amounted to a disaster of Biblical proportions—a disaster for them because it was their job to open the reply envelopes, process the checks, and enter the new names with the amounts of donations in a computer database.

Over the next 30 days, nearly $1 million in donations arrived in response to my mailing. The average donation was a little more than $13, which will give you an idea of how many reply envelopes showed up for these two elderly ladies to deal with.

Ralph did bring in some more workers to handle all this mail. He was ecstatic with glee. He told me that Pat Robertson called him daily for an update on the results.

"That's great, that's just great!" Pat would say upon hearing the day's tray and piece counts.

The profit on the mailing for Christian Coalition was about $400,000 as I had projected from the test mailing. And we had gained about 70,000 new Christian Coalition donors, just as I had projected to Ralph.

Thank goodness. Our friendship was still intact. In fact, I think Ralph liked me now more than ever.

If I loved direct mail before, I loved it even more after that. It was tremendously exciting. For me it felt like I had just hit a grand slam home run in the World Series.

I truly believe this mailing helped change history, because here's what flowed from that mailing:

Members of Congress started flooding Ralph with phone calls.

Some were outraged at how their votes were characterized in the 1.8 million Congressional Scorecards we had just mailed. They wanted corrections sent immediately to their constituents. Our position was that votes are votes, and unless we had made a mistake and recorded their votes incorrectly, the Scorecard would stand. Maybe next time they'll think twice before voting wrong on abortion, or school prayer, or gays in the military.

A few members of Congress were angry that we had included a vote on term limits in the Scorecard and questioned whether there could really be a Christian position on term limits.

That's a fair point.

There's certainly nothing in the Bible that would indicate

a Christian position on the term limits issue. But both Ralph and I wanted term limits for politicians, so we threw the vote on the Scorecard as a point of information for Christian voters.

Other members of Congress, presumably those who received favorable treatment in our Scorecard, wanted more Christian Coalition Scorecards distributed to their constituents, at least to those constituents who were conservative Christians.

The Christian Coalition also distributed some 40 million Voter Guides in conservative churches across America. These Voter Guides were distributed by local Christian activists on the Sunday before Election Day. I coordinated the printing and shipping of the Voter Guides to the homes of Christian Coalition activists and pastors across America who had agreed to distribute them in their churches.

The Congressional Scorecard and Voter Guide projects received the focused attention of the media. Liberal members of Congress were crying foul by saying their votes were mischaracterized. The Democratic National Committee filed a complaint with the Federal Election Commission, charging the Christian Coalition with violating election laws. All this media publicity helped reinforce the direct mail program and create momentum behind the Christian Coalition as a new major political force on the scene.

What we learned from the astonishingly successful direct mail program in the weeks and months leading up to the 1992 election is that there was an enormous market for the Christian Coalition, if the direct mail marketing was conducted properly.

After the election, we continued mailing prospect packages that were nearly as successful; and Ralph had me take over the regular housefile mail program as well.

In 1993 we mailed something like 12 million prospect packages and another 7 million or so housefile packages. As the housefile membership list grew and the Christian Coalition gained in power and influence, the increased media attention, even though much of it negative, just served to fuel

Christian Coalition's growth. Our donors did not mind at all that the liberal media did not like the Christian Coalition. Our donors interpreted the hysterically negative media coverage as evidence that the Christian Coalition must be effective by striking a nerve with liberals.

In the fundraising packages, we made heavy use of anti-Christian media slurs. For example, the *Washington Post* once called Christian Coalition's supporters "mostly poor, uneducated and easy to command."

Quoting this particular media slur in our direct mail helped underscore the need for an organized Christian voice that could effectively combat the anti-Christian bigotry that reigns in elite circles—for example, the need for Christian Coalition.

What the mostly liberal media did not understand was that every attack on the Christian Coalition only triggered more donations and strengthened the organization. We see this also with the NRA. The heavier the media attack on the NRA, the better it is for the NRA in terms of adding new members.

I believe the Christian Coalition, in combination with the term limits movement, was largely responsible in 1994 for putting both houses of Congress under Republican majority control.

This was the first time Republicans controlled both houses of Congress since the first Eisenhower Administration.

The Christian Coalition continued its Congressional Scorecard and Voter Guide distribution programs and waged an enormous "Get Out the Christian Vote" program.

In off-year congressional elections where voter turnout is low, a slight increase in Christian voter turnout can make a major difference in close races.

And that's exactly what happened in 1994. Republicans picked up 54 seats in the House and nine seats in the Senate, an historic seismic shift in the balance of power that forced President Bill Clinton to move significantly to the right.

After 1994, not one single liberal initiative passed in Congress; but a number of important conservative initiatives passed and were signed into law by President Clinton, including welfare reform and various spending restraint initiatives that produced the first balanced budgets in more than a generation.

The Christian Coalition deserves significant credit for this historic political sea change that occurred in 1994.

The success of the Christian Coalition depended on three key factors:

► The Christian Coalition had a brilliant leader at the helm, Ralph Reed. Ralph had a clear understanding of what the Coalition's mission should be: to transform a disorganized conservative Christian community into an organized political force.

► There was clearly a need, and a large constituency, for such an organization.

► Without a professionally run direct mail marketing program capable of building a significant donor file or membership list, there's no money, no organization, no organizeable constituency, and no influence. Politicans only listen to organizations that have a large base of supporters.

If any of these three elements had been missing, the organization would have gone nowhere.

This is important.

So often people come to me with an idea and ask if I can build them a large donor file that will support them and their idea.

I first ask myself, is the idea any good? By any good, I mean, "Do I agree with the idea and is there a market for this idea?"

If the answer is either "Yes" or "Maybe," I then ask, "If someone sends you a $10 donation, what will you do with it?"

If the answer is vague and not well thought out, I tell the prospective client, "No, I can't help you. Not until you can tell me specifically what you are going to do with a $10 donation."

With the Christian Coalition, the broad concept was to mobilize 40 million evangelical Christians into an organized political force.

But a general idea, even if it's a great idea, will not generate many contributions. People donate to specific, narrow projects that are easy to grasp.

In this case, the specific, narrow project was to distribute more Congressional Scorecards. "We're going to use your $10 donation to reach more Christians with these Congressional Scorecards," I would explain in my letter.

That's easy to understand.

That's an idea a reader can quickly grasp.

There is clearly a cost to this project. And I can easily see, not only how my $10 will be spent, but I can see how my $10 will have an impact.

My $10 donation isn't just going into some black hole somewhere. It will be used to cover the cost of printing and mailing more Congressional Scorecards, just like the one I have just now received in the mail.

You also need a charismatic leader with a vision.

That was Ralph Reed.

The donors want to see the organization they are supporting in the news.

If the only time donors hear about an organization is when they receive a letter in the mail, they wonder if the organization is real. This rule holds true more for political organizations than charities.

Ralph was a master of getting media attention—and the kind of media attention that communicated to his constituency that the Christian Coalition was effective and influential.

He was a regular guest on "Meet the Press," "Face the Nation," "Nightline," and the network news shows. Reporters constantly called Ralph to find out what the Christian Coalition was planning next, or what the Christian Coalition's position on an issue was. *Time* magazine put Ralph on its cover in the summer of 1996.

By then the Christian Coalition had nearly two million members and supporters and raised $27 million that year.

The Christian Coalition had become one of the most powerful lobbies in Washington, along with the big labor unions, AARP, the environmental lobby, and the National Rifle Association. A case can be made that the Christian Coalition was the most potent political force on the right in the mid-1990s.

In 1997 Ralph decided he wanted to move on and do something else. What he really wanted to be was a political consultant. His role model in this field was the late Lee Atwater, who was a genius political strategist who helped engineer Ronald Reagan's victories in the South and transform the South (which had voted solidly Democrat since the Civil War) into a Republican stronghold. Atwater was also the chief campaign strategist for George Bush the elder's landslide Presidential victory in 1988.

Ralph wanted to move on from his Christian Coalition post to become the next Lee Atwater. So he left the Christian Coalition in late 1997 to start his own political consulting and public affairs firm, which is now very successful. Ralph also ran for Chairman of the Georgia Republican Party and, of course, won. He was then the architect of a Republican electoral sweep in Georgia in 2002 that replaced an incumbent Democrat Senator and Governor with Republicans. The net result of this effort was to wrest control of the U.S. Senate from the Democrats. Everything Ralph does is successful. He is brilliant and a tremendous leader.

Once Ralph left for his new venture, new management came in to run Christian Coalition. They were very nice, well-meaning people, but they did not understand the organization's mission. They wanted to take Christian Coalition in a different direction. And they did not understand direct mail fundraising. They had their own ideas on how to conduct direct mail fundraising. As a result, the Christian Coalition, sadly, disappeared. But that's another story.

The point is, the Christian Coalition could not succeed without Ralph Reed, his vision, his energy, and his leadership.

The Christian Coalition also could not succeed without a state-of-the-art direct mail fundraising program capable of finding 2,000,000 members and supporters.

CHAPTER 4

The Economics of Direct Mail

The Value of a Donor

What counts is your cost to acquire a donor plus the future, sometimes called the lifetime value of the donor. I don't like the term lifetime value for the simple reason that I can't wait a lifetime to make a return on my investment. I prefer to ask, "How long will it take me to pay for acquiring a new donor?" My criteria is six months. Sometimes as much as a year, but no more.

Your criteria will depend on how much capital you have and how long you can wait to turn a profit on a new donor.

The value of a donor varies depending on the quality of the organization. In the commercial arena, I often tell magazines that I can almost always persuade people to try your magazine with my mailings. But it's up to the editor to persuade readers to renew their subscriptions by creating a great magazine that people feel they can't live without.

Similarly, I have great success persuading enough cold list prospects to contribute once to an organization. But then it's up to the organization, and its ability to deliver on promises made in mailings, to create loyal supporters.

Your Prospecting Program

Your direct mail program has two basic parts:

- The *prospecting* or *donor acquisition* program
- The *housefile* program—your list of people who have donated at least once to your organization

The purpose of your prospecting program is to build your housefile by persuading people to give to your organization for the first time.

The usual way to find donors for your housefile is to rent lists of names. You usually start by testing your letter to lists of donors who have contributed to similar organizations. The mailing list business is an enormous industry.

The great virtue of direct mail is that you can test an idea or cause in the mail for a relatively low cost.

The Prospect Test Phase

A typical test program for a direct mail prospecting package would be to try 10 lists. Let's say each list averages 100,000 donors. But you would never want to mail an entire list without testing it first. You would test no more than 5,000 names on a particular list. If that works, you might then try 25,000 or 50,000 names on that particular list and see if it still works.

The test is like taking a poll of a list. But it's much more accurate than a poll. By conducting a proper 5,000-name test of a 100,000-name list, you will get a very good idea of how the package will perform if you roll out to the entire list.

Think back to my discussion in the second chapter of how human nature is constant and fixed. The entire science of polling is based on the fact that mass human behavior can be predicted by conducting a survey of a tiny representative sample. A properly conducted poll of a few hundred voters will tell you, within a few percentage points, the results of tomorrow's national election.

The same principle holds true for small tests of direct mail packages.

To create a valid 5,000-name test, you will want to select every 20th name on the 100,000-name list you're testing. This is called an Nth name select in direct mail jargon, and it is critically important for creating a valid test.

If you do this, the results of your rollouts should track fairly well—assuming you're dealing with honest list brokers, which is always a problem in the list industry.

If a package works to a small test segment within a larger list, the entire list should bring back about the same response rate and same average gift on your rollout. Just always make sure you're rolling out to the same type of names you tested. You would not want to test $10+/last 12-month donors and then roll out to $5+/last 24-month donors and then wonder why your rollout crashed.

Make sure the names you are testing are exactly the same kind of names you're rolling out to: apples to apples. This is absolutely key. And learn the jargon your list brokers use to make sure you're talking the same language. When you order names, always be crystal clear in describing the names you want, and do it in writing, or you'll get burned.

The reason you would want to test probably 10 lists with test panels of 5,000 names each is that you'd want to give your package the best possible chance of success. If you try just one 5,000-name test of one list and the mailing fails, you wouldn't know if the reason for the failure is the package or the list. If the package fails to 10 lists that have proven to be good lists in the past, you know the problem is the package or the issue you're mailing on.

I usually test more than one package when launching a prospecting mail campaign.

Your prospecting program will likely lose money. Your housefile program will net money. The revenue shortfall you will likely suffer on your prospect program should be thought of as your cost to build your housefile list.

The question is how much of a shortfall should you be willing to suffer on your prospect program?

The answer is different for every organization.

But for a typical charity or issue-oriented organization where the average donation is between $15 and $20 on your prospect program, you can bring back 75 percent of cost and pay for acquiring a donor in about six months with housefile mailings, assuming you mail a fundraising letter to your housefile once a month.

If you bring back only 50 percent of your cost on prospect mailings, it may take you a year of housefile mailings to cover the cost of acquiring a donor.

If your prospecting program achieves a 2 percent response rate (two people contribute for every 100 people who receive a letter), you will gain 20,000 donors for every one million letters you mail.

This means you will need to mail at least five million letters to build a 100,000 donor housefile.

I say "at least" because you will have people who contribute more than once to a prospect program, even if you're rigorous about not duplicating prospect mailings against your housefile. I'll go into more detail on this phenomenon in another section and why I believe you should only undupe prospect lists against the best 20 percent or 30 percent of donors on your housefile.

Your Housefile Program

This is where the fun starts and the money starts rolling in. If your prospect program generated an average contribution of $15 to $20, expect your housefile program to generate 50 cents to $1 net income for each $10+ contributor you mail.

If you send a fundraising mailing to your housefile once a month, and if your housefile consists of 100,000 $10+ contributors who have contributed at least once in the past 18 months, your housefile mailings should be able to net $50,000 to $100,000 per month, assuming you mail your housefile once a month.

Net means revenue above and beyond the cost of the mailing.

You should send a fundraising mailing to your housefile at least once a month. Mailing a letter every 21 days is not too often. I'll explain why later.

A Basic Business Model for Your Direct Mail Program

So here's the basic business model for a direct mail fundraising program:

First, be sure you're using an experienced list broker who knows the market you're trying to reach. If you're trying to reach the Christian market, make sure your list broker specializes in Christian donor lists, not catalogues.

Good list brokers are worth their weight in gold because they should know the strongest lists in your market. Select, say, 10 lists to test. Test 5,000 names on each list for a total test mailing of 50,000 names.

Assuming the cost of your package is 50 cents apiece, that's an initial investment of $25,000 to find out if there is a market for your idea or cause.

Let's say your test mailing then brings in a total of $17,500. This means you are now down $7,500.

But you have not lost this money, because you find that five of the 10 lists you tested cover their cost on average, while the other five lists brought back half their cost. This is a great success because this means you can now roll out the package to five lists.

In effect you have paid $7,500 to find this information, crucial intelligence data that will allow you to bring millions of dollars into your organization over the next few years.

Let's say the five lists that work contain an average of 100,000 names each for the select you tested. This represents a rollout potential of 500,000 names.

You've struck gold!

Rollout or continuation is direct mail jargon for continuing your mailing to more names on the list.

You probably would not want to immediately roll out to all 500,000 names, even if you have a quarter million dollars lying around to spend. You would probably want to roll out to a third of these names and see if the results hold up.

This is called *pyramid testing*.

Over the next several months you mail all 500,000 available names on the lists you tested successfully. Your mailing brings back a 3 percent response and a $16 average donation. Your mailing has thus returned 48 cents per letter on a 50 cents-per-letter cost.

You are now $10,000 short of covering the cost of the rollout plus the $7,500 shortfall you suffered on the test, for a total shortfall on the program so far of $17,500.

So you're now down $17,500.

This is a blockbuster success!

Why? Because you have added 15,000 donors to your housefile from the rollout plus 1,000 donors from the test mailing for a total of 16,000 donors.

These donors should then generate 50 cents-per-name net income for your organization each time you mail them. If you send a fundraising letter to these names once a month, these 16,000 housefile donors should generate about $8,000 in net income per month for your organization.

Sample Direct Mail Plan

The Test Mailing

Cost **$25,000**
50,000 Letters
Test 10 lists (5,000 names for each list). Cost
includes printing, inserting, postage, list rental,
copy writing, graphics, and agency fee.

Income From Test **$17,500**
Number of donations: 1,031
Average gift: $16
Percent response: 2%

Profit/Loss . . . .**($7,500)**

Rollout

Situation: Five of ten lists tested covered their cost
on average. These five lists contain an average of
100,000 names in the selects tested, for a total
rollout potential of 500,000 letters. You will also
want to test additional lists for future rollouts.

Cost **$250,000**
500,000 letters
You might decide to mail this in three separate
stages over a 90-day period to make sure the test
results hold up.

Income **$240,000**
Number of donations: 15,000
Average gift: $16
Percent response: 3%

Profit/Loss from Rollout . . . .**($10,000)**

Total Shortfall (Test plus Rollout) . . . .**($17,500)**
Total Number of Donors Acquired 16,031

Estimated Monthly Net Income
From These Donors **$8,015**
This assumes you mail a "housefile" fundraising
letter to these donors once a month and each mailing nets 50 cents per name mailed on average.

Number of Mailings to Housefile Needed to Cover
the Acquisition Cost of Each New Donor **2.2**

As you can see, it will take you a little over two months to cover your cost to find these 16,000 donors for your cause if you mail a fundraising letter to your housefile once a month. After that, you'll have about $8,000 per month in net income from these contributors to spend on advancing your cause.

And while you're rolling out to 500,000 names on the lists you've tested successfully, you'll want to test new lists for more rollouts.

That, in a nutshell, is how you build a housefile.

Now, there are many nuances that I haven't gone into here that will further enhance your chances for success. For example, you'll want to test a number of different packages so that the success of your program does not depend on one package.

And there are many steps you should take with your housefile mail program to move the rate of return up from 50 cents net income per name mailed to 75 cents or $1 net income per name mailed, or perhaps even more.

The productivity of your housefile will depend a lot on what your organization is doing. You'll need to report your successes and victories to your supporters. And it will help tremendously if your donors hear about your organization in the news.

These factors can double and triple the returns on your housefile. For example, the NRA's returns for each name on its housefile will be far greater than for a gun organization we never hear about except through the mail.

So media visibility and the quality of work the organization is doing will have a major impact on returns from the housefile.

In addition, you can mail fundraising letters to your housefile more than once a month. I think it's fine to mail every 21 days without suffering much fall-off, if any, in net revenue for each letter you mail.

These changes can also dramatically increase the value of your housefile donors and thus change your business model, allowing you to spend more to acquire a new donor and thereby grow your housefile more quickly.

But these additional factors are for another discussion. I've outlined the simplest program above for illustration purposes only.

As a general rule for most organizations that are built through direct mail, I think a prospect program is successful if it returns 75 percent cost. At that rate, it will take six to eight months of housefile mailings to pay for each new donor.

Because prospect mailings typically lose money, it's important that at least part of the program you're raising money for is to send out more letters to educate the public about your issue and to mobilize them for action. For my prospect mailings, I often make the entire program the mailing. The letter will ask the reader to send a contribution to help me mail more of these "special reports," "more of these Congressional Scorecards, like the one you're now holding in your hand," "more copies of these books," or to "collect more of these signed petitions for delivery to Congress," or to "reach more people with this survey."

This is very important for prospect appeals in order to keep faith with the prospective donor. You must be scrupulously honest with everything you say in your letters. The only way you can be honest in your prospect appeals that lose money is if you say explicitly in your letter that mailing more copies of this package, hopefully millions of copies, is the program you're raising money for and is, in fact, a large part of what the organization does. This also is a very effective appeal. It so happens that issue-advocacy donors see the value of mail as a vehicle to educate the public about their issue.

In fact, you will have far more success raising money to send out more voter education letters on your issue than raising money through the mail to run TV ads on your issue. I'm not sure why, but testing shows this to be the case. I think it's because your direct mail donors like your letters and want more people to read them. Your letters are specific and concrete, something they are holding in their hand and can see for themselves. They can see the value of sending you $10, $15, or $20 to help you mail more of your direct mail packages so that others will better understand their issue. That, in summary, is how you mail millions of prospect packages, keep faith with your contributors, and build your issue-advocacy organization.

CHAPTER 5

40 Rules for Writing Successful Fundraising Letters

irect mail is a combination of science and art. Lists, techniques, database management. Any intelligent person can learn these things. Most people can even learn the basics of writing a pretty good letter. But very few people can write a great fundraising letter.

I can't teach you how to write a great letter.

But if you can write and if you have a good marketing sense, I can show you the basic elements of a successful fundraising package.

There are tried and true rules you'll need to follow if you want to write successful fundraising appeals.

Seven Words or Less

If you can't sum up your basic message in one seven-word (or shorter) sentence, your fundraising letter is probably doomed.

You should ask yourself: "Can I fit my central message on a bumper sticker?"

If not, stop writing. You'll be wasting your time and money.

The people you're writing to are very busy. They receive a lot of mail every day. They're thinking about things other than the cause you're writing about.

You need to get their attention.

If you can't convey your message in about three seconds, your letter is headed for the circular file. Don't ask your reader to try to figure out what you're trying to say.

You must be able to convey your main message instantly with headlines, on your reply form, in your P.S., and in the first sentence of your letter.

These are the places your readers will glance at first to decide whether they should keep reading or pitch your letter in the trash.

The Technique is Crucial

With few exceptions, packages work best that lead with the technique. Don't bury your technique on page two or three of your letter. I generally like the technique to be the first line of the letter. Not always, but usually—about 75 percent of the time, especially in prospect appeals.

Techniques are devices that get attention for your letter and reinforce your message, such as surveys, petitions, sweepstakes contests, etc. There are hundreds of techniques, often called gimmicks by my clients.

I'll cover techniques in detail later.

It's important to fit the technique to the message. Techniques should not be parachuted into the copy.

The technique should be integral to the entire appeal. If it's a survey package, build a case for the importance of the survey and the difference it will make. Make sure you report back to the donor later on the results of the survey and what you did with the results. At the same time, be careful not to distract from the need for a contribution. It's easy in survey packages, as well as other involvement device packages, to make the mistake of letting donors feel they've done their duty by completing the survey or signing the petition and sending it back without a contribution.

Sometimes the best technique is a very personal looking letter with a simple straight out request for money. Yes, that's a technique.

Don't make the mistake of relying on the technique to bring donations in. The technique merely gets attention for your letter. It helps get you to the battlefield. Then the battle begins to persuade the reader to contribute. If used incorrectly, a technique can hurt your appeal if it distracts the reader from your message. The technique must not only get attention, it must reinforce and underscore your message and the need for a contribution.

The First Sentence

The first sentence of your letter is the most important.

This is your lead.

This is the line your reader will look at first.

Your reader will decide to continue reading, or not, based on the first line of your letter.

Selecting your lead is a crucial strategic decision.

Do you lead with the issue? Do you lead with the technique? Do you look for a way to combine the technique with the issue in the first line?

The answer is not an easy one, but getting the answer right is absolutely essential to the success of your fundraising appeal.

As a general rule, I lead with the technique, especially with prospecting or donor acquisition mailings. I have not seen many successful prospecting letters that do not lead with the technique.

The purpose of the lead, as with the technique, is to intrigue the reader, to get the reader's attention, to pull the reader into your letter immediately so your prospective donor keeps reading.

Here are some successful lead sentences I've used:

▶ "I have sent you this $1 bill in a clear envelope because I had to make sure you would not overlook my letter."
▶ "Please complete the enclosed Report Card On The Bush Presidency."

- ▶ "Your membership dues for 2004 are now due."
- ▶ "It is my pleasure to inform you that you have been selected as a Donor of the Year for Virginia."
- ▶ "This is an emergency cry for your help."
- ▶ "I need your immediate help if I am to beat Hillary Rodham Clinton for the U.S. Senate."
- ▶ "I am writing to you with a proposal."
- ▶ "I am very anxious to hear from you regarding your support for 2004."
- ▶ "I hope and pray you're home when my letter arrives in your mailbox."
- ▶ "I need your immediate help if we're to survive the next 30 days and not close our doors."
- ▶ "Though you and I have not yet met, I have been told of your extraordinary commitment to...."
- ▶ "I have undertaken the extra cost of sending you this letter in a special USPS Priority Mail Envelope because I need your immediate answer to a very important question."
- ▶ "Please sign the enclosed 'Letter of Support' for President Bush and mail it back to me today."
- ▶ "You have been specially selected to participate in the enclosed survey."
- ▶ "I am honored to inform you that you have been nominated by Mr. John Smith of Sacramento, California, for membership in the President's Club."
- ▶ "I am updating my records and I need you to verify if your name, address and contribution record is correct."

Notice that most of these lead sentences ask the reader to take some action. At a minimum, the lead sets the stage for asking the reader to do something.

For example, the sentence "I am writing to you with a proposal" sets the stage for my asking the reader to "study the enclosed proposal" and, hopefully, support the proposal by sending a contribution. With few exceptions, however, the lead should either ask the reader to take some specific, well-defined action, or explain why you have done something unusual to get the reader's attention (such as enclose a $1 bill with your letter) or are sponsoring a sweepstakes contest.

The key to an effective lead is to get the reader's attention and draw the reader into your letter. It's a way to hit your reader across the forehead with a two-by-four. With your lead sentence, you're saying, "Pay attention now, this letter is worth reading. I have something interesting to tell you."

The most common fault I see from copywriters is that they bury the lead. They spend several paragraphs building up to the bottom line, kind of like an opera singer clearing her voice before the actual performance starts.

Often I'll find what should be the lead half-way down the first page, or even on the second page.

Opera fans don't want to hear the singer clear her voice before the performance. They want the performance. Your readers don't have time to try to wade through a lot of text to figure out what you're writing to them about.

The first line of your letter is not the place for pleasantries. Don't discuss the weather. Don't ask how they are doing. Get to the bottom line of why you are writing. Tell the reader what you want her to do: "Please sign the enclosed petition and mail it to me today. . . ." Or, "I am writing you with an emergency appeal for your help."

These are not complicated or especially imaginative leads, but they tell your reader immediately why you're writing. Err on the side of simplicity, not creativity. The more creative you are, the more confusing you're likely to be. Don't try to dazzle your reader with your creativity.

My favorite writer is Ernest Hemmingway. His sentences are so simple, clear, and to the point. Ernest Hemmingway would have made a great direct mail copywriter. Thank goodness he decided to write great novels and short stories instead.

The P.S.

After your reader has read the first line of your letter, the next place she'll likely look is the P.S. In fact, many people read the P.S. first, because they know that's where they will find the bottom line of why you're writing to them.

The P.S. summarizes the action you want your reader to take and restates the need for an immediate contribution. Try not to simply repeat lines from the letter, but don't depart from your theme either.

Keep the P.S. short and to the point. Remind the reader of the need for the rapid arrival of the contribution. I often include a specific date by when we need the contribution, restate the reason for why a contribution is needed, and tell why it's needed now.

The Cause

Techniques and first lines are essential for getting the reader's attention and persuading the reader to keep reading, at least for another sentence or two.

But far more important to the readers, in terms of convincing them to contribute, is the cause you're writing about. The cause or issue is the single most important factor in determining whether contributions will arrive in response to your letter. If you're writing to NRA members about what you're doing to protect Second Amendment rights, contributions will come in, even if your letter isn't especially good. But don't send even your best NRA fundraising letter to Sierra Club supporters.

Superb letter writing and execution will dramatically improve response to your letter but cannot overcome writing to people who don't care deeply about the issue you're writing about.

Put another way, you and your reader must agree first on the importance of the cause you're writing about. Once you've overcome this first hurdle, the battle for the contribution can begin.

The Project

If the cause is of paramount importance to your reader, the second most important factor in persuading your reader to contribute is the specific project you're raising money for.

Your potential contributors may be pleased to learn you care about the same cause, but they probably won't contribute until you explain exactly what you'll do with their $15 donation.

So, for example, let's say the mission of your organization is to help blind people.

Your reader may agree that's a nice idea, but wants to know exactly how. A good project might be to provide a trained guide dog for a blind person. This works because it's something specific and concrete, not vague and abstract. It's achievable. It's simple. It's easy to understand. It's clearly a need. And it's something that can be done immediately, as soon as the contribution arrives.

Helping the blind might be the mission or cause. But providing a guide dog for a blind person is the project—it's how you'll use my $15 donation.

People want to know exactly what you'll do with their contributions. They don't want their money to disappear into some black hole somewhere.

Assuming you and your reader both agree on the worthiness of the cause, your reader next wants to know what your specific project is: Why you need $15 today.

Don't Write a Sermon

The purpose of your letter is not to persuade your reader that you're right about an issue, or to convince your reader to care about your cause.

If you need to do this, you've lost the battle for the contribution before it even starts.

You should write to people you know agree with you.

For example, don't waste space persuading NRA members to care about the Second Amendment. You already know they care about the Second Amendment, which is why you are writing to them in the first place.

Instead, write about what you and your organization are doing right now to protect your reader's right to own a gun. Describe the battle raging in Congress, and how a vote on a key piece of antigun legislation is taking place in the next 21 days.

Write about how you need your reader to sign a petition to Congress and return it with a contribution immediately—a contribution you will use to bury Congress with millions of similar petitions in the next few weeks. Write about the advertising and media campaign you're planning, designed to generate a groundswell of public opposition to the antigun bill Congress will likely vote on in the next 60 days. Explain to the reader why you need contributions to fund this effort.

Discuss the need for an immediate response to your letter and the disaster that will ensue if contributions fail to arrive in answer to your appeal. Spend most of your letter describing precisely how you will use your reader's contribution.

Don't spend any time making powerful and compelling arguments for the right to own a gun. Save that for a magazine article or newspaper op-ed, not for a direct mail fundraising appeal.

The goal of your fundraising appeal is not to win converts. The goal is to find people who agree with you already and to persuade them to send a contribution, as well as mobilize them for action.

Your readers already know all the arguments concerning your cause. And they're already persuaded about the importance of your issue. What they may not know is why they should send a contribution to you instead of your competitor. Do not waste a single line of copy trying to convince your reader to care about your issue or to persuade your reader of the merits of your cause. Every line of your letter should instead be designed to improve your odds of getting a contribution.

Convey a Sense of Gathering Momentum

Discuss what you've achieved so far and your goals for the future. Include a timeline that shows precisely what you've been doing for the past six months, with specific accomplishments. Include a battle plan outlining precisely what you aim to achieve in the next 90 days. Demonstrate gathering momentum, like a building tidal wave or a symphony that will soon reach a crescendo. Paint a picture in the mind of your reader of how life will be different once you've achieved your goal.

Write to a Particular Person

Letters and packages should be written for a particular audience. If you're writing to people who have contributed $1,000, don't ask for $20. For those who have contributed $100 or more, spend some money and the necessary time on the package to make it as personal as possible.

Write as if you're writing to one person, not a million people. Reference specific information you know about the person in the copy in a way that makes sense, such as the amount of recent contributions, your thanks for past support, and the town and state of residence.

Referencing as much specific information you know about the person you are writing to will go a long way toward making your letter sound like a truly personal communication from one person to another. But do so in a way that makes sense. Don't go so overboard that your personalization looks contrived. Your personalization should be appropriate.

Use Direct Mail Language, Not Formal Grammar

Use regular conversational language in your letters. Don't write as your high school English teacher or your college English professor would want you to write.

I think my Ivy League Dartmouth education was actually

a hindrance to me becoming a successful direct mail copy-writer.

I had to unlearn some of the rules of grammar that had been hammered into my head for so many years. As the son of an English professor, this was especially difficult—and somewhat appalling to my father.

I try to write now as people actually speak when having a conversation on a street corner. I write my letters as I would write to my mom or a close friend. I now write at a sixth grade level, not because people are unintelligent, but because people simply don't have the time or patience to figure out what I am trying to say. They don't have time to unscramble the King's English.

Your mission is not to impress your reader with your intelligence. Your mission as a direct mail copywriter is to communicate your message as simply and directly as possible.

Always maintain the personal tone of your letter. Instead of saying "we" or "us" use the word "I." Always talk about what "you and I" can accomplish or how "you and I" can solve the problem. Letters should be one-on-one communications. The phrase "you and I" can be found throughout all my direct letters. It can sound redundant at times, but the "you and I" phrase is essential for making letters sound personal.

I think the best direct mail copywriters are people with blue-collar backgrounds who are used to talking with longshoremen, construction workers, and people at sports bars (where I like to hang out). The best direct mail copywriters are not people with Ivy League educations, or even any college education. A salesman who sells vacuum cleaners door to door and is used to talking with housewives everyday about his product would likely make an excellent direct mail copywriter.

A direct mail copywriter need not be able to deliver an esoteric lecture to a room full of college professors. In fact, anyone who can do that should probably select a field other than direct mail copywriting. A direct mail copywriter must know how to have a casual conversation with average, every-day folks who have everyday concerns and problems.

I remember once asking another direct mail copywriter if he thought the recent stock market crash would have a negative impact on returns to my mailings. He said, wisely: "Absolutely not. The people who send $10, $15, and $20 contributions in response to your letters don't have a big stake in the stock market. They are average hard-working, patriotic, churchgoing folks who care about America's future."

And sure enough, he was right. The 60 percent decline in the NASDAQ did not have any negative impact on returns to my mailings.

Direct and Clear, Not Illiterate

Don't be obsessed with the rules of grammar, but don't be illiterate either.

The rule is to be clear.

Instead of "such as," I use "like" because people don't use "such as" in casual conversation. "Like" is simple and clean. Instead of "requested," I say "asked for." I don't mind ending sentences with prepositions to sound more conversational and less pompous. "This is the information you asked for" is stronger than "this is the information you requested."

The phrase "the project you are raising money for" flows more naturally than the grammatically correct, "the project for which you are raising money."

I never use the phrase "to whom" or "for whom" in a direct mail letter, because people don't speak that way. I also split infinitives, much to the chagrin of my father, the retired Dartmouth English professor.

But you must follow certain rules of grammar for your sentences to make sense. For example, your subject and verb must always agree.

Never write: "As one of our very best supporters, I especially want to thank you for your recent contribution."

This is a badly misconstructed sentence. The writer does not mean to call himself "one of our very best supporters," which is what the sentence actually says. Instead write: "You are one of our very best supporters. And I want to thank you for your recent contribution."

I realize the rules of grammar say I must not start sentences with "And." But I did not want to use a comma because this would make my sentence too long and cumbersome. I also thought leaving "And" out made the two thoughts too disconnected. To avoid creating a long sentence, while also maintaining the connectivity between the two ideas, I decided to start the second sentence with the word "And"—a transition word that can help keep the reader reading.

Just because you are writing in a conversational style a sixth grader can understand does not mean direct mail copywriting is easy. Far from it.

Each word you select, each phrase and sentence you construct must be a carefully considered strategic decision.

Also, avoid using words with more than one meaning.

For example, the meaning of the phrase "Ben Hart's last book" is not at all clear. Does this mean "This is Ben Hart's last book" because he has just been hit by a bus and is no longer with us? Or does this mean "Ben Hart's most recent book"?

You want your reader's eyes to move easily through your letter. You don't want your reader to have to reread sentences in order to figure out what you're trying to say.

Following the basic rules of grammar helps ensure clarity.

But sometimes strict, fanatical adherence to the rules of grammar can make your letter sound stilted and off-putting, and it slows down the reader. Clarity trumps the formal rules of grammar, no matter what you're writing about . . . or "to whom."

Strike the Word "That" from Your Sentences

The word "that" is often unnecessary and usually weakens a sentence. Comb your letters for the word "that" and strike it out whenever you can. Your sentences will immediately sound stronger and more direct. "Which" is another weak word you should avoid whenever possible in your direct mail letters. You can't completely avoid using "that" and "which," but very often these words are superfluous.

Sometimes, however, I will start a paragraph with the word "which," or "that's." This can be a useful transition device. I'll sometimes start a paragraph by saying something like, "Which brings me to why I'm writing you today" or "That's what I mean when I say . . ." This can help keep your reader moving through your letter.

The Number One Reason People Contribute

A key factor that helps the direct mail fundraiser is this: The true reason most people contribute is that they are asked to contribute.

Public opinion surveys and other research confirm this is the Number One reason people give. "Ask and you shall receive," Jesus said. This maxim also applies to fundraising. The best fundraisers are those who are not the least bit shy or apologetic about looking someone in the eye and directly asking for a contribution.

The biggest single mistake made by amateur writers of fundraising letters is to neglect to ask for money or to bury the request so deep in the letter that it's easy to miss.

People contribute mostly because they are asked to contribute, and they will usually contribute the exact amount you ask for, not a penny more.

Make the Case for Why Your Reader's Contribution Is Needed Right Now

Urgency is a must in every fundraising letter. Your letter should have a deadline for response and should explain what the reader's contribution will achieve immediately when it arrives.

A deadline could be December 31st for an end of the year appeal, an election if it's a political appeal, Thanksgiving, Christmas, or other holiday for holiday-centered appeals. You should have a deadline date for matching grant appeals, a limited press run for premiums, such as books or fine art prints, and deadline dates for readers returning their completed surveys, signed petitions, and sweepstakes entry forms.

The strongest deadlines are specific dates—dates certain when something must be accomplished. But even if you don't have a specific hard deadline date in mind for the arrival of the contribution, your letter should clearly explain what the reader's donation will help achieve immediately.

You do not want your readers to feel they can put your letter aside, go on to something else, and come back to it later. You don't want your reader to think, "It does not appear essential for me to deal with this now, maybe I'll send a contribution tomorrow or sometime next week." You want your readers to feel they must act before they put your letter aside, because once they put your letter down, the odds they'll ever come back to it are cut drastically.

A reader putting your letter down is just like a potential car buyer leaving a car dealership. Once the customer tells the salesman, "I'll think about what you've told me and maybe come back later," the odds of this customer ever coming back to buy a car from this salesman are very low.

But urgency is not created by using a lot of frantic sounding language. Many writers think they are creating a sense of urgency by using the word urgent a lot, or other empty words like emergency, critical, and vital.

It's not that you should never use these words in your letters. But these words are grossly overused in most direct mail, and make the letter writer sound like a street corner huckster. You'll be far more persuasive if you just give good solid reasons for why contributions are needed today, right now, not next week or next month.

Most of your readers have a certain fixed amount of

disposable income they will use for contributions every month or every year. They want their contributions to make a difference right now, not sometime in the future. If your readers are not persuaded their contributions are needed now and will have impact today, they will send their contributions to another organization or charity that has a more clearly defined immediate need.

Reply Forms

Reply forms should look like reply forms. Make the dollar-ask section big. It's the most important line in the letter.

The reply form should include a headline that screams at the donor what you need money for.

The lead sentence, the P.S., and the reply form are the places the reader looks first. Of those who answer your letter, half will never read the entire letter. They will make their decision to contribute based on the first line, the P.S., and what they see on the reply form.

The reply form should contain all the action steps you want your reader to take.

If, in addition to sending a contribution, I want the reader to fill out a survey or sign and return a petition, I try to make sure the petition or survey is attached to the reply form. That

Figure 5.1

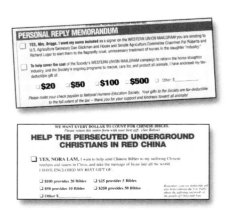

way the reader is less likely to return the survey or petition without also including a contribution.

Asking for a Donation

Try to make every sentence of your letter lead back to the need for a donation, but not in a heavy-handed way that will turn off the donor.

This is where creativity and brain power come in. The donor must not feel that the only reason for the letter is money, but at the end of the letter the donor must feel compelled to give. For example, a child writing home from camp and asking for money will be far more effective if she talks about the holes in her shoes and her wet cold feet than if she only asks for money.

Always discuss specifically why the contribution is needed.

And constantly connect the donation to what the donor is looking for—benefits to the donor, what will be achieved, and specifics about how you'll use the donation. Be sure to answer the question of why the donation is needed immediately—and the disaster or missed opportunity that will result if the donation does not arrive in a few days.

A request for a donation should be connected to something concrete, specific, and short term. But the letter must also contain a Big Vision and the prospect of achieving dramatic results. Give the donor a picture of how life will be different if the goal is achieved. Give the donor a negative picture of all the bad things that will ensue if the goal is not achieved.

Constantly connect the goal with the rapid arrival of the donation. In addition, I like to emphasize that I am not relying on any one person to shoulder the financial burden alone, that I am writing to others also. And that the key to success is for everyone to do their part and give what they can—whatever is right for them. That's how to get over the hurdle of persuading the reader that a $20 donation will really make a difference. It's best if you can say exactly what a $20 donation will buy, such as feed a hungry child in Ethiopia for a month.

Emphasize the Negative

Unfortunately, it's much easier and far more effective to raise money to stop something bad from happening than to raise money to make something good happen. That's because fear is such a powerful motivator to contribute. So be sure to remind the reader of the negative consequences of the contribution not arriving.

When writing fundraising letters for candidates, I paint a picture in the reader's mind of all the awful things that will happen if the opponent wins. It's much easier to raise money to stop bad legislation than to pass good legislation. And it's much easier to raise money to prevent a nightmare scenario that will change life as we know it than to raise money to build homes for homeless people. I am by nature an optimistic person. So it goes against my grain to constantly emphasize the negative. But I also want my fundraising letters to be successful.

Avoid "Double Stoppers"

Pages should not end with periods, if possible, especially on the first page. Periods are stoppers and tend to cause people to stop reading. Periods, of course, are unavoidable. But a period at the end of the page creates a double stopper.

Ellipses can help break up sentences and paragraphs and keep the reader's eyes moving through your letter.

The worst thing that can happen to a direct mail copywriter is for the reader to stop reading. Use every trick in your arsenal to prevent this catastrophe—the catastrophe of your reader putting your letter aside and going on to something else.

Underlining

Underlining key phrases in your letter will help catch the eye of your readers and keep them reading.

But don't underline too many phrases, or your underlining will lose its impact.

Think of underlining as similar to headline writing.

The phrases you underline should be mini-headlines. Your reader should be able to understand your entire appeal by reading only the underlined phrases, usually sentence fragments, hardly ever entire sentences.

Handwritten Notes

I will sometimes use handwritten underlining in blue or red ink, and even handwritten notes in the margin of my letters.

I love using handwritten notes throughout my packages: in the margins of the letter, on the reply form, and on the inserts.

Handwritten notes in red ink are sure to be read.

Scannability

Your letter, in fact your entire package, must be scannable — easy on the eye, with no large blocks of intimidating text. There's no greater stopper for a reader than to see a large block of undifferentiated text on the page.

Yuck!

Use bullets when you have a list of points.

Use indented paragraphs in bold to set certain paragraphs apart from others. Use subheadlines throughout your letter. Decide what the most important paragraph in your letter is, place it on the first page, and print it in red.

When you use an indented block paragraph for emphasis, keep it all on one page. Don't start it near the bottom of the page so it continues on the next page, or you'll destroy the effect. It will just look odd. It's best if your indented block paragraphs are somewhere near the middle of the page, so it pops out at the reader.

Short Sentences, Short Paragraphs, Short Words

I try to make every sentence a stand-alone headline that explains itself. That's not always possible. But it's a goal I strive for.

Use short declarative sentences.

When you select words, choose the shortest one. Instead of "allow," choose "let." Instead of "prevent" use the word "stop" if the shorter word will work just as well. Avoid four-syllable words whenever possible. Avoid unusual words (no Latin and French phrases). Write in plain English.

I'm not happy if I see paragraphs more than three lines in length in a direct mail letter. Generally, one sentence per paragraph is enough.

I often use one-word paragraphs, like "Why?" and "How?" . . . or brief phrases as entire paragraphs, such as "Please let me explain."

These very short paragraphs help break up the copy and make your letter scannable and easy on the eyes. Short paragraphs help keep the reader moving through your letter.

Your reader is far more likely to keep reading your letter if your letter is easy to read. Your language should be direct. Avoid multiclause sentences. Short declarative sentences are far more powerful.

Ernest Hemmingway understood this. Most writers don't.

Long Versus Short Letters

Testing shows that long letters usually work better than short letters. This is yet another example of how direct mail is "counter-intuitive."

Commonsense would seem to dictate that short letters would work better. Who has time to read a four-page or eight-page letter?

But all testing shows otherwise.

Long works far better than short 80 percent of the time.

A four-page letter will work better than a two-page letter. An eight-page letter will work better than a four-page letter.

This is a general rule. I'll tell you about some exceptions in a moment.

The reason is this: About half the people who answer your

letter with a contribution will have read every word. The other half who answer will have scanned your appeal. The scanners read the first line, the P.S. and the reply form, your headlines and perhaps some of your underlined phrases. Your scanners don't need a long letter.

But half your contributors want all the information before they make a decision to contribute. These people can't get enough information. And if you fail to answer all their questions, they won't contribute.

You must write for both audiences: Your scanners as well as those who can't get enough information.

Of course, there comes a point of diminishing returns.

A 16-page letter is overkill in most cases, and may drive your cost up too high, though I have written a number of very successful 16-page letters. The fact that it's 16 pages is enough to get a reader's attention, and suggests that the writer must have a lot of important things to say. Generally, a 16-page letter will outpull an eight-page letter, but not enough to make up for the increased cost.

But there are important exceptions to this rule.

Membership renewal notices should be short and look more like invoices than letters. A one- or two-page letter works best here and also keeps your cost low.

If the cause does not need much explaining, a short letter will work best.

For example, if the President of the United States is writing to his supporters asking for contributions for his reelection campaign, he does not need a long letter. The need is obvious. It does not require explaining. Everyone knows who the President of the United States is. Everyone knows political campaigns cost money. Besides, a Presidential election is in the news everyday. In a case like this, a long letter will be a distraction and likely depress contributions.

Long letters will almost always work best in prospecting. Since, in a prospect letter, you are writing to people who have never contributed to your organization, more explaining will be needed to persuade your reader to contribute.

Your housefile program should be a mix of long and short letters. Long letters are not as important for your housefile because your housefile supporters already know who you are and what your organization does.

Even for your housefile mailings, long letters will generally out-perform short letters. But you can't send a long letter every time you write. The long letter would start to lose its impact.

Far more important than whether your letter is long or short is the project you are raising money for. If the project is not compelling, it won't matter whether your letter is long or short.

The length of your letter should be determined by how much you have to say. The rule is to answer all the questions your reader might have. If this requires eight pages, write eight pages; if it requires four, write four.

Don't waste words.

Make the message simple and compelling. Don't bore the reader. Pull the reader through the copy. The easiest step a reader can take is to stop reading and go on to something else.

Your reader will know if you're not saying anything of much importance. Every word should count. Every word, every phrase, every sentence should have a purpose. All superfluous words and sentences should be ruthlessly cut. But don't cut copy just to make your letter fit into two pages or four pages either. Tell the whole story.

But there's another side benefit of the long letter. A very long letter, eight pages or more, is attention-getting in itself. It adds weight and heft to your package. Kind of makes your No. 10 envelope, stuffed full of paper, feel like a brick when it arrives in the mailbox. "I wonder what's in here?" your readers will ask themselves.

Don't write an 8- or 12- or 16-page letter just to do it. Make certain you really have enough to say to fill up all this paper. But the attention-getting aspect of a very long letter is a factor to consider. Many of my most successful direct mail packages land with a thud when dropped on a kitchen table.

Your USP—
Unique Selling Proposition

What is it that's different about your organization?

What is it that your organization does that no other organization does?

If I were to start a competitor to the NRA, I would not start an organization that does exactly what the NRA does.

I would try to figure out what needs to be done in the Second Amendment arena that the NRA isn't doing. I would try to find a task that needs doing that no one else is working on.

Perhaps I would try to be even more hardcore and purest on the Second Amendment issue than the NRA. By taking this approach, I would never become as big as the NRA, but I might become 20 percent or 10 percent the size of the NRA. And that would be a worthwhile achievement.

Or I might set up a Second Amendment Legal Defense Fund to defend gun manufacturers against liability lawsuits launched by the antigunners. I would try to find some niche to dominate and become known for some niche not occupied by the NRA.

It would be hopeless to try to compete directly with the NRA, as hopeless as it would be to try to compete with Coca Cola by launching an imitation cola.

Yes, I'm aware that other companies have done it.

Pepsi did it successfully with many billions of dollars in advertising. Of course, Pepsi will never surpass Coke. Pepsi will always be the No. 2 cola drink, and that's not bad. But even Pepsi emphasizes its differences with Coke. Pepsi is "less syrupy," has a "cleaner, more refreshing taste," "is chosen by 70 percent of people in blind taste tests," and is for a "younger generation"—or so the company claims. Pepsi never says it is the same as Coke, but rather claims to taste better than Coke.

But most of us don't have billions of dollars to compete with the Coca Colas of the world, so we need to do something different, something that's clearly not being done by some other organization that's a lot bigger and richer than we are.

We need to carve out a unique role so we can have a Unique Selling Proposition (USP) in our direct mail appeals.

I don't want to see comment mail coming back in response to my mailings that say, "But this job is already being done" by some other organization. I want to see comment mail that says, "Thank goodness someone is finally taking on this crisis."

Of course, your USP must be a difference that's both needed and sellable. No point in having a USP no one wants, like diet pizza.

But that's another discussion.

Sell Just One Thing

Never try to sell two things in a fundraising package or any marketing mail package. The mind can grasp one thing, at most. You would never want to say, "You can donate to help cure cancer and rescue abused animals."

Ask for money for one concept, one project, one cause. And be as specific as possible. You would never want to say, "Donate to help cure diseases." You'd want to say, "Donate to help cure cancer." Narrow is the gate to paradise. Focus your message like a laser. And keep it simple.

This is Direct Marketing Principle 101. This rule applies equally to fundraising and commercial appeals.

By the way, catalogues are not an exception to this rule.

Catalogues, of course, sell more than one thing. They sell many different items.

But successful catalogues are really selling one overreaching idea or theme. Successful catalogues sell one image, one theme, one concept. And all the products should fit into that theme, or USP. So, in the final analy-sis, even catalogues must sell a single, narrow overarching theme to be successful, and not try to be all things to all people (for example, Sharper Image, LL Bean, Lands End). The more a catalogue company diverts from its single easy-to-understand theme, the quicker it will fail, for example Sears.

Lawn, Not Lawn Seed

People first want to know what it is exactly that you are try-ing to achieve. What is the end result of all this hard work and the contributions you're taking in?

They don't want to hear about your organization. They don't want to hear about process. They want to know: How will my life be different once this work is completed?

They want to know first what their lawn will look like after all the expense and all the work is finished. Don't start by showing your prospective customer what seed you plan to use and how much it will all cost. Instead, show your prospec-tive customers a picture of what their lawns will look like.

The same principle holds true for fundraising.

You won't have much success raising money to pay salaries—even though everyone knows salaries must be paid. Focus on the end result.

Of course, you will also need to paint a believable picture of why your plan will succeed. So your letter may get into why the lawn seed you're using is absolutely the best, and why this kind of seed will generate the most beautiful, most durable lawn.

But don't lead with a picture of the lawn seed. Lead with a picture of the lawn—the end result, why your reader's life will be different once the project is completed.

Another way to think of this principle is: don't focus on your needs or your organization's needs. Focus on your reader's needs and on what your reader wants. Your reader does not care one wit about your organization, except to the extent that your organization is the right vehicle to achieve your reader's goals.

Paint a Picture with Your Words

"My goal is to bury Congress with an avalanche of these petitions over the next 30 days."

That's a lot better than, "My goal is to deliver hundreds of thousands of these petitions to Congress in the next 30 days."

An avalanche is a much stronger visual image than a large number, which is too abstract.

Or, how about this: "We have delivered so many of these petitions to Capitol Hill in the last few weeks that members of Congress are literally wading through these petitions to get to their offices."

Instead of closing your letter with a dry and unmemorable line like, "I hope to hear back from you soon," why not say something like this: "I will check my mailbox daily for your reply to my letter, which I hope will arrive in the next few days."

This creates a clear visual image of you anxiously waiting by your mailbox every day for a response and a sense of urgency not present in a standard close of most letters.

Consider telling a shocking story if you have one—but only if it's brief and truly shocking. Stories will lose the attention of your reader if the story isn't especially compelling. And few stories are compelling enough. Including stories in your direct mail letters is risky.

I prefer to examine every sentence in my direct mail package to see if I can make the sentence more vivid, stronger, and to see if I can do a better job of conveying fast-moving events, action, or urgency without using clichés.

Clichés destroy urgency and undermine credibility. Clichés roll off the reader's mind like drops of water falling on rocks in a rainstorm and leave no impression whatsoever.

Notice in my previous sentence that I did not fall into the trap of saying, "like water rolling off a Duck's back"—a cliché your mind would have just skimmed over and hardly noticed.

Clichés are lazy language. Work hard to come up with fresh new images your reader won't easily forget. Use language to jar your reader, language and images your reader can't ignore. Think of your reader's mind as your canvas, to be used by you to paint a vivid and lasting picture.

By painting a picture with your words, I am most definitely not suggesting using flowery language. Quite the opposite. Use strong action words. Be direct and clear. Don't use the passive voice.

Comb though your copy for clichés, and get rid of them. I'm sure some enterprising reviewer will comb through every line of this book and catalogue the clichés and lazy language I've no doubt used throughout these pages. It's not easy to follow the rules one advocates. It's what makes writing so difficult.

But the rules of effective writing are no less valid, even though we constantly fall short of the mark. Yikes, that's a cliché! So, "avoid clichés like the plague." Uggggh!

Oh, well. You get the point.

Emotion Is a Must

People contribute in response to direct mail letters mostly out of impulse. They contribute because their heart, far more than their brain, told them to contribute. They contribute because the letter, the package as a whole, hit an emotional chord with the reader.

With this rule in mind, which of these two sentences do you think is the stronger?

```
"350,000 people die of cancer every year."
```

Or

> "I'm sending you a photo of my little eight-
> year-old friend, Jimmy, who died from cancer
> today."

Reciting statistics and numbers is death to direct mail fundraising copy. Statistics are impersonal. It's one thing to say six million Jews died in the Holocaust. It's quite another to watch "Schindler's List," read the *Diary of Anne Frank*, or visit the Holocaust Museum in Washington, D.C., where you will see, hear, read, and feel the stories of actual people.

Statistics leave no impression on the brain.

Statistics leave the reader uninvolved.

Now you may want to include a few statistics in your direct mail letter to back up some of your claims. Your letter does need to make at least some appeal to the brain part of your reader, not just the heart.

But statistics and numbers will not move your reader to contribute. A stunning, heart-wrenching story about a real person will. The right story about an actual person will shock the reader's senses and move your reader to pull out her checkbook. Copy aimed at the heart will always out-pull copy aimed at the mind.

Jesus knew this. He used parables, stories that made his points. He did not approach us with data.

Remember, your goal is not to win a debate with your reader. Your readers already agree with you, or you would not be writing to them. Your goal is to move their hearts and tug at their emotions in such a way that they will send a contribution.

But if you feel you absolutely must use a statistic in your letter to show the magnitude of the problem, try something like this:

> Imagine if the September 11th attack on Amer-
> ica happened 100 times a year.
>
> Imagine terrorists flying planes into our
> buildings, killing 3,000 people twice a week.

```
Yet that's exactly what cancer is doing:
killing 6,000 people every single week.
```

This is far more powerful than simply saying "350,000 people die of cancer every year," because here you are connecting a number to an actual event you know your reader has experienced.

You are giving meaning to the number.

September 11th was a shocking event for every American. It was an emotional event.

Now you are pointing out that cancer causes just as catastrophic an event, but more than 100 times a year, every year.

By connecting your appeal to an event like what happened on September 11th, a catastrophic event we all experienced, you are providing a graphic visual image of the horrifying carnage cancer leaves in its wake each day. You are tapping into your reader's emotions. You are getting your reader involved, in a personal way, to show the magnitude of the crisis you are writing about.

Is Your Cause Presold?

You will have a very hard time convincing people to contribute money to help solve a problem they have never heard of.

People will contribute to help find a cure for cancer, or Alzheimer's, or heart disease. Everyone is well aware of these diseases. Almost every family has been affected by the devastating impact of these diseases.

No need to waste much copy persuading people these diseases are an enormous problem for almost everyone.

If the problem is generally understood, you just need to persuade your reader that your organization is uniquely positioned to have some measurable impact in solving the problem. Your solution to the problem must be easy to understand, and it must be believable.

But if your audience has never before heard of the problem

you're writing about, forget it. The alleged disease you're describing might indeed be very serious, might even be poised to kill millions of people. But if your readers don't know about it, you might as well write your letter in hieroglyphics. You'll have about as much success.

The cause or issue you're writing about must be presold in people's minds.

Your readers will need to have a solid understanding of the problem from reading newspapers and watching the news. If the major news networks are not talking about the problem you're addressing, if your readers have seen nothing about the problem in the magazines and publications they usually read, if their friends and family members have never mentioned the problem, your hurdles as a copywriter will be just too difficult to overcome. You won't just be paddling upstream. You'll be trying to paddle up a waterfall.

Listen to Your Market

The results of your prospect mailings might well indicate that your mission or purpose is not quite right.

But it could be that only a subtle shift is needed in your mission to attract more supporters and build a very large housefile. Or perhaps you just need to rethink the project you're raising money for.

A great example of this was my work for Judicial Watch.

Judicial Watch was originally established to keep a watch on the judicial system: corrupt judges and abuses in our courts.

Well, there wasn't a big market for that.

But when Judicial Watch Chairman Larry Klayman started filing lawsuits against the Clinton administration for corruption, contributions poured in.

Judicial Watch quickly changed its focus to cleaning up corruption in the Clinton White House instead of cleaning up corruption in America's courts. Soon Judicial Watch was able to acquire more than 400,000 donors and raise upwards of $25 million a year from direct mail to pursue President Clinton and other scoundrels in the Clinton administration.

So pay close attention to what your market is telling you, which can be found in the results of mailings. By testing many different projects and approaches, you will discover your market and what your market will readily support. Sometimes a subtle change can make all the difference between failure and success, like turning a screw just 10 degrees to the right.

When Apple computer started putting its computers in brightly colored boxes, that made all the difference in sales. Apple computers started flying off the shelves.

Who would have thunk it? Aren't people just interested in computers that work?

Sure people want computers that work. That's a given. But apparently people also want computers that look pretty, hip, and high tech.

Cosmetic appearance was important for selling computers.

Other computer companies quickly followed suit, putting their previously drab looking computers in new, brightly colored boxes.

Successful nonprofits, like any business, must listen to what the market is saying, and be willing to make changes based on what the donors are telling us. This does not mean completely changing your mission. Often, the required adjustment for success is a slight shift in focus—something like putting your perfectly good computer in a brightly colored box, like Apple did.

Write for Seniors: Young People Don't Contribute

Your contributions through the mail come from people over the age of 60. You'll go broke trying to convince young people to contribute. There are a number of reasons for this.

Young people are worried about their careers and providing for their families. They're under tremendous financial pressure and have little disposable income. Even very successful young people in their 20s, 30s, and 40s are just being pulled in too many directions to sit down and read your letter. They have kids and jobs, too little time, and they're worried about money. They rightly believe their No. 1 responsibility is their family. Charities and political causes are nice, but they can wait. The screaming baby who needs a diaper change can't.

Senior citizens, especially retirees, have time on their hands. The kids are grown. They've moved into smaller, more manageable homes. For better or worse, their lives are pretty well set. They have time to think about other things. They even have time to peruse the mail.

I used to be concerned that all my direct mail contributors were getting older and would soon die. And that would be the end of direct mail, the end of my business. But I no longer think that's the case. The current generation of senior citizens will be replaced by the next generation of senior citizens, whose children will also be grown, whose lives will also be settled, and who also will have some more time on their hands to read the mail.

Most people just are not in a position to contribute to causes until they are about 60. And so most don't. Your mailings, no matter how compelling, will not change that fact of life. So don't go broke trying to persuade young people to contribute to your cause.

Some of my colleagues worry that direct mail fundraising may die as an industry because the next generation, even when it reaches 60, will be more used to the Internet having grown up in the media age of instant gratification.

I don't believe these pessimists.

When TV came on the scene, did that mean the end of radio?

No.

Will the Internet mean the end for newspapers? No. People will always want their newspaper.

And people will always check their mail. They just won't answer it until the kids are grown and out of the house.

Essential Differences Between Prospect and Housefile Letters

With letters to your housefile, you are talking to friends. With prospecting or donor acquisition appeals, you are writing to strangers.

That's the key difference. You must write your letters with this difference in mind. You must always understand who your audience is.

Strangers who have never contributed to your organization probably don't know much, if anything, about what your organization does. So you'll need to do a lot more explaining.

Very likely, your letter will need to be longer. Many of my prospecting letters are eight pages. You also may need more inserts and enclosures for your prospecting appeal. I usually pack my prospecting appeals with testimonials, a lift note from a luminary, perhaps a premium or gift, and often not just one involvement device, but sometimes several. In addition to a survey, I might include a petition for the reader to sign. The sheer weight, thickness, and heft of my prospect appeals provoke curiosity by the recipient and ensure the envelope is at least opened.

"I just received another one of your Ben Hart Brick Packages in the mail," one of my direct mail competitors told me recently. "I always know a Ben Hart package when I see it because it's just so darned heavy."

Significantly, under nonprofit postage rates, you can go up to 3.2 ounces with your package and still qualify for paying the lowest postage rate—unlike with First Class mail where postage rates go up for each additional ounce. This gives writers and creative people great latitude to load up prospect packages with all kinds of material reasonably cheaply, paying little more than the cost of the additional paper and printing.

There's something about a lot of material stuffed in an envelope that conveys a sense that the organization is serious.

Your housefile letters don't need to be as long, as a general rule, because you are writing to people who have already supported you. They are friends. Asking your housefile to renew their membership makes sense, and should be done with a short one or two-page letter. But a membership renewal notice would not be appropriate for a prospect appeal.

Even if you decide to write a long housefile letter, which I often do, and load up the carrier with a lot of supplemental material, the kinds of material you include will be very different from a prospect package.

The most successful housefile packages are those launching a specific compelling new project, through a project that deals with the same problem or cause the organization was set up to address. A prospect package would much more likely make an appeal focusing on the organization's core mission. To use a commercial marketing analogy, your prospect appeals would try to sell "Coca Cola" (the proven winner) first, before attempting to sell a new soft drink or some variation of Coke, such as "Caffeine-Free Coke" or "Diet Coke."

The challenge with prospecting is to find one theme, one issue that works, and then stick with it. This becomes your control package. Until another package proves more successful than your control, you stick with your control. Successful control prospect packages can mail for years, even decades, sometimes virtually forever, hardly ever changing a word.

With housefile appeals, the challenge is to always come up with new angles and new reasons to write to the same people but still on the same theme or issue that built your housefile. If your housefile was built on Coca Cola, don't try to sell them TVs.

Another big difference is that prospect appeals, at least those that mail millions of copies, are usually generic "Dear Friend" offset letters. The only component that's personalized is the reply form, which shows through the window and flies the package.

This problem does not apply to limited circulation prospect appeals to highly select lists of people who contribute $50 or more to similar organizations. For these kinds of gold-plated lists, you can afford to send highly personalized appeals, and you should.

But for your mass-market appeals where you are striving to get an average donation of $15 or $17, you'll likely need to use a generic "Dear Friend" style form letter. The reason is cost. Personalizing the letter will add about a nickel to your cost, and just isn't worth it in most cases, particularly if you are anticipating a $16 average gift and a 2 percent or 3 percent response rate. You should always test this proposition, but that's what most large-scale direct mailers have found with their prospect programs.

Since you don't know very much about contributors on lists you rent for your prospect program, you won't know whether to ask your reader for $10, $20, $50, or $1,000, because you don't know what each reader typically contributes. So you'll need to offer a range of giving options, usually stretching from $15 to $1,000. The same string of suggested giving amount options are typeset on the reply form and sent to every prospective donor. "Can you send $15, $25, $50, $100 or perhaps even more?" are lines you will find in most mass-market prospecting appeals.

This, of course, undermines the personal feel of your prospect letter.

With housefile letters, I often ask for just one amount, calculated on the reader's previous giving history. I'll usually reference the amount of readers' previous contributions in the text of the letter. And I'll thank the readers for all their past support. I can't do any of this with most mass-market prospect appeals, because I don't know very much about each person I am writing to. I'm lacking the information I need for effective personalization.

But even with all these limitations hampering your prospect appeal, such as a lack of information about the reader and the requirement to keep the cost of your package low, there are steps you can take to make your prospect letter sound somewhat personal.

For example, you can mention, at least vaguely, how you got your reader's name. I'll say something like: "You and I may not have met personally yet, but your past activities tell me that you are politically active...."

Somewhere on the first page, I will say something like, "Before I explain further, please let me introduce myself. My name is John Smith. I am writing to you because...."

This sounds like something I might say in person if I wanted to introduce myself to a stranger.

I might also apologize for the impersonal form letter, but explain that "I am trying to cut costs so I can reach as many patriotic Americans as possible with this urgent call to action concerning...."

This is making lemonade out of lemons, that is, taking what should be a negative—an impersonal form letter—and turning this into a good thing—an effort to cut costs so I can reach more people on this urgently important issue.

I'll even admit that I'm sending a copy of this letter to hundreds of thousands, perhaps millions, of Americans as part of our national campaign to mobilize a nationwide grassroots army to pressure Congress to pass or stop some piece of legislation. This helps provide justification for the generic, non-personalized prospect letter.

You should not ignore the pink elephant in the room.

In the case of your prospect letter writing, the "pink elephant in the room" is the fact that the letter typically isn't personalized. I think it's a good idea to explain why. Cutting costs so you can reach more people with the vital information in the letter is a good reason. This explanation also demonstrates honesty to your reader because it's obviously the truth. You are candidly admitting a shortcoming. This helps give credibility for the rest of your appeal.

Some Important Additional Tips

Cartoons and drawings don't work. The exceptions to this rule are Christmas and other greeting card packages, packages that might contain a fine-art print, artwork on address labels (a commonly used technique). Still, never use cartoons to make your point.

Humor doesn't work in direct mail fundraising. Money, and asking for money, is a very serious topic.

Photos are often a great help. A photo can be worth a thousand words, especially if the photo shows what you say you're doing in your letter. Photos can also tug on heartstrings.

Direct mail involves trade-offs. You can't put everything you want to in the package because of cost. As much as deciding what to include, you must decide what to leave out.

A fundraising appeal should not look like commercial mail. It should look homemade and amateurish. The slicker the mailing looks, the worse it will do.

A fundraising appeal should talk about past successes. Potential donors want a track record. Testimonials, a letter from a celebrity, or newspaper clippings on the organization are all good devices for establishing *bona fides*. Donors want to know what you did with their donation last month before they send another donation this month.

How Much Should You Ask For?

This goes to knowing who your readers are, knowing your audience.

For housefile letters, I know what people are used to giving from their previous giving history, which has been faithfully entered into a computer database as past contributions have come in. If a reader's "Highest Previous Contribution" (HPC in direct mail jargon) is $1,000, don't ask this person for $20. Not only would asking a $1,000 donor for $20 drastically decrease the amount of money your letter would raise, but you risk insulting your reader by telegraphing your ignorance of your reader's previous contributions to your organization.

If your reader's HPC is $100, I would likely ask for $100 again. Or I might try to make the case for sending a $150 or $200 contribution as part of an upgrade strategy, especially when writing to people who have contributed to the organization more than once. For a membership type of appeal, I might ask for less than their HPC, perhaps half of their HPC in an effort to maximize the rate of response.

The key point is to base your contribution request strategy on the previous giving history of the donor. You can ask for more or less than HPC, but have a reason for requesting the amount you're asking for. Have a strategy in mind. I'll almost always explicitly state my reason for asking for the specific amount right in the letter.

I might say something like:

```
You have generously sent this amount before.
I'm hoping you can contribute this amount
again.
```

Or

```
I'm basing my request in part on what you have
contributed so generously before and in part
on what we need from each of our very best
friends and supporters to fully fund this cam-
paign if everyone I am writing contributes.
```

Or

```
I am asking our friends and supporters who
customarily contribute $100 to send $100
again, and those who customarily send $50 to
send $50 again. That way I know I'm not asking
anyone to send more than they can comfortably
afford. If everyone contributes what they can,
we will have the funds we need to carry out
this campaign.
```

Notice how explicitly stating how you arrived at the amount of the contribution request adds to the personal feel of your letter. The reader understands you are writing to many people, and that you are asking many others to chip in with a donation, but the reader also feels you are speaking directly and personally to the reader as an individual. You are answering the question as to why you are asking for this particular contribution amount. The amount you are requesting is not just a number pulled out of the air.

Rather than key your ask strategy off your reader's HPC, you might sometimes use Most Recent Contribution (MRC) as the basis for calculating how much to ask for, or perhaps an average of their three MRCs. I generally prefer using the reader's HPC as the key piece of data guiding me as to the level of contribution I request. But whether you decide to use HPC, MRC, or an average of their three MRCs, the crucial point is to base your request on what your reader customarily contributes.

When you are prospecting, you often don't have this information. All you might know is that the names on this list you're renting contributed $5 or more to some other organization in the last 18 months. In this case, you don't have the information you need to tailor the ask amount to your reader's previous giving history. You'll need to offer a string of giving options, typically ranging from $10 or $15 to $500 and "Other $_____." This certainly undermines the personal feel of your prospect letter, which is often an offset, generic "Dear Friend" style letter anyway. But you have little choice.

One way to get around this problem in your prospecting, at least partially, is to find out what the average contribution of the list you are renting is likely to be and to ask for that amount. You can find this out by testing the list or checking the past performance of the list if you've rented it before. Let's say the average contribution for a particular list is $14. Ask for $14. If the average contribution on the prospect list you're mailing is $50, ask for $50. The weakness of this approach is that you'll be leaving larger contributions on the table, because people tend to contribute what you ask for, not a penny more. So, when prospecting, test this approach against offering your reader a wide-ranging string of giving options.

The Purpose of Graphic Art

Graphic art and appearance is crucial to the success of a direct mail package, but not to make the package look pretty.

The purpose of graphic art is to enhance the central message of a package, not to dazzle people with fancy graphics.

So often I've seen graphic art actually obscure the message of a direct mail piece.

Graphics should enable your reader to grasp the message of your package in three seconds or less. Simple layouts are best. Not only are they far less costly to produce, but simple is more effective. In direct mail fundraising it's plain Jane, not the prettiest girl at the party who wins.

Words, not graphics—not even pictures, are the most powerful way to communicate ideas. If you use photos, they are to reinforce your words. Photos may or may not be useful in your appeal, and can help you get the attention of your reader. But it's the copy that does the selling. You can sell without pictures; you can't sell without words. The Bible has no pictures, only words, and it's the best selling book of all time.

Of course, you want your packages to look good. But for fundraising, as opposed to commercial mail, the packages should have a homemade, amateurish look to them. Otherwise the donor thinks you're spending too much money on the mailings. Plus, what makes fundraising mail work is that the letters should look like they are coming from an individual and should be as personal as cost allows. Fundraising letters should not look like they are coming from a corporation.

Also, make every effort to change the look of your packages. Try not to fall into a rut of making everything look the same. Use different borders and layouts while being careful not to allow the graphic art to overwhelm the headlines.

For your letter, use an old fashioned typewriter type, such as Courier or Prestige fonts. You can use the desktop publishing fonts like Times Roman and Helvetica for other enclosures and inserts, but not for the letter.

The look and feel of your packages can be changed dramatically simply by using different colored and textured paper stocks. Use a variety of envelope sizes, and keep up with all the formats that are available. Varying formats, carrier envelopes and paper colors will do a lot to make packages look different. I often mail letters in boxes, tubes, clear envelopes, manila folders, bubble packs, sometimes even between two pieces of cardboard stapled or taped together. And there are all kinds of self-mailer formats.

New formats and ideas are coming out all the time. Visit lettershops to find out what others are mailing. Meet with printers and envelope manufacturers to find out what's available to vary the look and feel of your packages.

Write a Package, Not Just a Letter

The letter is the heart of your package. The letter is certainly the most important element of your package.

But your package contains other key components, including a contribution or reply form, a reply envelope, and a carrier, at a bare minimum.

I almost always include a variety of inserts, perhaps photographs, a sheet of testimonials, a budget, a track record of the organization's achievements, or some item that the reader will find useful, such as a bumper sticker, a booklet, or a list of action steps the reader can take to help achieve the goal outlined in the letter.

I will draw attention to and explain the various inserts in the letter.

The key point here is this: Every element of the package must lead the reader back to the reason you are writing. You need contributions *now* to achieve some specific goal. No matter what element of the package the reader picks up, the reader should be hit over the head with the same message. Don't have different messages and different themes conveyed with your inserts. With every direct appeal, you must market one and only one concept, one

Big Idea. The purpose of every element of the package is to underscore the one single overarching reason you are writing.

Some inserts can reinforce different aspects of the one Big Idea you are selling. For example, testimonials and track records show the reader that you have a long history of achieving what you set out to achieve. You can document your successes.

But testimonials and track records must be directly on point with the theme of your letter. If you're writing about what your organization is doing to find a cure for cancer, don't insert a track record on your success with assisting hospitalized veterans. Any insert or enclosure that is off point, even slightly, will distract and confuse your readers, can undermine your credibility, and will depress returns.

The Outer Envelope: The Competition for Attention

You can write the greatest fundraising copy in the world, but if no one notices your letter in the mailbox, if it just looks like all the other junk mail, your appeal is doomed.

Big consumer product companies know this, which is why they spend so much money, time, effort, and research on packaging. They want their product to stand out on the shelf in a supermarket. You want your letter to stand out in the mailbox.

Chapter Seven on "Techniques" will give you many ways to make sure your appeal is noticed by your readers.

I pay a lot of attention to the outer envelope or carrier, also called the wrapper on self-mailers. Getting the recipient of your letter to open your envelope is the first battle you must win with your reader.

When people sort their mail, they generally put them in three piles: personal letters from friends and relatives; bills they must pay by a certain date; and commercial junk mail.

Most commercial junk mail, including fundraising solicitations, will go into the trash. A few pieces of bulk rate or non-profit rate mail will be kept if they look intriguing.

Since everyone reads personal letters from friends and relatives that arrive with First Class postage, your best strategy is to send your letter with First Class postage stamps and make your envelope look like it contains a personal letter from a friend. These letters should arrive in a nonwindow closed-face envelope. A handwritten address on the carrier is best of all.

Everyone who receives such an envelope will open it.

This is great for your very best donors, those who you think will contribute $50 or more. But the problem with sending a First Class letter to most of your housefile, and for prospect appeals, is cost. It's just too expensive to send a First Class highly personalized letter to donors whose average contribution is $15 or $20 and who have only a 3 percent or 4 percent chance of responding.

For these folks, you have no choice but to send them bulk rate or nonprofit rate mail, which knocks 10 to 20 cents off the cost of your lowest rate First Class letter.

When you're sending bulk rate or nonprofit rate mail, you must come up with other ways to entice people to open your envelope.

Usually the best way is to create a sense of mystery and intrigue. Sometimes the most effective strategy is with no copy or teaser at all. Just a blank envelope, not even an address. Another strategy is to make your envelope look like an important government document, as if it might be from the IRS or the Department of Motor Vehicles. "Monitored Delivery" is a phrase I sometimes use on my outer envelopes. "Financial Documents Enclosed" is a phrase I sometimes use if the package contains a budget document or prospectus.

As a general rule, headline-style teaser copy broadcasting what's inside the envelope is hazardous. Extensive testing shows most teasers depress response. One reason is that headline-style advertising copy on outer envelopes telegraphs to the reader that this is advertising or fundraising mail, that it's junk mail.

But a really good teaser can sometimes outperform a mysterious carrier. A teaser I used stated in big bold red type: "At last . . . a Christian Alternative to AARP!" This worked better than all other outer envelope approaches I tried with this particular prospecting appeal.

Why?

Because there were millions of Christians out there who were interested in a Christian Alternative to AARP. Enough senior citizens were peeved enough with AARP's consistently liberal lobbying activities that this opened up a market for a conservative Christian alternative. I mailed millions of copies of this letter for the Christian Seniors Association. But even here, the mystery carriers worked almost as well.

Using a headline on the outer envelope to grab interest is a risky proposition. When in doubt, I'll use the far safer strategy of creating a sense of mystery.

In most cases, I don't like to put the name of the organization on the outer envelope, even for housefile appeals to my most loyal supporters.

Not only does putting the name of the organization on the carrier envelope advertise that this is probably a fundraising solicitation, it also tells the reader that this is not a personal letter from a friend. It screams that this is an institutional mailing, which automatically places the letter in a second, third, or even lower category of importance.

Think of the psychology of envelope opening this way.

Is a child more excited at Christmas to see a pile of presents wrapped in colored paper hiding what's inside all those boxes? Or would the child prefer to arrive at the tree on Christmas morning and see all her presents in plain view with no pretty wrapping paper?

It's far more exciting to have no idea what's in all those boxes. Children are delirious with delight as they frantically rip off all that wrapping paper to find out what's hiding inside.

I think the same psychology is at work in designing outer envelopes for your direct mail appeals. More often than not, you will do better by creating a sense of mystery and intrigue with your envelopes—but not always.

There's also a lot to be said for that one unwrapped present standing under the Christmas tree if it's an especially wonderful present, a present that will create excitement by itself, even though not wrapped—perhaps a shiny red bicycle.

I agonize for hours, sometimes days, over what to put on my outer envelope. Is the cause compelling and exciting enough to broadcast what's inside with a headline-style teaser? Or should I stick with the far safer mystery strategy.

Ninety percent of the time I will opt for creating mystery with my outer envelopes.

However, don't use the mystery strategy if you're fortunate enough to have your letter signed by a celebrity or famous person. In that case, you'll want to advertise that the envelope contains a letter from a celebrity. Do this by putting the famous person's name in the upper left corner of the carrier. Make the envelope look like it contains a personal letter from the famous person. The outer envelope should be designed to look like it's the famous person's personal stationery.

But please heed this word of caution. Be careful here not to run afoul of postal regulations. If you want to mail under nonprofit postal rates, you must not include the address of the organization along with the name of the celebrity. It's not important why, just know that you can't. Instead, print the

Figure 5.2

name of the celebrity by itself in the upper left corner of the carrier with no return address. Also, use a meter, not a nonprofit stamp.

For some reason, you're not required to include the organization's name or return address on the carrier if you use a meter to preserve your nonprofit postal rate, but you are if you use a nonprofit stamp. Go figure. Since postal regulations are changing all the time, it's always safest to take your carrier design to the post office for approval before printing it if you're concerned about mailing the package under nonprofit postal rates.

The Reply Envelope

Pay attention to the reply envelope. Put text on reply envelopes reminding the reader to "please use this reply envelope to send your contribution" or some text to remind readers what action steps you want taken and to draw attention to the reply envelope. Never pass up an opportunity to remind the reader of the need for a donation.

Remind the reader what else to include in the reply envelope besides a contribution, perhaps a survey or signed petition. Remind the reader to "please be sure to sign and date your contribution check," which is another way to remind the reader of the need for a contribution. Make the reply envelope as big as possible. People don't put large checks in tiny reply envelopes. I sometimes like to fold the reply envelope to draw attention to it. Sometimes I put graphics on the reply envelope to approximate the look of a USPS Priority Mail envelope or FedEx envelope.

For more generous donors I'll actually include a USPS Priority Mail reply envelope. Or I'll affix First Class postage stamps to the reply envelope to emphasize the need for a reply. If you decide to spend the money to affix First Class postage to the reply envelope, be sure to use at least three stamps that add up to the First Class postage rate, never just one stamp. I like to use as many as eight stamps on the reply envelope to draw the reader's attention to the reply envelope.

Most direct mail packages I see miss an opportunity to use the reply envelope to underscore the need for a contribution and a rapid response. Sometimes I list benefits on the back of the reply envelope: "Your contribution of $15 or more will entitle you to receive...."

I believe focusing special attention on the reply envelope can boost response 20 percent.

BRE or Non-BRE Reply Envelopes

You should constantly test whether business reply envelopes (BREs) or just plain preaddressed reply envelopes work better. My test results go back and forth, and vary depending on the organization. The advantage of the BRE is that the donor doesn't need to hunt for a stamp to respond, and you only pay the post office for those BREs that come back.

Anything you can do to make it easier for the donor to answer your letter is a plus.

Commercial mailers almost always use a BRE.

The disadvantage for fundraising mail is that a BRE can come across as too institutional and undermines the personal look of the letter. Remember, fundraising mail should have a homemade amateurish look to it. The slicker fundraising mail

Figure 5.3

looks, the worse it does as a general rule. It starts to look like junk mail.

Also, with survey packages or other involvement device packages that generate a lot of nondonor responders (often four nondonors for every donor), you may not want to pay the postage on every nondonor BRE you receive. So you'll want to conduct regular testing to determine the cost-benefit of including a BRE, or not. Lately I've been using mostly non-BRE reply envelopes, where the donors need to affix their own postage to send a donation. But I'm getting ready to do another round of testing to see if I should move back to BREs for all, or most, of my fundraising mail.

Track the Results

Carefully follow the results of your package. Look at donor to nondonor ratios. Are there too many nondonors? That will tell you something about the package. Is the average gift too low for a particular group of donors, for example, a $28 average gift from those who usually give $50 or $100? How are different lists performing? Should the package be written differently for different lists? Usually the answer is "Yes." Is the package performing well to low-dollar names, but not as well as it should to high-dollar names?

These are questions you should constantly ask about every package. Every package should undergo a rigorous autopsy.

CHAPTER 6

Getting the Most
From Your Housefile

How Often Should You Mail
to Your Housefile?

I scratch my head in amazement at how many charities and nonprofits mail fundraising letters to their supporters only once or twice a year.

The notion here is that "We don't want to wear out our welcome with our supporters."

What a catastrophic mistake this is!

Do Nike, Coca Cola, and McDonald's only hit you with one or two ads a year for fear they might wear out their welcome in your home?

No. They hit you with ad after ad until you can't get their ads out of your mind. You find yourself humming their theme songs and repeating their slogans to yourself. Above all, you buy their products. You buy their products because their ads have hammered out a space in your brain. You can't get their ads out of your mind.

My six-year-old daughter, Victoria, saw a box of Oxiclean detergent on the shelf in the grocery store. She asked, "Mom, are we going to buy Oxiclean?"

"Why?" her mom asked.

"Because bleach destroys your clothes. Oxiclean cleans your clothes," Victoria answered.

No telling how many times little Victoria had seen the Oxiclean ad. I'm sure it was many, many times. She knew the ad's exact slogan by heart. At age six, she might not have been able to read the words on the box, but she certainly recognized the design of the box, which immediately prompted her to repeat the ad's slogan: "Bleach destroys your clothes. Oxiclean cleans your clothes." That's what an advertiser wants. The advertiser had achieved its goal with little Victoria with relentless repetition of the same ad and the same slogan.

Now I can't get this slogan out of my mind: "Bleach destroys your clothes. Oxiclean cleans your clothes."

I'll bet you'll be thinking all day about this phrase now too. Sorry about that.

Relentless, mind-numbing repetition is the key to effective advertising. Effective advertising is a form of brainwashing.

When you think sneakers and sports attire, and now athletic equipment, you think Nike. When you think soft drink, you think Coke. When you think fast food hamburgers, you think McDonald's.

If you're running a nonprofit organization, you need to think like these companies. You need to think: "How do I become the Coca Cola of my issue?" whether your issue is curing cancer, abolishing the IRS, or banning handguns. You want your organization to become synonymous with your cause—like Kleenex is to tissue paper or Xerox is to copiers.

You do that by mailing often to your housefile.

And you do that by mailing as much prospect mail as you can possibly afford.

As with all advertising, there does come a point of diminishing returns. But I submit that 95 percent or more of nonprofits do not send enough mail to their housefile.

They worry about offending donors and burning out their list. This is a misplaced concern.

Your supporters send contributions because they support what you are doing. They like you. They want to hear more from you. They want to know about the progress you are making. They want to know about your successes. They understand that you rely on contributions to fund your operations.

If you go to church on Sundays, wouldn't you be surprised if the collection plate was only passed around once or twice a year?

No church could operate for long with that approach.

In every church I've attended, the collection plate is passed around every Sunday, sometimes twice on Sunday, if there is a special need. And no one is offended because everyone understands that a church needs contributions every week to operate.

Direct mail is like passing the collection plate from afar.

A direct mail letter is a collection plate arriving in your mailbox.

In my housefile letters, I usually prepare my reader to expect more letters to arrive in the coming weeks and months, updating them on the organization's activities. I'll mention an important breaking development that I'll keep the supporter informed about as details become clearer.

In addition, I always explain in my housefile letters how the organization I'm writing for relies on regular, faithful support. I hammer this point home over and over again.

I explain how thankful I am for every donation we receive, but that operations and projects of the charity are funded primarily by those who make a commitment to send regular donations.

If some of your donors express irritation at the frequency of mail, you can always flag those donors and mail to them less often. You will certainly receive a few of those kinds of complaint letters. But that will be a very small percentage of your donors. Your supporters contribute to you because they believe strongly in what you are doing and they understand the importance of your cause.

If your supporters only hear from you once in a while, they will conclude that maybe your projects are not so important after all. They will then find another charity that is doing the work they thought you were engaged in.

Your Battle for Market Share

Here's another important fact of life.

Your supporters have a certain amount of discretionary money every year that they will contribute to something.

They will contribute this money to causes they care about no matter what—whether they receive your mailings or not.

Your mailings are the only opportunity you have to persuade these people to send part of their annual charitable contribution budget to you. If your letter does not arrive, their contributions will go into someone else's reply envelope.

Those organizations that mail infrequently to their housefile begin to lose their housefile to other organizations, just like McDonald's would lose its market share to Burger King if it stopped advertising. If you mail infrequently to your housefile, your housefile will get weaker, not stronger. Frequent mailings will actually serve to strengthen your housefile by reinforcing the impression in the minds of donors that you are doing a lot, that you are an organization that's on the move and gathering momentum.

In this respect, a nonprofit is no different from any other commercial business. You are in a competition for market share and customers. We just call our customers donors.

Make Your Organization Part of Your Supporter's Regular Routine

Another iron law of marketing is that people are creatures of habit.

I always buy Crest toothpaste.

I don't know why. I just always have, I guess because my mom bought Crest when I was a kid. I know I need toothpaste. I know this toothpaste works. And Crest is well known because of relentless advertising over many decades.

It would take some effort to persuade me to switch to another toothpaste. Other companies are spending billions of dollars to persuade people to use their toothpaste instead of Crest.

But they aren't having much impact on me because I'm used to Crest. I'm comfortable with that brand.

People who have chosen to contribute to your organization instead of your competitor would prefer to stick with you. To switch their allegiance to another organization is to admit that they had made a wrong decision to support you—in effect, to admit a failure.

It's very difficult to change people's buying patterns, because this means moving people out of their comfort zone.

Most people are creatures of habit.

But you will lose your customers (donors) if they lose sight of you—that is, if they stop receiving mail. Or if they receive mail so infrequently that you are no longer a part of their regular routine, no longer a part of their everyday life.

If your organization is supported by direct mail contributions, your donors should receive a mailing every two weeks or so—if not a fundraising letter, a newsletter or some communication. You can send a fundraising letter to your housefile every 21 days. You must constantly put your organization in front of your supporters—just like Nike, Coca Cola, McDonald's and every successful corporation that depends on the average consumer for business.

This is such a basic principle of marketing that I am stunned at how few nonprofits understand it.

Of course, there is a point of diminishing returns. If you mailed a fundraising letter to your housefile every day, your donors would not have enough time to respond to one mailing before getting hit with the next letter.

I think 21 days separating housefile appeals is best. With three weeks separating appeals, your letters won't step on each other and you'll be able to maximize net income from your housefile.

But aside from your fundraising appeals going out every 21 days, you can also send a newsletter and email alerts on a breaking issue of importance to your supporters, telephone thank you calls and thank you gifts. All these additional (non-fundraising) bonding programs will also help make your organization an important part of the daily, or at least weekly, lives of your supporters.

The Value of "Multigivers"

Your mailings to donors who have contributed more than once to your organization (multigivers) will be at least three times more productive than mailings to those who have not yet sent a second contribution (single givers).

Of the donors you find with your prospect program, you are doing well if you can persuade 60 percent to contribute again. For me, the most depressing aspect about direct mail fundraising is that nearly half the folks who contribute to a prospect mailing will never contribute to your organization again.

But the good news is that those who do contribute again (those who become multigivers) will usually stay with you as regular supporters for a very long time.

That's another reason you want to mail often to your housefile, at least once a month.

You want to identify your multigivers as quickly as possible, because multigivers are at least three times more productive than those donors who have not yet sent a second contribution.

A mature housefile is far more productive than a new housefile for the simple reason that you have identified your core of multigivers—your regular, faithful supporters.

In addition, you stop mailing regular housefile mailings to most of those who have not contributed in 18 or 24 months, which slashes the cost of your housefile mailings. That's why an older housefile with a lot of multiple donors will often generate $1, $2 or even $3 net income for each name you mail, compared to a new housefile which will generate between 40 and 60 cents in net income for each name you mail.

The older the housefile, the more productive it will be for each letter you mail.

For this reason, I consider the prospect program to really have two parts. There's the prospect program to your outside lists, designed to find your first-time donors.

But then there's the prospect program to your housefile that's aimed at persuading your first-time donors to send a second contribution. In this sense, your multigivers are your true housefile, because these are folks who clearly like what they see from your organization and who have made a conscious decision to continue supporting you. They have chosen to join your family.

The 80/20 Rule

With the above discussion in mind on the immense value of your multigivers, another way to think about this is the "80/20 rule"—which means 80 percent of your *net* income from your housefile will come from the best 20 percent of your supporters.

These are your super multigivers. These are your diehard supporters—folks who contribute frequently, including some who contribute nearly every time you ask.

These people should be treated very differently from everyone else on your housefile. They should receive highly personalized letters that don't look mass produced. Instead of spending the usual 40 or 50 cents on a letter for the bottom 80 percent of your housefile, you might spend $1, $2, $3, or even $5 per letter when writing to your very best donors.

The best 20 percent of donors on your housefile should receive thank you phone calls in addition to thank you letters and emails, as well as regular updates on your activities.

Many of these donors should receive handwritten thank you notes instead of the mass-produced thank yous you're sending to the rest of your housefile. Your top 20 percent of donors should receive thank you gifts (calendars, lapel pins, etc.), Christmas cards, and invitations to meetings. These donors should be treated like the dear friends they are to you and your cause. The top 20 percent of donors on your housefile are the lifeblood of your organization.

Those who send a contribution of $500 or more should immediately be placed in an even more special category.

As a general rule, someone who has never met you, but who sent $500 or $1,000 in answer to one of your letters, is capable of giving ten times that amount if they meet you in person. As soon as that $500 or $1,000 gift arrives, that donor should receive an immediate thank you phone call. And during the course of this phone call, schedule a one-on-one personal meeting. Building this relationship will be well worth the price of a plane ticket.

But don't make the mistake of stopping to send these folks your fundraising letters.

I am incredulous when organizations stop writing to donors who give $500, $1,000 or more—out of fear of offending these donors with too much mail. These major donors are on your housefile list because they answered one of your direct mail letters. They are direct mail responsive. They support you because they like what they read in your letters.

But you should spend more effort and money on your major donors. Spend money to personalize every page. Write to them as you would write to a personal friend. Give these donors personal attention. Consider sending letters FedEx or in a USPS Priority Mail envelope. I'll further develop this last point later in this book in Chapter Eight.

How Much Should You Spend on a Letter?

When calculating cost, determine first to whom you are writing.

You can spend more when writing to someone who customarily contributes $100 than you can when writing to someone who contributes at most $15. You might spend $2 or perhaps even $4 on a package to a $100+ contributor, $1 or as high as $2 when writing to a $50 contributor, while you should not spend more than about 50 cents when writing to $10, $15, and $20 contributors.

The key is to calculate your expected response rate and the average expected gift. Each housefile is different and varies in responsiveness, so I can't give you hard and fast rules here. But you can know your likely average gift from the donor's giving history. You also know each donor's likely chance of answering your letter from past results of your mailings. So a 5 percent response rate and a $100 average gift will produce a very different financial picture from a 5 percent response rate and a $15 average gift. In this instance, you could spend $2 to write to the $100 contributor, but should only spend 40 cents to write to the $15 contributor.

But some types of packages and techniques historically generate 10 percent response rates, but are more costly to produce. Still, the extra cost is worth it because it will drive up the response rate. Always ask: Will an increased response rate justify the additional cost? And will the additional cost produce a higher response rate?

Also, risk/reward analysis is a key factor in determining how much extra cost you want to add to a package.

Pushing response rates up 2 percent for your $100+ contributors is very different from pushing response rates up 2 percent for your $15 contributors. Because there are far fewer $100+ donors on most housefiles, and the return is far greater for these folks for each letter you mail, the risk/reward is far more favorable here than for the $15 donor.

In other words, invest your money in the high end of the file, the top 15 to 20 percent of your contributors. The returns will be far greater, the risk far lower.

The "Thank You" Program

Common courtesy requires you to thank people for their gifts. Your thank you program is also essential to the success of your overall direct mail fundraising effort.

Your contributors will expect to receive a thank you note for their contributions. Of course, there is a cost to sending thank you notes. I generally do not send thank you letters for donations under $10. It's just too expensive to thank donors who contribute less than $10.

I'll make an exception to my *"no thank yous for contributions less than $10 rule"* if my mailings are asking for less than $10. Some charities do just fine asking for $8 in their prospect campaigns. In this case, you would want to thank anyone who gives $5 or more, because these donors are basically just contributing what you asked for and will likely contribute more in the future.

Your thank you note should mention the amount of the donation sent and explain to the donor specifically what you used the contribution to achieve.

If possible, include a news clipping about your activities with your thank you note, especially powerful if the news clipping is about the project you were raising money for. If you don't have a relevant news clipping, include an insert outlining your progress or track record. This will show donors that their decision to contribute was a good one—a wise investment.

I don't like including a reply form with my thank yous, because then the thank you note begins to look like another fundraising appeal. The donor should feel she has been thanked with your thank you note, not set up for another ask for money.

For this reason, I also don't like thank you receipts, which are sent by many large charities. I don't feel I've really been thanked if I receive a machine-generated thank you receipt in return for my donation.

A thank you should look like a personal letter or note. The more personal and homemade-looking, the better.

I usually include a return envelope with my thank you letter, but with no specific ask for money, except perhaps a general statement in context of thanking the donor about how the organization relies entirely on voluntary contributions to fund its projects. The contributions that come back in these return envelopes will usually be enough to pay for the entire thank you program.

I realize that including a return envelope with your thank you note tends to undermine somewhat the warm fuzzy feeling of appreciation you are trying to create with your thank you. But as long as there is no contribution reply form, no heavy ask for money, and no reference to the return envelope in the letter, your thank you will still come across as a true thank you and not as just another fundraising solicitation.

The reality is, the organization needs money to operate. A thank you program is costly. And simply throwing a return envelope in with your thank you letter will allow you to cover the cost of your thank you program.

For first-time donors, consider sending a more elaborate welcome package. When you first join the NRA, you receive a large bubble pack with a shooter's cap and an NRA magazine. The NRA gives you several magazines to choose from. And you also receive a thank you note that gushes appreciation, welcomes you to the NRA family, outlines your benefits of membership and describes crucial upcoming battles in Congress concerning attacks on your Second Amendment rights.

Your thank you note should be sent immediately after the donation arrives. No more than a day or two should pass before your thank you note goes out. If too much times passes, your donor (especially a first-time contributor) likely will have forgotten about the donation and quite possibly have forgotten about your organization. But a rapidly arriving thank you note will make a great impression.

For donations of $50 or more, send a handwritten thank you on a heavy note card. I know some women who have made a cottage industry of writing handwritten thank yous on note cards.

Those who contribute $100 or more should receive a personal phone call thank you from the letter signer or someone closely associated with the organization. Your extra effort in thanking your donors properly will reap huge returns down the road.

Your relationship with your donors is just like your other personal relationships. The more you put into a relationship, the more you will get back in return. Thanking your donors in thoughtful and creative ways is much more than just good manners, it will dramatically increase the returns on all your housefile mailings. You should spend as much time and effort coming up with new and imaginative ways to thank your donors as you do asking for contributions.

My longtime friend Morton Blackwell runs an organization called the Leadership Institute that trains young people how to become effective activists for the conservative cause. He conducts programs to teach young conservatives how to manage political campaigns, get jobs in government, become chief-of-staff for a congressman, start a conservative student newspaper and become a journalist. His organization raises in excess of $10 million a year, all from voluntary contributions. He also harvests honey from beehives as a hobby. Morton sends jars of his honey to his best donors every year for a Christmas gift and as a thank you for their support over the past year.

Now that's the kind of thoughtful thank you donors will remember. And it sure pays off for Morton.

Newsletters

Every nonprofit organization should have a newsletter, at least those organizations that seek donations through the mail.

Like your thank you program, your newsletter is designed to bond your donors to your organization. The purpose of the newsletter is to describe in detail how your organization is using the contributions you are receiving.

A newsletter should also include information that you know will be of interest to your supporters. If the purpose of your organization is to cure cancer, have a regular feature in your newsletter on how to reduce the risk of getting cancer — though this feature should be secondary in importance to articles on how you are using contributions effectively to achieve the organization's purpose.

A newsletter can also include a regular feature article about a particular donor. This is a great way to thank a special contributor, as well as emphasize the need for contributions. People like reading human interest features about particular people. That's the whole idea behind publications like *People* magazine.

Newsletters should also include letters from contributors, especially letters and testimonials on how great your organization is. Include letters from contributors in your newsletter to communicate to your donors that you care what they think and that they have a voice in your organization.

Your newsletter can be monthly or quarterly. This decision will be governed in part by how much news you have to report.

Just make sure you have a regular schedule for your newsletter. A newsletter that arrives sporadically with no set schedule gives the impression of a haphazard organization. If you're a subscriber to *Time* magazine, you would be irritated if some weeks your magazine arrived on Mondays, other weeks Wednesdays, other weeks Fridays, or did not arrive at all some weeks.

So set a schedule for your newsletter and stick with it, at least until you decide to make a conscious change in the schedule.

As with every other aspect of your direct mail program, your newsletter schedule should be a conscious decision, not simply allowed to drift with an "I'll put out a newsletter when I can get to it" attitude.

A newsletter should be scannable and easy to read: no long articles with a lot of text. Newsletters should include photographs that show what you are doing with contributions.

Newsletters demonstrate to your donors that your organization is real and doing real things.

A lot of thought should be put into what's in your newsletter. It's far better to have no newsletter at all than the wrong newsletter.

Your newsletter should also include a reply form that

encourages a contribution, and possibly a cover letter that explains why contributions are needed. Your newsletter program should generate net income for your organization, though not as much as a regular fundraising appeal.

Instead of newsletters, some large nonprofit organizations have institutional magazines. AARP's magazine is one of the largest circulation magazines in the world. It's sent free to all AARP members and is paid for by advertisers who want to reach the seniors market. AARP's magazine is an enormous profit center for AARP.

Most nonprofit organizations are not large enough to justify a monthly institutional magazine. But every direct mail-supported nonprofit organization needs a newsletter.

How to Handle Lapsed Donors

Lapsed donors are former donors who have not contributed in the past 12 or 18 months. For lapsed donors I generally don't like to send them special lapsed donor or "why hast thou forsaken me?" letters for the simple reason that I don't like to remind people that they've stopped supporting my organization. I just send them successful prospect packages. This approach has the added merit of making my lapsed donor program much easier to manage.

I will also find out what kinds of packages lapsed donors have responded to in the past, and send the same kind of package. If I know that a lapsed donor answered a survey package in the past, I'll send a survey package—of course, on the same issue as before.

When you think about it, a "why hast thou forsaken me?" or "where have you gone?" letter is not the kind of letter your lapsed donors have ever answered in the past (at least as far as you know). Send your lapsed donors the kinds of packages you know they have answered. If you know from their past history that they like Coca Cola, don't try to sell them Pepsi, or worse, chocolate milk.

CHAPTER 7

77 Techniques to Increase Response

The purpose of the technique (sometimes called a "gimmick" by my clients) is to get attention for your letter and reinforce the message of your appeal. I always review my list of techniques before I sit down to write a fundraising appeal.

Many of the techniques and strategies described below can and should be combined. Each technique has many variations. But here's my basic list.

1. The Survey Package

Including a survey almost always improves response in a direct mail package. A survey is so valuable as a direct mail technique that just about the only reason you would not include a survey in your direct mail package is that you simply can't include a survey in every fundraising letter you write, because that would just look silly. And eventually your surveys would not be believable.

But I'm starting to question even that assumption.

I'm starting to assume you should include some kind of survey—even if only two or three questions—in almost every direct mail fundraising letter, at least for issue-advocacy and political appeals.

Why?

Apparently, people, especially those who have strongly held political beliefs, want to express their opinion, on whatever subject.

I think this truth relates back to why direct mail fundraising works in the first place.

People contribute to direct mail fundraising appeals because they want to make a difference.

They know perfectly well that their $15 donation is not going to solve the entire problem. But they believe it will do some good.

It seems almost arrogant for an organization to ask for a donation but then not show any interest in the opinions of the donor. Why not ask for their opinions? Why not make some effort to find out what your supporters actually think?

Surveys work especially well for political causes. Political cause supporters are faithful voters. They know their vote will make only a very tiny difference, if any difference at all. But they vote anyway, out of a kind of patriotic duty. They vote also because they have strong opinions.

The survey technique harnesses this desire for your political issue supporters to express themselves. They know their $15 donation is needed to help advance their cause. But they want their opinions to count as well.

There are many ways to construct a survey package.

Do you lead with the request for a donation? Or do you lead with the request to fill out the survey?

This is a key strategic question the copywriter must answer. The answer is not an easy one.

Essential to a successful survey package is that the survey not come across as an afterthought. The importance of the reader participating in the survey must be essential to the entire package. You must make the case for the importance of the survey. You must explain why completing the survey is worth the reader's valuable time. You must explain exactly how you intend to use the results of the survey, and how this survey will make a difference in advancing the cause the reader cares about. You must make the survey look impressive with graphics and layout, which helps convey its importance. You must explain why this particular survey is different from other surveys the reader may have taken part in or read about in newspapers.

You are asking for the reader's time by asking her to fill out this poll. That's as serious a subject as asking the reader for money. Be sure to ask intelligent questions in the survey. Ask questions that will hit the reader's emotional hot button, but the questions should not come across as loaded. Don't insult your reader's intelligence with excessively biased questions. Your readers will recognize a poll that is not serious and pitch it in the trash.

Be imaginative in naming and packaging your surveys. Ballot, Census, Questionnaire and Poll are variations you might use. Have a good reason for your survey. Putting your survey in booklet form or putting your survey in its own separate envelope inside the carrier are ways to make your survey look impressive and serious. Be sure your Contribution Reply is part of the survey document; otherwise you'll receive too many surveys without contributions.

If constructed properly, the survey serves four important goals of your direct mail appeal:

1. You give readers an outlet to express their opinions in a way that holds out the promise of making a difference.
2. Your survey questions should reiterate the essential points of your fundraising letter in Q&A format. Design your questions so they will elicit a strong emotional response pertaining to the topic you're writing about, but not loaded or obviously biased questions (this is the tricky part).
3. You'll find out what your supporters actually think. Many surveys you'll receive by return mail will also include handwritten notes from your supporters. Study these notes as well as answers to the survey questions to

discern a pattern of concern that will help you write more powerful fundraising appeals to this audience in the future.

4. The survey will act as an involvement device that will draw your reader into your package and increase the likelihood of a contribution. In fact, including a survey will almost always increase the number of contributions you will receive in response to your letter.

There are exceptions to rule four above. Rare though they may be, there are some occasions when including a survey will not increase contributions to a political issue appeal.

That exception usually involves raising money for a towering political figure—such as the President of the United States.

Including a survey in a reelection letter signed by, say, the President of the United States, would likely depress results. Better in that case just to send prospective donors a one-page note. Better in that case to dispense with virtually every conventional direct mail fundraising rule, technique and gimmick. Better in that case just to make the letter as personal as possible, as though it was penned by the President's own hand on his personal letterhead. That would be such a powerful appeal

Figure 7.1

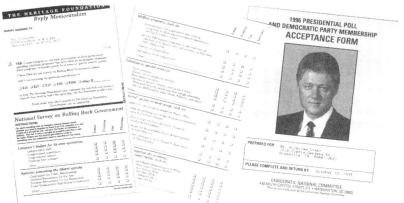

that including a survey would just take away from the impact of receiving such a letter.

When writing direct mail fundraising letters for New York City Mayor Rudy Giuliani, I tested a survey package with a letter signed by the mayor against just a simple two-page fundraising letter also signed by the mayor. The package without the survey won hands down, because the letter was signed by a big name political celebrity who clearly needed money for his campaign. In this case, he was running for Senate against Hillary Rodham Clinton before Giuliani had to drop out because of prostate cancer.

Everyone knew who Giuliani was. Everyone knew he was running for Senate against Hillary Clinton. This was the most watched and covered Senate race in the nation. Everyone knows money is needed to win such a campaign. So there was no need to underscore these obvious pre-sold points with a survey, which might only distract the reader. There was no need to gild the lily.

The copywriter must always answer the question: "What is my strongest lead?" Is it the issue I'm writing about? Is it that I have a huge celebrity letter signer? Or do I need to lead with a survey, or other technique, to get the reader involved in my letter, because otherwise the reader will just tune out, crumple up my letter and throw it in the trash?

Ninety-five percent of political issue fundraising packages will be strengthened by including a survey—and by making the survey a major part of the package. The direct mail department at the Republican National Committee tells me a membership appeal letter with no survey is their strongest prospecting package. I'm skeptical. Maybe there's something wrong with the way they are constructing their survey packages. Surely, including a well-constructed survey with their membership appeal would improve their returns.

I find including a survey to be essential for almost all of my direct mail prospecting packages for political issue organizations. Usually a survey will perform significantly better than a petition, better than postcards, better than almost any other single involvement technique. I think the reason is people would rather be given the opportunity to express their own opinions than be told to sign someone else's opinion, such as someone else's words on a petition, even if they agree with the petition. A survey gives the reader nothing to disagree with. It's merely an outlet for the reader to express her own views. I think that's why surveys work so well, and will always work well.

Human nature will never change. People will never get tired of filling out surveys, polls, and ballots.

2. Petitions to Congress or Other Policymakers and Decisionmakers

This technique is a key staple for a political lobbying organization, such as the National Rifle Association, the National Organization for Women, the Christian Coalition or the American Conservative Union.

The idea is to swamp Congress with petitions and letters demanding passage of legislation of concern to the organization's supporters, or to defeat legislation that is antithetical to the mission of the organization.

Asking the reader to sign and return a petition with a contribution will almost always boost returns, especially from low-dollar contributors—those who are likely to contribute $10, $15, or $20. Petitions are especially good for prospect packages where you are trying to maximize the number of responses to your mailing.

A petition is an ideal involvement device to draw the reader into your letter. By asking your reader to sign and return a petition, you are getting on the reader's good side by not immediately starting your letter with a plea for money. The text on the petition also dramatizes the importance of the issue you're writing about. Your reader is almost certain to read the text on the petition before she decides to read your letter.

A petition is a document that should be returned to the

Figure 7.2

organization in the reply envelope along with, hopefully, a contribution. You inform the reader that: "I will deliver your signed petition to your congressman on your behalf, along with tens of thousands of similar petitions we are now collecting."

You should state a specific goal for your petition drive, perhaps 100,000 petitions on this issue delivered to Congress within the next 90 days—something like that.

With petition packages, it's crucial that the petition drive be real, not just an involvement device to get the reader to respond. You should describe the petition drive in a fair amount of detail. You should explain exactly what the petition drive will achieve. The petition should look impressive to get the reader's attention. The petition should look like an official document. The letter should clearly state that contributions will be used to collect and deliver more of these petitions, as well as bury Congress with an avalanche of letters, postcards, telegrams, phone calls, emails, faxes, and messages demanding immediate passage of this legislation.

This allows the mailing itself to become part of the program you are raising money for. In effect, you can raise money to send out more of these letters and petitions and still keep faith with the donor, because you have explained that this is exactly what you are doing with the contributions. This is especially important in prospecting where you might not even recover the cost of the prospect mailing. In all prospecting, part of the program you are raising money for must be to fund the mailing itself. For this reason, a petition drive is a great technique for a prospect mailing.

Petition packages have many different forms and variations. Some petitions are attached to the reply forms. The advantage of this is that the donor is less likely to return the petition without the reply form, and presumably without a donation. By keeping the petition connected to the reply form, the donor will feel a little guilty returning the petition and the contribution form without a donation. Conventional wisdom in direct mail fundraising is to keep the involvement device, including petitions, attached to the contribution form.

I have a mixed view on this rule.

An impressive stand-alone petition looks more like an official document. It looks more like you are serious about the petition drive you are describing in your letter. It looks less like a gimmick designed to get your reader to respond. It looks real and less junky. I like petitions to look something like an official government document.

Lately I have had better results with stand-alone petitions than with petitions that are connected to the contribution form. But this is something you should always test, because what's true today might not be true tomorrow in direct mail.

Petition packages come in all shapes and sizes. Petitions can be directed to specific members of Congress, the President of the United States, or any policymaker who has decision-making authority over the issue you care about. Mailings can contain one petition or many petitions. I've sent fundraising letters with an entire stack of petitions for the reader to sign and return.

With petition packages you will receive a large number of responses with no donation. One donation for every three or four responses is not unusual.

This brings up a key point.

If you use the petition or postcard technique, be sure the technique does not distract the reader from sending a donation. This is a big mistake copywriters often make with petition packages. You don't want your readers to feel they've done their jobs just by returning the petition or mailing the postcards.

The petition itself should reinforce the need for a contribution. For example, the letter should stress the need for contributions to fund the petition drive you are describing. The text of the petition should paint a dire picture of the disaster that could ensue if the legislation is not passed, stopped, or whatever the case may be. I will often mention in the petition that the signer is a supporter of the organization. On the reply form I might suggest that a minimum contribution is needed to cover the cost of sorting, processing, and delivering the petition. The reply form should be constructed and written, so that it will be psychologically difficult for the reader in good conscience to return a signed petition without a contribution.

But even if you take all these steps, you will likely still receive more reply envelopes with no donation than replies with a donation. But that's okay, because now you have all these non-contributor supporters on your list. These become excellent prospects for donations in the future. I would immediately send your non-donor supporters a letter thanking them for signing and returning their petition, describe to them what you've done with their petition, and make your case again for the need for a contribution. You should be able to net money by mailing effective letters to your non-contributor petition signers and responders.

With petition and action device packages, I often give the reader an entire list of possible actions they can take:

► Write your own letter to your congressman
► Phone your congressman
► Email your congressman
► Fax your congressman

- ▶ Write a letter to the editor of your local newspaper
- ▶ Confront your congressman at a local town meeting
- ▶ Schedule a meeting with your congressman

I usually put these additional optional action steps on a separate sheet of paper. Be sure to include all possible information with your action steps, such as relevant phone numbers, the mailing address where you want letters sent, etc. You want your action steps to be easy for your reader to carry out.

Offering your reader an entire menu of actions shows that you are serious about getting results, not just donations. In addition, Congress and the media will take any organization seriously that can generate this much activity. Be prepared for shrieks of outrage from Congress if you start locking up their switchboard with phone calls and swamping their mailrooms with letters, petitions, and postcards. If members of Congress must wade through letters and petitions just to get to their offices, you've done your job, and Congress will pay attention to your issue. This will put your organization on the political map.

So there are a lot of side benefits to the petition and action step packages, besides just receiving donations. These packages can have a major impact on policy.

But, again, be careful in your letter not to give your readers the impression that they are off the hook for a donation if they take all your suggested action steps. Always come back to the need for a donation.

3. Postcards to Congress

Ask your reader to sign and mail postcards to Congress.

This is especially strong if you match the reader's name to their actual congressman and two senators. There are computer programs that will do this for you. These congressional match computer programs can help further personalize and strengthen many of your legislative action mailings, including your survey and petition mailings.

Figure 7.3

In postcard mailings, usually I ask the reader to mail the postcards themselves, using their own stamps. Sometimes I ask the reader to return the postcards to the organization for delivery. Postcards are really just another variation of the petition package.

If I ask readers to mail the postcards themselves, I always ask them to return the reply form telling me they have mailed their postcards. That way, I tell my readers, I can track the number of postcards hitting Congress. For the mailing to be successful, it's crucial for the reader to return something to the organization. I'll often put a Postcard Mailing Verification Receipt on the contribution form for the reader to fill out and return. You don't want your readers to just mail their postcards and think they've finished their jobs. You also want them to send the reply device to you, hopefully with a contribution.

For my best donors, the top 15 percent or so of a housefile, I might also paper clip stamps for the reader to affix on the postcards on the front of the letter. I'll explain that I've done this so the readers won't need to waste time hunting for their own stamps. This is a real attention-getter and further strengthens the involvement technique and impressiveness of the mailing.

4. Enclose a Copy of the Bill You Want Congress to Pass

The best direct mail appeals are essentially show-and-tell presentations. You communicate most effectively by showing while you are also telling, explaining, and describing.

For legislative action organizations you should always, or whenever possible, enclose a copy of the specific bill you want Congress to pass.

Be sure the actual number of the legislation, such as H.R 234, is prominently displayed, not just on the bill you've enclosed, but also on the reply form, the petitions, or postcards you want your readers to sign and throughout the package.

Enclosing a copy of the actual bill shows your reader that this legislation is real and on the legislative calendar, and indicates that a big battle in Congress is looming in the next few weeks. I'll often put handwritten notes, underlines, and yellow highlights on the bill to draw the reader's attention to certain aspects of the legislation or to stress particular points.

If the legislation has a bureaucratic, unimpressive name, rename the legislation for the purpose of the package so your readers will understand exactly what the bill will accomplish. Bills I've enclosed in packages include the Voluntary Prayer in School Amendment, The Boy Scouts Protection Act, The Defense of Marriage Act, The Tax Relief Act, The Balanced Budget Amendment, the Term Limits for Congress Act, and the Repeal the Death Tax Act.

Not all of these bills made it into law. In fact, most did not. But it's clear from the names of these bills what they were trying to achieve.

Critical to successful direct mail campaigns is for the solution to the problem to be simple. Right or wrong, most people believe the easiest step to fixing many problems is to pass a new law. For conservatives, it's mostly to repeal bad laws or stop some horrific new law from passing. Legislative action is always an easy-to-understand solution or is at least a partial solution to whatever problem concerns an organization.

Of course, the solution must be something your supporters strongly desire. It should involve an issue your organization was specifically established to address. But that's another subject covered elsewhere in this book. The key point here is that lobbying to pass specific legislation is a tried and true strategy for generating impressive returns on your mailings.

When you think about it, there are really only two ways to solve political problems in America. There's the election solution. We can elect the right people to public office, and we can defeat those with whom we disagree.

Or we can generate massive public pressure on Congress to pass, or not pass, legislation. Electing the right people to office is a long-term solution that does not yield immediate results. Election years are the only time you can raise significant money for candidates and elections. But legislative battles are taking place all the time. The results of legislative battles are nearly immediate and often have far-reaching impact.

Legislative solution packages have always been among my biggest mailers. If the issue is right, and if it's especially contentious and in the news a lot, I can often mail millions of legislative solution or legislative action appeals.

Legislative action packages can include petitions you want your reader to sign and return for delivery to Congress; postcards you want your reader to sign, stamp, and mail to Congress; or a survey for your readers to fill out and return to the organization for tabulation and processing. These packages are all about getting your readers involved in the issue and mobilizing your readers to personally lobby their elected representatives in Congress.

In addition to sending postcards and signing petitions, you should also include a sheet of additional action steps your reader can take to help pass or defeat a bill. Ask your readers also to call and write their congressman.

And always come back to the need for a donation, which you'll use to contact and mobilize millions of Americans by mail and with ads to swamp Congress with hundreds of thousands of petitions, postcards, telegrams, letters, phone calls, faxes, emails, and messages demanding immediate passage of the bill.

Not only are these packages effective fundraisers, they can have a major impact on Congress, and can be a deciding factor in determining whether the legislation passes or is defeated.

5. Letter of Encouragement

Ask your reader to sign a Letter of Encouragement to someone under attack. A Letter of Encouragement looks a lot like a petition.

The Letter of Encouragement works well if the object of the letter is in some way linked to the need for money. Raising money for a legal defense fund would be a good place to use a Letter of Encouragement to support a courageous figure who is under heavy attack by the media.

People like to support underdogs and people under attack for standing up for principle. A Letter of Encouragement underscores the underdog nature of the cause you are raising money for and helps you paint a sympathetic picture of the person who is under siege for doing what is right.

Another variation is to ask the reader to sign a Letter of Thanks to someone who has taken a courageous stand or perhaps to a hospitalized veteran. As you write your direct mail packages, you'll think of all kinds of variations.

6. Pledge or Letter of Support

Ask the reader to sign and return the enclosed Pledge or Letter of Support.

This is effective for packages raising money for a high-profile candidate. A presidential campaign is ideal for a Pledge of Support package, or a high profile senate or governor's race.

Figure 7.4

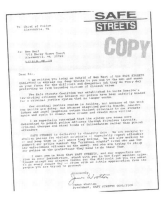

The idea here is to give your reader an opportunity to let powerful figures know the reader supports them. The psychology behind this technique is to give the reader a chance to get on the good side of the perceived powerful figure.

When raising money for an anticrime organization, I asked the reader to sign a Letter of Support that would be delivered to the reader's local police chief. This was very successful, because most people want the police to know "I'm one of the good guys." There's also a sense on the part of the reader that perhaps I'll get some special treatment or favor from the powerful person if I sign this Pledge or Letter of Support. The reader might think: "Maybe I'll get invited to a fancy party at the White House," or "Maybe the police will drive by my house more often just to make sure everything is okay if I sign this Pledge of Support."

The Pledge of Support is a powerful technique in the right package. The other great feature is that a Pledge of Support implies the need for a donation. After all, you can't be much of a supporter if you don't send a contribution. And a Pledge of Support certainly implies that you will be a loyal contributor in the future.

In your thank you letters, be sure to thank donors not just for their donation, but also for signing the Pledge of Support. This underscores the donor's commitment. Remind the donor in your thank you letter that success depends on not just one donation, but on regular donations and loyal, long-term support. Thank the donors more profusely for their Pledge of Support than for their actual contribution, because their pledge implies support that is ongoing, not just a one-time event.

7. Enclose a $1 Bill With Your Letter

Enclosing a $1 bill with a letter is a great way to get a reader's attention.

If you're using a standard closed-face envelope, fold the $1 bill over the top of the letter so it's the first item your readers see when they open the envelope. If you're using a window envelope, you should paper-clip the $1 bill to fix it in place and have at least part of it show through a window, as a kind of teaser. I'll sometimes even use a clear outer envelope so the reader is sure to see the $1 bill.

My $1 bill letter will begin something like this: "I have taken the unusual step of enclosing a $1 bill with my letter because I had to think of a way to get your attention for a matter of urgent importance."

This is honest and straightforward.

I've seen copywriters come up with convoluted reasons for why they're sending $1 bills. But I believe straight forward honesty is always the best policy in direct mail fundraising. "I have enclosed a $1 bill because I had to think of a way to make my letter stand out in your mailbox" is also a good way to start your $1 bill letter.

You'll then want to say you can't afford to lose any of these $1 bills and that you will be thankful if the reader returns the $1 bill with a donation. Explain also that you hope the reader will return the $1 bill even if not sending a contribution. A great feature of the $1 bill mailing is that the technique and your explanation for sending the $1 bill allow you constantly to explain the need for a contribution.

You'll want to repeat your reason for sending the $1 bill in the P.S. Try something like: "I knew it was risky for me to include a $1 bill with my letter. But if I have succeeded in getting your attention for this urgent matter, it was well worth the risk."

And you'll want to repeat the reason for the $1 bill again on the reply form. I sometimes start the reply form by saying something like: "Thank you for explaining why you sent me the $1 bill as a way to get my attention for your letter."

Don't forget to include two options on the reply form reminding the reader to return the $1 bill. One check box should say something like: "I am returning the $1 bill you sent me with my donation. The second check box should say: "I'm sorry I cannot contribute. But I am returning the $1 bill you sent with your letter because I know you cannot afford to lose this money."

In the text of my letter, I sometimes even apologize to the reader for perhaps being too hokey or gimmicky by including a $1 bill. But I then go on to explain that, "Over the years I have found that including a $1 bill really does get people's attention and significantly increases contributions."

I usually say, "Because some of our loyal supporters have reacted negatively to me sending $1 bills in the mail with fundraising letters in the past, I only do this when the need is truly urgent ... and this is certainly one of those times."

Also, I add reassuringly: "Sending $1 bills with a fundraising letter once in a while has proven in the past not to be a waste of money, since most friends and supporters I write are gracious enough to return the $1 bill, even if they can't also send a donation."

Again, straightforward honesty and complete explanations are always the best policy and will help diffuse objections.

The great benefit of this straightforward and honest explanation for the $1 bill is that it allows you to stress the urgency of the need for financial help. But the need better be truly urgent, or your $1 bill mailing will crash and burn. Your supporters will sense if you are crying wolf.

Always keep this crucial point in mind.

Like all techniques, enclosing a $1 bill with your letter will not ensure the success of your mailing. What's most important is the project you're raising money for.

Techniques, such as the $1 bill described here, will help get the reader's attention for a moment. But the success of your letter will depend on the cause and project you are raising money for. Most importantly, you must explain to prospective donors precisely what you are going to do with their donations.

8. Enclose a $1.50 or $2.50 Check With Your Letter

The check mailing works according to the exact same principle as the $1 bill mailing, but it's less costly and risky.

In deciding who receives $1 bills and who receives $1.50 or $2.50 checks, I employ the 80/20 rule. The top 20 percent of a housefile can receive a $1 bill, the bottom 80 percent should receive a check, which is far less risky than a $1 bill, because very few people will actually take the trouble to cash a $1.50 check. Remember, you're not out the money until the check is cashed.

I almost never use $1 bills for prospect mailings, because it is too easy for people just to pocket the cash; but I use a lot of $1.50 and $2.50 checks in my prospect mail.

Figure 7.5

With your check mailings, put "CHECK ENCLOSED" in official looking sans-serif type on the carrier envelope. Make the package look like this might be some kind of refund, perhaps from the phone company. I like to have part of the check along with "Pay to the Order of" show through the window of the envelope. You'll be printing your own checks. I usually make the check part of the reply form, detachable with a perforation.

You'll need to meet with your bank to get the proper specifications on your checks. Your bank will likely require the use of magnetic ink for the account number that is printed on the checks. It's a bit of a complicated process, but it can be well worth the effort, because enclosing a check with your letter will usually significantly increase returns.

9. Clear Envelopes

Sending a fundraising letter in a clear envelope is a great way to get attention for your letter. Enclose something impressive and attention-getting in your clear envelope, perhaps a $1 bill (combining the clear envelope technique with the $1 bill technique outlined above). Bumper stickers, books, an American flag, and impressive premiums are also good items to put inside clear envelopes.

Even if I don't have an attention-getting, front-end premium available, just using a clear envelope is often attention-getting enough. As with the $1 bill technique, I usually start my letter off by saying something like: "I am sending this letter in a clear envelope as a way to get your attention. . . ."

This is always a great explanation for doing something a little peculiar and attention-getting with your mailing.

10. Coins (Penny, Nickel, Dime, Various Combinations)

These are just variations on the $1 bill/$1.50 check techniques described above. Coins should show through windows and

Figure 7.6

are an effective way to get your letter opened. Coins work best for charitable appeals, such as helping the homeless or feeding hungry children. Coins allow you to underscore your point that "we can feed a hungry child" for just "a few pennies" or the "cost of a cup of coffee" a day.

Again, ask your reader to return the coins along with a donation. Explain to your reader that you can't afford to lose these pennies, which we need back to "feed a hungry child."

11. Seasonal and Holiday appeals

Especially for charitable causes, you can often build your entire appeal around a holiday. This is effective for such causes as helping the homeless, feeding hungry children, disaster relief, helping hospitalized veterans, and supporting our troops serving in dangerous war zones overseas.

People are in a charitable mood during holidays, especially Thanksgiving and Christmas. Letters built around delivering a toy to an impoverished child for Christmas or a turkey dinner to a homeless person for Thanksgiving are powerful appeals.

Combining your Christmas fundraising appeal with a Christmas card the donor should sign and return for delivery to a child in need, if that's your cause, or a hospitalized soldier, if that's your cause, will further strengthen your fundraising appeal.

Depending on the cause, you can build similar appeals around Easter, which is great for Christian charities. For charities assisting hospitalized and disabled veterans, be sure to build patriotic appeals around July 4th, Veterans Day, and Memorial Day.

For appeals built around patriotic holidays like July 4th, I like to include an American flag decal, usually with a patriotic slogan like "God Bless America," "Proud to be an American," "United We Stand," or "I Support Our Troops."

I'll ask the prospective donor to "please be sure to display this decal on your car or in some prominent place where others will see it as an expression of how grateful we should all feel to be Americans." This is especially effective for helping disabled veterans appeals.

I've sent out millions of these stickers over the years. I feel satisfaction seeing these stickers and decals on cars everywhere.

Even for noncharitable causes, such as political campaigns and issue appeals, if you're sending a letter during a holiday, be sure to mention the holiday. Christmas cards are a great way to thank your donors for all their support during the past year.

12. Annual Support to Raise Next Year's Budget

This letter should be mailed in November or December and is built around raising next year's entire operating budget.

The letter starts off saying something like: "I am now putting together our operating budget for the coming year, but I can't finalize this budget until I hear from you."

You explain that this is an annual letter aimed at raising enough in donations to cover all fixed monthly operating costs for the coming year.

The letter goes on to remind the reader of all the great things the organization has done over the past year and then describe all the great things you're planning for next year.

The letter then discusses the fixed monthly operating costs that must be covered, such as rent, phones, electricity, office supplies, computers, office equipment, salaries for staff, and all the typical costs any business must cover to continue operations.

You explain that charities are no different from businesses in this respect. These fixed monthly bills come due and must be paid.

You further explain that you hope to cover all these unglamorous fixed monthly operating costs for the year with this one letter, and that this will require a "near 100 percent response from our best friends and supporters."

In this sense, the Annual Support letter is very similar to a Membership Renewal letter. Some organizations (like AARP) are better suited for Membership Renewal appeals. The more strictly cause-oriented organizations are better suited for Annual Support letters. Annual Support letters are best for donors who are passionately committed to a cause. Membership Renewal notices are best for audiences that are more concerned about keeping their membership benefits or if there is prestige and perceived exclusivity attached to membership.

Some organizations are hybrids of membership and cause-oriented organizations. The NRA is a good example of a hybrid. The NRA offers valuable benefits for its membership: a magazine, a shooter's cap, a membership card, discounts on ammo and shooting ranges, etc.

The NRA is also a cause: "Help us protect your Second Amendment right to own a gun." This is a great combination because the NRA can mail a mixture of cause and membership appeals. The Sierra Club is another very effective hybrid. It's a single-issue organization ("Help Protect Our Wilderness") with membership benefits and a membership that is every bit as passionate about their cause as NRA members are about their Second Amendment rights.

13. Membership Appeals

Send your supporters an attractive plastic membership card with the supporter's name prominently embossed in gleaming gold type on the front, like an American Express card.

Membership card appeals can be effective for both prospecting and housefile mailings.

Housefile membership appeal programs are usually a series of at least three mailings, starting in November of each year. The first mailing is called a prebill. It looks a lot like an invoice. The first line will say something like: "Your annual voluntary membership dues are now due."

Don't make the mistake of asking the reader "if" they would like to renew their membership in your organization. Assume they will. And simply state that: "Your voluntary membership dues are now due" or "I am writing to remind you to send your American Conservative Union membership dues for 2004."

I often write "STATEMENT ENCLOSED" on the carrier over the widow, which gives the impression that this might be a bank statement or an electric bill.

A few paragraphs in the letter on what the organization has planned for the coming year are also important. But the

Figure 7.7

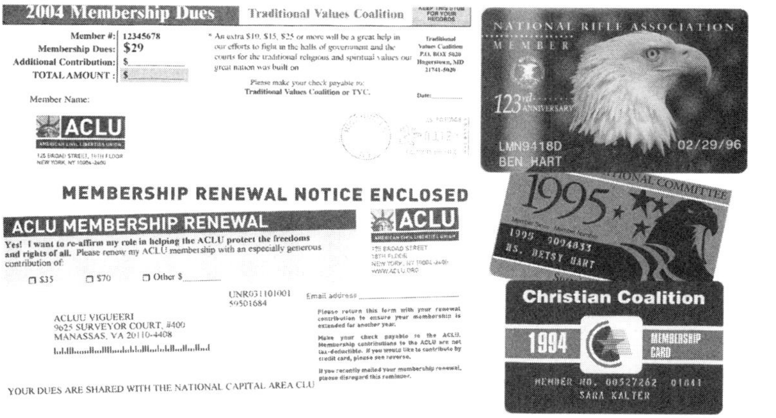

key trick here is that a membership dues prebill mailing should resemble a bill. People will pay it along with their other bills.

The other great virtue of the prebill mailing is that it's inexpensive. Most prebill mailings are one sheet of paper, with a perforated reply slip, a return envelope, and a window carrier. That's it.

Be sure to mention in your prebill letter that their personalized embossed membership cards will be arriving in the mail in the next few weeks.

Two weeks after the prebill, the personalized membership embossed plastic membership card should arrive, with another letter and perforated reply slip. The letter should remind the member/supporter to be sure to send in their voluntary membership dues if they haven't done so already. It's important for the plastic membership card to look impressive, like an American Express card. It's great if you can mention the date they first became a member or supporter of your organization.

Six weeks later, mail a postbill to those who have not renewed their membership dues for the coming year. I like to print postbills on pink paper that shows through the window of the carrier envelope.

This really gets people's attention and is very effective. Though be prepared for some negative comment mail, which you can always answer with a letter apologizing for any undue alarm you may have caused with the mailing, but also explaining how you had to get their attention with pink paper because their continued membership is so important.

This usually diffuses any anger over making your pink postbill look like a "payment past-due" notice.

There are a significant number of people on most housefiles who will respond only to membership appeals and never to fundraising appeals. They will always renew their membership, and that's it. They will never send another donation until the next membership dues renewal notice arrives.

That's why organizations like the Republican and Democratic National Committees are always looking for new excuses to mail membership dues appeals. They create new membership clubs with additional membership benefits and different more prestigious looking membership cards.

There are people on these housefiles who are carrying three or four different membership cards in their wallets for the same organization, but corresponding to different clubs within the organization. The clubs have names like President's Club, Founders Club, Inner Circle and Executive Committee and are intended to create a sense of prestige and exclusivity.

This approach works well for organizations like the Republican or Democratic National Committees, which are, in effect, selling donors access to policymakers and powerful people in Washington. The prospective donors are told that if they join one of these exclusive clubs, they'll be invited to Washington to meet with key lawmakers, including perhaps even the President of the United States, if they contribute at a certain stratospheric level.

14. USPS Priority Mail BRE

Including a USPS Priority Mail reply envelope with your mailing is a great way to emphasize urgency and the need to receive contributions back immediately. Draw the donor's attention to the special USPS Priority Mail reply envelope on the first page of your letter. Mention it again in the P.S. and again on the reply form.

Use text early in your letter that says something like this: "I have included a special USPS Priority Mail Reply Envelope to ensure the most rapid possible arrival of your contribution. I have even covered the $3.40 postage cost for you. That's how important it is that I receive your contribution in the next two or three days."

I'll go on to explain that all they need to do is "drop your USPS Priority Mail Reply Envelope in the nearest mailbox today, and the Post Office has assured me that your contribution will reach me in about two days."

All this emphasizes the urgency of the matter and the need for a speedy reply.

Of course, for this mailing to work, your need must be truly urgent. Like all techniques described here, this one too will wear thin with your donors if it's over-used and abused.

Also, be sure to use a BRE version. Otherwise your donors will have to go to the post office and pay the $3.40 in postage.

15. USPS Priority Mail Carrier

Using a USPS Priority Mail envelope as a carrier for your mailing is costly but effective for your higher-dollar donors. But, unlike the USPS Priority Mail BRE described above, the postage cost applies for every letter you mail, not just the reply envelopes that come back. This pushes the cost of your mailing up to at least $4 or $5 per letter you mail. You can afford to mail this only to your best donors, those who have sent you at least $100 in the past 12 months.

I like to start the letter with copy that reads something like this: "I have gone to the extra expense of rushing you this letter in a special USPS Priority Mail Envelope because it's urgent that I hear back from you in the next two or three days."

Since you're spending so much on the carrier with this mailing, you should also invest extra money in the letter.

Personalize every page of your letter. In your personalization refer to the amount of the reader's most recent or highest previous contribution. Find a way to mention the city and state the reader is from. For example, I might mention that "You, Mr. Smith, are one of our very best supporters from the Great Falls area in Virginia."

Write a letter that indicates you know this person and consider this person a friend. Gush thanks in your letter for all her past support. Apologize for the need to request an immediate contribution, but explain you have no choice because of the urgency of the matter. And put your letter on cream or ivory stock and heavier paper to give your letter a high-quality look and feel.

When writing personalized letters, base the amount of the contribution you request on the donor's previous giving history. Don't ask a $100 donor for $1,000 and don't ask a $1,000 donor for $100. Never ask donors to move far out of their comfort zones. It's okay sometimes to try to ask for a little more than the donor has contributed before, perhaps even double the amount of their highest previous contribution. But don't ask for 10 times more than the donor has ever contributed in the past.

Also, for high-end packages like this, I like to ask for one specific amount. This shows you've given some thought to how much you actually need from this person. When you give the contributor many gift amount options on the reply form, you undermine the personal nature of the letter.

16. Imitation of a USPS Priority Mail Carrier

You can only afford to use a USPS Priority Mail carrier and reply envelope with your very best donors. So what do you send the other 80 percent or 90 percent of supporters on your housefile?

I like creating quasi "knock-offs" of the USPS Priority Mail carrier.

Figure 7.8

I've developed a stable of carriers and reply envelopes that look a lot like post office products but aren't. I can mail these carriers at the low bulk or nonprofit rate.

You can't use the same wording as the post office's carrier. And you'll need to be careful to make your carrier look not so much like the post office's product that the post office prohibits you from mailing it or requires you to pay the same postage rate as the official post office product. You should always clear a carrier—especially a questionable one—with the post office before you print it to make sure you can mail it at the bulk or nonprofit postage rate.

17. Three-Envelope, Three-Month Pledge

This mailing contains three reply envelopes for three consecutive months, such as an envelope for June, July, and August. The letter asks the donor to pledge contributions for each of the next three months.

You'll need a good reason to ask for a three-month pledge.

One reason I've used is that the head of the organization is working so hard on a particular project (a project of keen interest to the donor) that he won't have much time to attend to his usual fundraising duties. Yet the organization's regular monthly costs must still be covered. The only way to cover these costs is for the organization's best friends and supporters to commit to contributing for each of the next three months, after which the crucial project should be completed.

Another reason for a three-month pledge is the usual fundraising summer slump most charities suffer. The letter notes that, because so many people are traveling in the summer, it becomes difficult to reach our friends and supporters in a timely way by mail. And many people don't answer their mail as faithfully during the summer. You explain to your supporters that a three-month pledge from our best supporters will help carry us through the summer, a difficult fundraising period.

The three-month pledge is actually a donor upgrade

Figure 7.9

strategy, because the letter gives the reader two basic options. Send the entire suggested three-month contribution at once, using one reply envelope (the biggest one), or send the first month contribution in the biggest envelope marked June and keep the July and August reply envelopes in a convenient place for mailing the second and third contributions every 30 days or so until the three-month commitment is completed.

A significant number of donors will send the entire contribution representing the entire three-month commitment all at once. You will have thus upgraded these donors.

Three reply envelopes, representing three consecutive months, appears to be the optimal number for this kind of a program. I've tried five envelopes, but this does not work nearly as well. Three months appears manageable to most people, while five months and five reply envelopes is too daunting.

The three-reply envelope technique has several advantages that also help fuel the mailing.

First, the three reply envelopes emphasize the need for a contribution, or a series of contributions.

Second, the three reply envelopes provide a conversational springboard that lets you naturally flow into the urgency of the project that needs completing and funding.

Third, the three reply envelopes technique is an attention-getting device just by itself. The three-envelope package is a technique that allows you to spend almost the entire letter talking about the need for donations without seeming too heavy-handed.

I've had tremendous success with the three-envelope, three-month pledge package. One three-envelope housefile mailing I wrote netted $1.4 million for an organization whose housefile was in the 300,000 donor range.

This can be a blockbuster letter.

But the reason for the three reply envelopes and three-month pledge request must be a good one. You must make a strong case for why your readers should make such a heavy financial commitment to your organization at this particular time, a greater financial commitment than they've ever made before.

18. Matching Gift

Ask one or several of your major donors if they would be willing to make their next donation a matching gift challenge grant. That is, they will match every gift that comes in over the next, say, 60 days, up to some maximum amount. We'll say $50,000 for the purpose of this discussion.

You then explain the matching gift challenge grant program in your next housefile letter. The power of this appeal is that "your $20 gift now is really worth $40" to your organization "because every dollar you contribute in response to this letter will be matched dollar for dollar." In other words, "your contribution of $20 now will have twice the impact it normally would because ..."

The first sentence of my matching gift challenge grant letters is usually something like, "I have some great news."

I like to include two facsimile checks in matching gift packages. The checks are made out for an amount the reader

Figure 7.10

has previously contributed. I'll ask the reader to return one or both of the facsimile checks with their matching contribution. Graphics for your facsimile checks are important to get your reader's attention and underscore the Matching Gift program.

You want your facsimile checks to look like real checks, signed by the generous donor who is contributing the challenge grant and made out to the organization. Be sure to print "Facsimile Check" on each check and include copy telling the reader the checks are for illustration purposes only and are not cashable. You never want to confuse your donors.

You also need a time deadline for when the matching gift challenge grant expires to add urgency to your appeal. Have a specific deadline date. Mail your letter 21 days before the deadline date. Don't give readers more time than this to respond or they'll put the letter aside and forget about it.

Deadline dates for all your fundraising appeals must be imminent, not somewhere over the horizon. Your letters must always make a compelling case for why it's important for the readers to stop whatever else they might be doing and send a donation today, right now, before they put your letter aside—not tomorrow.

19. Photos and Snapshots

I often include stand-alone photos and snapshots with my letters. This is more powerful than a printed newsletter with the same photos because stand-alone snapshots are more personal and attention-getting. When you receive a letter from a friend or relative, don't you appreciate it if the envelope includes a photo of a new baby, or of the family, or of something noteworthy going on in the life of the letter-writer?

You can be 100 percent sure of one thing: stand-alone photos and snapshots will be looked at. I will put a note of explanation in blue handwriting on the back of each photo.

In direct mail fundraising, the photo should show something being accomplished by you and your organization. For political fundraising letters, I might include snapshots of the candidate on the campaign trail, or with his family. For issue-oriented cause organizations, I might include snapshots of the head of the organization delivering truckloads of petitions to Congress, perhaps with members of Congress standing there watching. Or I might include a photo of the head of the organization at a press conference behind a bank of microphones, with reporters shouting questions. For feed hungry children type charities, I would include snapshots of the head of the charity or letter signer delivering food to children.

I don't like including horrifying snapshots, such as photos of children actually starving. Some fundraisers do this. I don't. I much prefer photos showing the problem being solved, children with smiles being helped by the organization. I think readers are turned off by shocking photos showing some horror. You don't want your reader to be repulsed by your package.

Photos should show exactly how you are using donations to solve a problem—whether it's passing legislation in Congress or feeding hungry children. Your reader already knows children are starving. Now your readers want to know exactly how their $15 donations will improve life for a child. Use snapshots to show how. Use snapshots to show that a $15 donation will truly make a difference and won't just disappear into the organization's general operating fund.

And photos should not be professionally taken. They should be the kind of snapshots you or I might take. They should look amateurish. This communicates authenticity to the reader and adds to the personal feel of your letter.

20. Certified Return Letter

Put certified letter postage on reply envelopes to communicate the urgent need for an immediate response and an immediate contribution.

The first line of your letter should say something like this:

```
Dear Mr. Smith:

  I have taken the extraordinary step of
enclosing a reply envelope with $2.37 of
CERTIFIED MAIL postage affixed because I need
to hear back from you in the next two or three
days. Here's why.
```

After you provide the reader a few paragraphs of explanation, be sure to draw the reader's attention again to the Certified Mail reply envelope by saying something like this:

```
  Mr. Smith, I have enclosed a return envelope
with CERTIFIED MAIL postage already affixed
because I wanted to make sure I got your undi-
vided attention for just six minutes.

  And I pre-paid the $2.37 cost of the CERTI-
FIED MAIL postage on your reply envelope
because I wanted to communicate to you how
urgent it is that I hear back from you no
later than Tuesday, June 21st.
```

If you use this approach, be sure the reason truly is urgent. Don't cry wolf.

I'll use the Certified Return Letter technique for candidates when the election is perhaps just six weeks away. I'll discuss the need for immediate money to put more ads on the air in the final few weeks of the campaign, something like that, something the reader will easily understand.

The big downside of the Certified Return Letter is the huge cost. You'll need to pay the full Certified Letter postage on every reply envelope you mail. As of this writing, that postage is $2.37 per return envelope. So you can only afford to do this for your very best supporters.

Because I'm spending so much here on the reply envelope, I'll paper clip the reply envelope to the contribution form for added emphasis. I will also mail this package first class. So we're talking here about a very expensive package, nearly $4 a letter.

But the Certified Return Letter has proven to be very effective for me when writing to loyal established donors who have contributed $50 or more in the recent past to fundraising letters.

At most, I'll use this technique to a housefile once a year. I won't use it unless the need is truly urgent—and even then, only if I feel the reader will easily see and understand the urgency. In other words, the need must be urgent to the reader, not just the writer. A lot of things might be urgent to me, but not necessarily urgent to the reader. Copywriters must always learn to distinguish between what's urgent to the organization and what's urgent to the reader. These are often two very different things.

Make sure you clearly understand this difference when deploying the Certified Return Letter technique, or you will lose a lot of money and anger your supporters, all in one fell swoop.

21. Outgoing Certified Letter

I am not a fan of this technique.

I hardly ever use it. But it can be very effective, so I feel obliged to mention it here in a book on direct mail fundraising.

Here you will put certified postage on the *carrier* envelope.

This will require your reader to actually go to the post office to pick up the letter. The reader will go to the post office window with the slip of paper she received in her mailbox announcing the arrival of the certified letter.

The reader is very nervous because certified letters almost always contain bad news. Have you ever received good news in a certified letter?

Maybe you're being sued. Maybe your driver's license has been suspended. Or maybe the IRS wants to audit your tax returns. Whatever it is, good news almost never arrives via certified mail. So your reader rushes to the post office in a panic to find out what's in the letter. Or some readers put off going to post office because they're just too scared to find out what's in this mysterious certified letter.

Can you see why I absolutely despise this technique?

A certified letter is guaranteed to be opened and read by your prospective donor, who is angered, but at the same time relieved that this is just a fundraising letter.

But the letter is now being read—which is always the first battle the copywriter must win with the reader.

The first line must be a profuse apology for requiring the prospective donor to leave the house and go to the post office to pick up this letter.

This apology must then be backed up by a true emergency of near life-threatening proportions. The emergency must be real. The emergency must be something the donor will easily understand. The emergency must be so dire that your supporters will forgive you for frightening them with a certified letter and for requiring them to leave the comfort of their home to pick up your letter at the post office.

If the emergency is not truly dire, you will likely lose half your supporters. So think very carefully before sending your loyal supporters a certified letter appeal.

Be sure to have a heartfelt thank you letter ready to mail to everyone who contributes to your certified letter, complete with a restatement of your apology along with a restatement of the dire emergency that prompted the certified letter. Be sure also to have a letter ready for those who responded with no contribution, just an outraged complaint about the certified letter. And have another letter of apology ready to mail to those who did not respond at all to your certified letter.

For me, certified letters are too risky, except in the rarest of circumstances. You risk losing half your housefile if your emergency is not convincing enough to outweigh the inconvenience your supporters experience by having to physically go to the post office. For me, it's a risk not worth taking.

I also believe successful fundraising programs are ultimately about building relationships with your supporters. An inappropriately deployed certified letter can destroy that relationship and trust you are working so hard to develop with your donors. I think a certified letter is the direct mail equivalent of a nuclear weapon. It's a very powerful weapon in your arsenal, but you should hope and pray you never have to use it because the collateral damage is so high.

Maybe there should be a law against direct mail fundraisers using the certified letter for fundraising purposes. I've seen this technique used far too often for phony emergencies, which gives direct mail fundraising a terrible reputation and badly damages the credibility of legitimate direct mail fundraising appeals.

22. Handwritten Letter on Note Paper

Computers can now imitate your exact handwriting.

This allows you to create a personalized fundraising letter in the handwriting of the letter-signer.

Produce the letter on monarch-sized note paper. Make sure the handwriting is easy to read, clearly legible. My handwriting is very bad. So I would hand print my letter if I were the letter signer.

This technique is especially powerful if the letter signer is well known or is a celebrity.

George W. Bush, when he was running for president in 2000, sent a one-page fundraising letter on personal note paper to Republican contributors. The letter was computer generated in his handwriting.

Though most readers could tell he probably did not sit down to write each separate letter himself, the letter created an impressive visual effect. It was the kind of letter people might frame, even knowing it was computer generated. It looked real enough.

As a fundraising appeal, this letter certainly got the reader's attention. As you might expect, this was one of the most successful fundraising letters ever mailed. Of course, it was mostly powered by the fact that George W. Bush was the signer. But its handwritten appearance certainly helped returns.

23. Handwritten Letter on Yellow Legal Paper

This is just another variation of the handwritten letter on note paper.

I might use yellow legal paper if the letter signer is a lawyer writing about a case or raising money for a legal defense fund. A letter written on yellow legal paper might include figures and calculations.

I've seen copywriters who will claim the letter signer is traveling and did not have access to regular letterhead, and so wrote the fundraising letter on yellow legal paper.

The problem with this approach is that it's fundamentally not truthful. Even if the signer is traveling, does he really want the reader to believe the letter could not have been transmitted back to the office and put on letterhead? Besides, thousands of copies of this letter are being mailed to the housefile or to prospective supporters. The letters have to be printed to be mailed and could easily be printed on regular organization letterhead.

The best policy is always tell the truth.

I like my standby reason for doing something peculiar. Much like my dollar-bill mailings, I would say something like this:

> I wrote this letter on yellow legal paper, and decided to send it to you this way instead of on regular letterhead, because I thought it would get your attention.
>
> I must confess, I just liked the way the letter looked on the informal yellow legal paper, so I thought I'd just send it to you this way.
>
> Like always, I try to think of ways to make my letters stand out in your mailbox. I make a special effort to do this when the reason for my letter is especially important...and this is certainly one of those times.

Most copywriters spend too much energy trying to think up phony convoluted reasons for doing something unusual in their mailings. But our readers are intelligent people who can smell a snow job.

It's so much easier just to tell the truth. And it's so much more effective. By admitting the truth, even if somewhat embarrassing, you actually establish credibility for the rest of your appeal. Consciously or subconsciously the readers say to themselves, "That makes sense. I'm not being conned here. I think I'll read further, with less skepticism than I otherwise might."

If you make one false statement in your letter that the reader can detect, your reader will discount every other claim you make.

I don't use this yellow legal paper technique very often. I find it comes across as too contrived. But it can be effective and often improves returns.

Direct mail copywriters must always find ways to get the reader's attention and create curiosity that compels the reader to read. Producing a fundraising appeal on yellow legal paper is another arrow in a copywriter's quiver.

24. Reproduce Pages From a Diary

The heads of nonprofit organizations should keep diaries of their activities relating, obviously, to the cause they're raising money for. This applies to candidates for elective office as well.

This will help the direct mail copywriter enormously in writing effective fundraising letters. The copywriter will have a far better feel for what the letter signer is doing each day to advance the cause of the organization.

Every so often, I like to reproduce pages from the diary to include with the fundraising letter. This is a little like the handwritten note concept. But diary pages are especially intriguing. Who can resist reading pages from someone's diary if they land in your lap?

Again, it's best if the handwriting in the diary is neat and easy to read. But the phrases can be just sentence fragments and brief statements which paint a picture of a tremendous amount of activity and extraordinary impact.

25. Long Letter in Tiny Envelope

And I mean a very tiny envelope, smaller than a monarch-sized envelope.

This is yet another attention-getting device. People will open a tiny closed-face envelope stuffed with paper to find out what's inside. I think this is a variation on the concept that the best gifts come in small boxes. The reader will definitely be interested to find out what could possibly be in such a tiny envelope.

Envelopes like this are not an off-the-shelf product. They need to be specially manufactured. The letter I put in the tiny envelope is usually eight pages, which further accentuates the odd appearance of the entire package. But because the sheets of paper are so tiny, an eight page letter for this package is equal to about three pages for a conventional package.

Personalizing the letter is important to the success of these packages. I'm a big fan of the tiny envelope package. The tiny envelope package works best for a loyal well-established house-file.

Consider using a handwritten letter with your tiny envelope. And consider using handwriting to address the carrier. Computers can reproduce the handwriting of the letter signer.

I would not likely use a tiny envelope for prospecting, because it's expensive, and because the format does not allow the writer enough paper to fully explain the cause and project.

26. FaxGram

This is similar in construction to the Western Union Authorization appeal. But instead of promising to send a Western Union message to the decisionmaker on behalf of the reader, you promise to send a FaxGram to the decision-maker.

Create your own FaxGram graphics to get the reader's attention — official-looking graphics that convey seriousness, authenticity and urgency.

As with the petition and other action-device packages, I like to include an entire menu of additional action steps the letter reader can take to help pass or stop the legislation, or achieve the objective outlined in the letter.

27. HomemadeGram

Make your letter look something like a competitor to Western Union by developing your own graphics. It's best if the graphics appear on every component of the package: carrier, letter, and BRE reply envelope. I like to use colored paper (yellow or orange for all components) and have pin feeds going down both sides of the letter and the reply.

This appeal generally works best for a housefile. And it's important for the need to be truly urgent concerning some breaking development or emergency that will be easy for the reader to understand.

Figure 7.11

Here's an example of what I'm describing:

MRS. SMITH:

  I AM WRITING YOU 21 DAYS BEFORE ELECTION DAY.

  NEW POLLS SHOW THE RACE DEAD EVEN, 46 PERCENT
TO 46 PERCENT WITH 8 PERCENT UNDECIDED.

  I MUST RAISE $43,565 IN THE NEXT SEVEN DAYS
TO KEEP MY TV AND RADIO ADS ON THE AIR.

  PLEASE SEND AN IMMEDIATE CONTRIBUTION OF $50
IF YOU CAN.

  IF THAT'S TOO MUCH, PLEASE TRY TO SEND $25,
LIKE YOU GAVE BEFORE.

```
   I AM ONLY WRITING MY VERY BEST, MOST LOYAL
SUPPORTERS.

   IF I DON'T RECEIVE A NEAR 100 PERCENT
RESPONSE TO THIS EMERGENCY APPEAL FOR HELP,
I'LL HAVE TO PULL MY ADS OFF THE AIR.

   I CAN WIN THIS ELECTION. BUT I NEED $43,565
IMMEDIATELY. I MUST HEAR FROM YOU BY OCTOBER
15TH.

   PLEASE RUN OR DRIVE TO THE MAILBOX WITH YOUR
DONATION RIGHT NOW. PLEASE USE THE SPECIAL
POSTAGE PAID REPLY ENVELOPE TO MAIL YOUR CON-
TRIBUTION.

   MY ADS ARE WORKING. I'VE CLOSED A 10 POINT
GAP SINCE MY NEW ADS STARTED RUNNING TWO WEEKS
AGO. I MUST KEEP THESE ADS GOING UNTIL ELEC-
TION DAY TO WIN.

   BUT I CAN'T KEEP MY ADS ON THE AIR UNLESS I
HEAR FROM YOU AND EVERY LOYAL SUPPORTER IN THE
NEXT FEW DAYS.

   IF YOU ACT TODAY, AND PUT YOUR DONATION IN
THE MAIL BEFORE 5:00 P.M., YOUR DONATION WILL
REACH ME IN ABOUT 48 HOURS. AND I'LL BE ABLE
TO KEEP MY ADS ON THE AIR.

   THANK YOU FOR ATTENDING IMMEDIATLY TO THIS
URGENT MATTER.
```

Have computer-style pin feeds running down both sides of the letter and a tear-off reply slip. The letter should be on yellow paper. The graphics of the letter should match the graphics of the carrier and reply envelope. Use a BRE for this appeal. Try to keep your appeal to one page of copy so that you can maintain the look and feel of a telegram. Write in the same terse staccato style you would expect in a telegram. Be brief and to the point. Use all capital letters, as you would also expect in a telegram. This appeal does not work well if the need requires a lot of explanation.

28. Cryptic Note

I don't use this technique often. But it can be very effective if used at the right time for the right reason.

The closing days of an election may be a good time for a candidate to use this technique. A cryptic note is written something like this:

```
Dear Mr. Smith,
   I urgently need you to send a $50 donation
today.
   I cannot explain why right now. If I were to
explain why, this could tip my hand to my
opponent and he would be able to take counter-
measures.
   I will fully explain why after the election.
   You will see how urgent this matter is when I
reveal all the details to you later.
   We are in the closing days of the campaign.
   I will be so thankful if you will just trust
me and put your $50 donation in the mail right
now, before you put my note aside and go on to
something else.
   Thank you so much for understanding,
                          John Doe
                          Candidate for Congress
```

Put your cryptic note on a personal note card or personal monarch-sized letterhead. Since you'll only be sending your cryptic note to your best donors, include a reply envelope with multiple stamps affixed totaling the first class postage amount. Stamps on the reply envelope help communicate urgency, an expectation of a response, and adds to the personal look and feel of the appeal.

A cryptic note will work only to your loyal supporters. You will need to have established a great deal of credibility with your donors for a cryptic note to be effective, but it can be very effective in the right situation.

Be sure you really have a good reason for a cryptic note, because you will need to explain your reason later, in your thank you letter. If your reason falls flat, if it's not a true emergency, if your reason for secrecy turns out to be bogus, you will inflict serious damage on your housefile. Do not cry wolf with your cryptic note. In fact, do not ever cry wolf with your direct mail solicitations.

Think very carefully before you send a cryptic note. Do not insult the intelligence of your supporters. You cannot repair lost credibility with your housefile. Your donors support you because they trust you. They believe what you tell them. Do not destroy that trust with an ill-conceived cryptic note.

29. Certificate of Appreciation

Sending a frameable Certificate of Appreciation is a great way to thank your donors. The certificate should be impressive, resembling a college diploma. It should be on heavy paper with a decorative border, and with the name of the donor in large print right in the center.

This technique allows you to gush thanks on your donors for all their past support. The certificate should also include text describing the organization's mission, the logo of the organization, and it should be signed by the head of the organization.

On the reply form, ask your donors to indicate whether their certificate arrived in good condition with their name spelled correctly. And, as always, be sure to ask again for a contribution to support the organization's ongoing work.

Figure 7.12

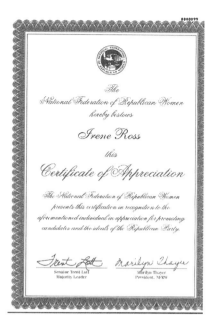

For your very best donors, those who contribute $1,000 or more, consider sending the certificate in an actual frame and in a box.

Certificate of Appreciation packages are not going to be your biggest revenue producers, average at best. But they are a great way to thank your supporters and cement their loyalty to your organization. I'm a big fan of well-done Certificates of Appreciation, because I believe they dramatically improve the overall results of future housefile appeals. It's also just good manners to thank your supporters in a meaningful way.

30. Wall of Honor

Create a Wall of Honor at your national headquarters for those who have given your organization $1,000 or more. Take a photo of the engraved name on your Wall of Honor and mail it to each of your $1,000-plus givers. What a great way to cement the loyalty of your very best contributors!

Believe me, this will be well worth the expense and effort.

Anyone who's giving you $1,000 or more loves what you are doing. Over time, each of these donors may be worth $20,000 or more to your organization. Wouldn't it be worth spending some time and effort to show these wonderful loyal supporters of yours that their support has been noticed, and, indeed, is permanently memorialized on a Wall of Honor? Invite your supporters to your headquarters to see your Wall of Honor.

The most popular war memorial in Washington, D.C., is the Vietnam War Memorial. It's popular because the name of every person who died in that war is forever etched in those black stone panels. There's an eternal quality to names engraved in stone or metal.

There's no greater honor than for athletes to be admitted to the Hall of Fame of their sport. Admission to the Pro Football Hall of Fame means your achievements in football will never be forgotten. Your Wall of Honor for your best contributors can approximate this feeling. It's like a Hall of Fame for those who have contributed the most to the growth and success of your organization.

Promote the Wall of Honor to your $100-plus donors. A rule of thumb is that someone who contributes one amount through the mail, with no special prodding, can be persuaded to contribute ten times that amount. Offering to permanently engrave a donor's name on a "Wall of Honor" is a persuasive inducement to achieve $1,000 donor status.

An effective mailing is to give your better donors a status report as to where they stand concerning being forever memorialized on your Wall of Honor. The purpose of the mailing is, for example, to alert donors who have contributed $735 to date that a contribution of just $265 will qualify them to have their names permanently engraved on your organization's Wall of Honor.

Some of your donors will have achieved near Wall of Honor status simply by faithfully contributing in $15 and $20 increments over the years. These donors are not likely to contribute much more than that in answer to your letter, but alerting these faithful lower-dollar supporters as to where they stand with regard to having their name engraved on your Wall of Honor is effective encouragement for them to continue their loyal support.

Other benefits to these $1,000 donors should accrue as well. I discuss these benefits in the section on giving clubs—benefits designed to keep your supporters giving faithfully, hopefully at even higher levels.

The Wall of Honor strategy creates a sense not just of appreciation and thanks, but also an atmosphere of prestige and exclusivity. Honor, prestige, and exclusivity are powerful incentives to contribute. That's why universities like to name buildings after their best donors. Colleges tell a super-rich alum: "Give us $50,000,000 and we'll name a building after you." The alum agrees. A building is built and named after him. He is now assured his name will be remembered long after he's dead and gone.

Your Wall of Honor can create that same feeling for your supporters. You should constantly promote your Wall of Honor in your quarterly newsletter and even write feature articles on your newest Wall of Honor inductees.

31. Extensive Proposal

This is constructed like a business plan or prospectus for investors.

I use it to launch a major project for an organization. It includes an introduction explaining the need for the project and what you hope to achieve. It should include reasons as to why you think this new project will be successful in achieving the organization's goal, or, far more importantly, the donor's goal.

Your proposal will also include a detailed budget, line item by line item, with descriptions accompanying each line item or section. The impression you want to convey is that you have put a great deal of thought into this project and into the funding that will be required to put the entire battle plan in place. The document should look impressive.

For your best donors, consider putting this document in a see-through plastic binder to give it a serious, heavyweight look. The proposal should be at least 16 pages in length, at least the version you send to the best 20 percent of your supporters. Remember the 80/20 rule! That is, 80 percent of your housefile net income will come from the best 20 percent of your givers.

At the end of your proposal, be sure to include another appeal for a contribution, similar to your letter. Consider putting handwritten notes in strategic locations throughout your proposal.

As always, include a cover letter with your proposal—the fundraising appeal.

Send your proposal in an impressive envelope. Consider a USPS Priority Mail envelope or even FedEx for your best donors, or at a minimum a 9" x 12" closed-face carrier clearly marked First Class with a green-diamond border. I've even mailed especially thick proposal packages in a cardboard box, which our production department has labeled "Ben's pizza box mailing."

Send less costly versions of the proposal to your lower-dollar givers. But keep it in a 9" x 12" carrier. You would never expect to receive a serious proposal, business plan, or prospectus in a No. 10 envelope.

I have raised many millions of dollars with impressive proposal packages over the years. It's always among my most successful mailings. But make sure you are serious about carrying out your proposal and have a realistic chance to make your proposal a reality in relatively short order. Your supporters will expect updates on the status of the project in subsequent letters.

It's fine if you go back to your supporters with budget shortfall letters explaining that you have fallen short of funding your entire proposal and need additional help. Budget shortfall appeals can be very successful. But never follow your dramatic proposal mailing with something completely different, as though you never mailed this impressive proposal. That's one of the fastest ways to alienate your housefile.

So, before you send your proposal package, be sure you are prepared to demonstrate with specificity the project's achievements in future letters to your supporters.

Indeed, you should be doing this with your entire housefile program. Your housefile letters should not be stand-alone events. Your housefile letters should tell an ongoing story to your supporters, referring to previous letters and describing in detail precisely what has been achieved with all the donations you've received.

32. FedEx

Consider sending your fundraising package FedEx.

Because of the high cost, only use FedEx for your high-dollar donors, those who have sent a contribution of $200 or more and who have given more than once.

To save on cost, use FedEx's two-day delivery service instead of overnight. FedEx is always coming out with new products, such as FedEx Ground to compete with UPS, which may also reduce your cost.

Anything with FedEx on the carrier will be opened.

As with all techniques, be sure you explain your reason for sending your letter this way. With the FedEx technique, you'll want to make sure the need is clearly urgent and that there is a time deadline that is rapidly approaching.

Your opening line should say something like:

```
Dear Mrs. Smith,
  I have undertaken the extra cost of rushing
you this letter Federal Express because ...
```

And your reason better be a good one, or you'll irritate your supporters for wasting money on such an expensive mailing.

For your very best supporters, consider also including a FedEx return envelope, complete with your organization's name, address, and FedEx account number already filled in for your contributor. FedEx will charge you only for the FedEx reply envelopes that are actually used by your readers.

UPS is a less costly alternative to FedEx. And a USPS Priority Mail letter is the least costly product that will give your mailing an authentic express delivery look. The USPS Priority Mail letter arrives no more quickly than regular first class mail. But that's fine, because what you are after is an official express delivery look that will ensure your reader opens your package.

33. Express Delivery Knock-Offs

You can't afford to send a FedEx package (or even a less costly USPS Priority Mail letter) to more than about 10 percent of your best contributors on a typical direct mail housefile.

So what do you send the other 90 percent?

Our agency has developed all kinds of FedEx knock-off carriers that create the impression of an "express delivery" package, but which can be mailed at the nonprofit or bulk rate.

It's important to keep coming up with new "express delivery" appearing carriers so your readers won't recognize it as "junk mail" when your letter arrives in their mailboxes for the third and fourth time.

Make your knockoff express delivery carrier a large envelope, at least a 9" x 12". I've tested express delivery graphics on a standard No. 10 envelope, and it provides little if any lift over even a blank carrier envelope. Knockoff express delivery

Figure 7.13

graphics on a standard No. 10 window carrier just come across as junk mail. Most effective is to use a heavier paper stock for your knockoff express delivery carrier, so as to approximate the cardboardish feel of the Post Office's Priority Mail letter.

Of course, cost is always a consideration, especially when mailing to low-dollar donors and prospect lists, which usually include a lot of $5 and $10 givers. So it may not be cost-effective to use a cardboardish paper stock for your knockoff express delivery carrier. As always, you'll need to test and crunch your numbers.

Be very careful to design your knockoff express delivery carriers in such a way that you won't be sued by FedEx or some other express delivery company. Avoid using a name for your product that is similar to FedEx or UPS, or any other express delivery company, or you will be contacted by attorneys for these companies who, at a minimum, will demand that you cease and desist. And make sure the carrier you come up with passes muster with the post office. Have your knock-off express delivery carrier cleared by the post office before you start printing large quantities.

I will also often use the knockoff express delivery design I've come up with for my BRE return envelope and on the reply form, so as to give my package a unified look and feel and to make it appear even more like a new FedExish product. For these packages, use a BRE. Enclosing a reply envelope that requires readers to find and affix their own stamps destroys the official FedExish look and feel you are trying to achieve for your package.

34. Taped "Announcement" and "Reminder" Phone Messages

It's very inexpensive now to phone your donors with a 30-second taped message. You can do this for about six cents per completed call these days (depending on the volume of calls).

You can use a taped 30-second message to alert your supporters that you are sending them a very important letter that will arrive in the next day or two. This is a precall. Don't give away too much about the specific contents or topic of the mailing. Create a sense of mystery. Just describe what the letter looks like so your supporter can keep an eye out for it. Stress that the letter is of great importance, perhaps concerning some major announcement that will make national news. The taped message should be from the letter-signer. It's especially helpful if the letter and the taped message is from a well-known celebrity or luminary.

Think of your precall like a super-charged teaser.

But instead of graphics or a headline on a carrier designed to provoke interest and curiosity, you're phoning your reader, which is an especially potent strategy for making sure your letter is noticed and opened when it arrives.

Just make sure the letter you're sending really is newsworthy and important. As with every direct mail technique, pick your shots carefully. Don't abuse your most potent techniques through overuse; and tailor your technique to the type of appeal you're sending.

You can also use the 30-second taped message a few days after your letter has arrived (in a postcall) to remind your readers to answer your letter. Skillful and carefully timed use of a 30-second taped message precall and postcall will often boost returns 15 percent to 25 percent.

I also sometimes use the taped message just to thank donors for supporting the organization. At six or ten cents a call, this is far less expensive than a mailed thank you letter—though I would never use the taped thank you phone call in lieu of a mailed thank you note. I would use the phone call *in addition* to a regular thank you note.

Very often your supporter will not pick up the phone to hear your 30-second taped message. Caller ID and other phone-screening devices are making it very difficult for telemarketers these days, and I'm glad about that. But that's fine for your 30-second taped message. You just leave your taped message on the answering machine or voice mail. In fact, that's even more effective, because voice mail messages are often saved and listened to several times, creating repeat impressions on the mind of your supporter.

35. Enclose a No. 2 Pencil

I'll sometimes enclose a No. 2 pencil with my survey packages. Printed on the pencil will be the organization's name and address. The survey package will be constructed to look like an official test, like an SAT, with round circles next to the answers the reader will need to color in with a No. 2 pencil. The instructions will explicitly ask the reader to use the No. 2 pencil.

The virtue of this approach is that it underscores the importance of the survey by making it look so official. The pencil also bulges the envelope, virtually guaranteeing the envelope will be opened.

The conventional wisdom in direct mail is that getting your envelope opened is half the battle. That's not quite true.

Most envelopes are opened and then the material promptly discarded. Including a No. 2 pencil with your survey package will pique your reader's curiosity long enough so you can begin the battle for the contribution. This device gives you an excellent chance to get to the battle. Most direct mail packages I see never make it to the battle, never penetrate the reader's consciousness.

36. Put More Than One Stamp on the Reply Envelope

In letters to the best 15 to 20 percent of donors on a house-file, I'll affix first class postage stamps to the reply envelope. This significantly enhances the personal look of your communication and commands the reader's attention.

But if you're going to spend money to put first class postage on the reply envelope, be sure to use more than one stamp. I'll often affix five stamps on the reply envelope, adding up to the first class postage amount.

The purpose of affixing all these stamps is to call attention to the fact that a reply is called for. It acts like a billboard. You've missed an opportunity to create this billboard effect if you use only one stamp. I also want the stamps to be a little

Figure 7.14

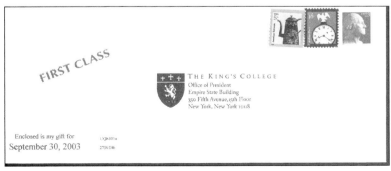

askew, not perfectly neat and straight. This further adds to the personal look of the appeal.

This rule also applies when you're affixing first class postage to your carrier envelope. If you use a meter or just one stamp, you've wasted the money. Create a billboard effect. Draw attention to the first class postage by using many stamps.

37. Paper-Clip Stamps to Your Letter

Paper-clipping stamps to your letter is another way to command your reader's attention.

Explain what you want your readers to use the stamps for. Perhaps they should use the stamps on the reply envelope. Or perhaps they should use the stamps to mail the enclosed postcard or letter to their congressman. Have some reason.

The psychology here is a lot like enclosing a $1 bill with your letter. It gets your reader's attention because it's an odd thing to do. But, as with every technique and every odd thing you do to get attention, provide an explanation that makes sense. Anyone can get attention by doing something odd. If you run down the street naked, you will get attention, but it may not be the kind of attention you want.

38. Wife Letter

For election campaign appeals, letters signed by the wife of a candidate can be a very strong technique, but only to loyal supporters. You would not want to use this strategy for a prospect letter.

The virtue of a wife letter is that it allows the wife to say things about the candidate that the candidate cannot say. The wife can talk about how hard the candidate is working, the long hours he's spending on the campaign trail, what this has meant to the family, how much he cares about the issues he's fighting for, what a great husband and father he is, etc. A wife can make the kind of emotional appeal that would be inappropriate for the candidate to make about himself.

Figure 7.15

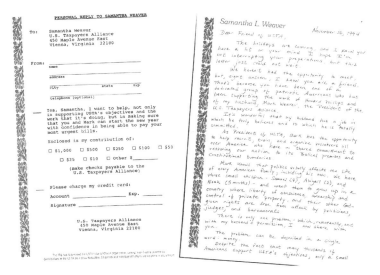

A wife letter should be self-deprecating. She should say something like: "I've never written a letter asking for money before, but my husband Jim is on the campaign trail right now and cannot write to you himself. I know that the campaign is in desperate need of funds, so I told Jim I would write to you and other loyal friends to ask for help."

The child of a candidate can also be a good letter-signer, because a child can say things about the candidate and campaign from a child's perspective. People will always read a letter from a child.

Wife letters should be feminine looking, printed on pastel colored, even pink or raspberry paper in an envelope that looks like it might contain a Hallmark card. I know I may be sounding a bit sexist right now. But my role here is to tell you what works. Also, use a feminine-looking handwritten font to address the envelope. Computers can now replicate the letter signer's actual handwriting. Including a family photo with the wife letter will further strengthen your appeal. Good photos will strengthen many fundraising packages.

By the way, if the candidate is a woman, a letter from the husband won't work nearly as well. I know what I'm saying is "politically incorrect." But facts are facts and results don't lie. Your readers just don't expect to read heartfelt, "cry on the page" letters from husbands of candidates.

39. Debt-Reduction Letter

This is an essential staple of almost all my housefile programs.

Virtually every organization, even the most successful, has debt. So almost every organization can truthfully mail a debt-reduction letter at least occasionally to its supporters.

My rule is that if you are not running at least a slight debt on your prospect program, you're not mailing enough. And you're stunting the growth of your organization. So almost all organizations, especially those that are growing, always have a debt they need to take care of.

Debt-reduction appeals should only be mailed to your multi-givers, those who have demonstrated loyalty to your organization. Mail something else to those who have given only once. Your one-time givers don't care about your debt. They just want the problem solved that your organization was set up to address. And they don't care very much about any financial problems your organization might have.

But your loyal supporters—your multigivers—care about you. They feel a personal bond with you. They've been receiving letters from you for perhaps years, and they'll want to help you out of your, hopefully, temporary financial crisis.

But don't mail debt-reduction appeals too often. Once or twice a year is enough. More than that, and even your most loyal supporters will start to wonder if you're being responsible with the money they're sending you. After a while, you'll cut even your own child off if you think your loved one is squandering money. Your supporters want their donations to be used for the cause your organization is supposed to be advancing or the problem your organization is supposed to be solving. But they won't mind an occasional debt-reduction letter, if the reason for the debt is a good one.

I'm a believer that most debt-reduction letters should be relatively short—not my typical eight-page manifesto that I often write for prospect appeals or for large new projects to the housefile.

The reason is that you are sending this letter only to your most loyal supporters, perhaps the best 40 percent of donors on your housefile. These people are with you. They know what you do. They don't need the mission of your organization explained. If you give a good reason for the debt, if you show that the situation is temporary, and if you prove that the debt is not the result of financial mismanagement, your supporters will give.

I like two-page debt-reduction letters. If you have to go longer to explain the reason for the debt, perhaps the reason is too convoluted for your supporters to follow. In that case, your debt-reduction letter will fail.

A debt-reduction letter should be as personal as possible, on personal letterhead. A monarch-sized carrier and letterhead helps make the letter look more personal. And the carrier should be closed face, not a window carrier. Your letter should come across as a communication from one person to another, not a communication to the masses. Your letter should be emotional. You should bleed on the page.

Your letter should be a cry for help. In fact, I sometimes headline my debt-reduction letters "A Cry for Help" so that the reader will know exactly what this is.

For political organizations, right after an election is a good time for a debt-reduction appeal because of all the money the organization has spent to win the election, thus depleting its coffers. In this case, you can use the debt-reduction letter as a springboard to talk about all your great achievements and election victories—effective for political action committees, assuming there are victories to talk about. In this case, clearly the debt is not the result of financial mismanagement, but is the result of using contributions effectively for what they're supposed to be used for.

After all, your donors are not sending you money so you can build up a big savings account either. Spending the money on what it's supposed to be used for—achieving documentable results—is always a great reason for a debt.

I might say something like this: "I thought long and hard about going into debt. I considered what was at stake in this election. And I did not want to wake up the morning after the election with John Kerry as the new president-elect and wonder, could I have done more? So I made the decision to buy another $543,000 of TV ads in four key battleground states where I knew the election would be won or lost."

I'll sometimes talk about an enormously successful membership drive the organization has just completed, for example, a prospecting campaign which almost always produces debt—a membership drive that will ultimately make the organization even more powerful and influential but has caused a temporary financial crunch that could require layoffs of dedicated staff and cutbacks on key projects if I don't receive a strong near-100 percent response to this letter.

I might also talk about a budget shortfall, a letter describing how we have fallen short of funding a project budget outlined in my previous letter. I am therefore sending this follow-up letter to close this budget shortfall so I won't need to scale back our plans.

There are all sorts of great reasons for a debt-reduction letter. Make sure your reason is easy for the reader to grasp. And give just one reason for your debt, not many reasons, or you'll come across as grasping for straws. One reason is always more believable than many reasons. Is a teacher more likely to believe a child who gives just one good solid reason for forgetting his homework, or a child who gives ten reasons? One reason is always far more believable. And be scrupulously truthful. Your reader knows when you're blowing smoke.

After an election, candidates, successful or not, mail almost all debt-reduction appeals, but they're a special case. After an election, there's nothing else for candidates to write about except retiring debt from their campaign. The trick here with each letter is to continuously provide status reports on your debt-retirement efforts and to package your debt-retirement appeals many different ways. In the case of debt-retirement letters for candidates, I'll bleed on the page on behalf of all the printers and small business people to whom the candidate still owes money.

I can speak from personal experience. I'm still owed tens of thousands of dollars from political campaigns long over, which is why I've learned to be very careful about any political candidates I take on as clients. It's no fun to call the campaign office after the election to see about getting your bill paid only to find that the phone has been disconnected.

40. Enclose Copies of Invoices that Must be Paid

This can add fuel to a debt-reduction appeal.

All of us can sympathize with the feeling of dread that comes with staring at a stack of bills you can't pay. Be sure your letter describes how your loyal vendors, mostly small business people, went out on a limb and extended you significant credit because they trusted you to pay your bills, and because they believed in your cause and what you are trying to achieve.

Explain how you have always managed to pay your bills in the past, which is why these small-business people were willing to give you such favorable credit terms. Explain how, not only will your organization's credit be damaged if you fail to pay these invoices by a specified date, but that some of these hard-working small-business people could go bankrupt or could be hurt very badly. Obviously, you'll need to craft your appeal to fit the facts of the situation, but you can see the general drift.

Including copies of actual invoices that must be paid by a certain date helps show your reader that this is a true problem with potentially ruinous consequences for real people, including your organization and the cause your donors care about.

This appeal is most effective for the most loyal 40 to 50 percent of your active housefile. This is obviously not an effective prospect appeal. Nor will it work especially well for your low-dollar givers who have only contributed once to your organization or campaign. But it should produce a very strong response from your loyal supporters.

41. Summer Slump

Summer-slump appeals are similar to debt-reduction appeals, though not as dire in tone.

Like a debt-reduction letter, this is mailed to your best supporters and is usually two pages—a relatively short letter.

Your letter explains that summer is a time when donations always drop. People are typically on vacation and enjoying nice weather. They are visiting their grandchildren, having barbecues and are not answering your letters as faithfully as they do during other parts of the year. The bottom line is: "Your donation is needed to help get us through this three-month summer slump." Consider combining a summer-slump appeal with the three-envelope, three-month pledge technique described earlier.

As with all your fundraising letters, be sure to describe the consequences of failing to make up the revenue shortfall that will occur if your readers neglect to answer your summer-slump appeal. Discuss programs you'll need to cut back or cancel if your letter is not answered. Describe specifically what will happen if you're forced to scale back or cancel your programs designed to advance the issue or cause your supporters care about. "We won't be able to deliver enough turkey dinners to homeless families for Thanksgiving." Or, "We won't be able to collect and deliver enough toys to hospitalized children for Christmas." Or, some horrendous piece of legislation will pass "if we're forced to cut back our nationwide grassroots lobbying campaign."

42. Annual Report

Every publicly traded corporation in America must produce an Annual Report for its shareholders. Charities and nonprofits should, too, and combine it with a fundraising letter.

Your Annual Report should be an impressive looking document that explains how much money the organization took in, where it came from, and how it was spent. It should include photographs, pie charts, and graphs showing the organization's growth—copy describing all your programs and accomplishments, and testimonials about your organization's effectiveness.

An Annual Report mailing is the opposite of a debt-reduction mailing, because an annual report seeks to communicate the rock-solid strength and astounding growth of your organization. Your annual report tells your supporters they are part of a winning team.

Your Annual Report should be mailed in a large envelope, a 9" x 12" or even larger.

Your Annual Report mailing will not be your best revenue-producing letter of the year. The annual report tends to distract your readers from your letter and reply form and undermines the urgency of your appeal. But not every letter you send should be an emergency, or else letters describing true emergencies won't be believed.

Your Annual Report mailing is designed to make your supporters feel good about the donations they've sent you over the past year. It's meant to reassure your supporters that the contributions they've sent were a good investment. Of course, your letter should remind your readers of the need for ongoing support, and that the money needed to fund vital projects comes entirely from voluntary donations.

Your Annual Report mailing is an important tool for cementing the loyalty of your housefile, which, in turn, will significantly improve results from your subsequent fundraising appeals throughout the year.

The reply form should include an "Annual Report Delivery

Receipt" that the supporter marks and returns to indicate they've received your Annual Report in good condition. As always, the reply form should also include a prominent contribution section.

43. Name and Address Labels

This falls into the category of premium mailings, in which you enclose a gift with your fundraising letter. In this case the gift is a set of 30 or so labels with the reader's name and address printed on them for use on the reader's personal letters and correspondence.

The gift is inexpensive. It will likely only add a couple of pennies to the cost of your mailing, depending on volume. But address labels are attention getting because there's nothing more attention getting than for readers to see their own names.

There's one way I can guarantee that you will read an entire book, and that's if I give you a book that's about you and your life with your name emblazoned across the dust jacket. Is there any doubt you would read such a book? Including a set of personalized address labels commands the reader's attention, because someone went to the trouble of actually printing the reader's name and address on these labels and then sending them to the reader.

For a little extra cost, you can put decorative gold foil on each label, which seems to enhance the value of the labels in the mind of the reader. I'm not exactly sure what it is about gold foil, but all recent tests indicate that adding decorative gold foil to your name and address labels dramatically improves results. Perhaps it's that glittering gold conveys importance, prestige, and value. Maybe it's that the gold foil shows that the letter sender put some extra thought into designing these attractive and personalized name and address labels. Whatever it is, there's something in the human psyche that responds positively to sparkling gold foil, even if the recipient knows the gold foil has no monetary value.

I think we see that in how women respond to gold. Most women I know would much prefer a yellow gold necklace to a necklace made with white gold, or even a platinum necklace, which has greater monetary value. There's just something about that glistening gold color that creates a giddy feeling in most people.

Sometimes I'll also include the organization's logo on the address label, sometimes I won't. It doesn't appear to make much difference either way to results. The main thing is that address labels are an inexpensive personalized gift anyone can use and will appreciate. Most important, from your point of view, this is another device that will help draw your prospective donor into reading your letter, or at least start to read it. Whether your reader decides in the end to send a contribution will still depend, as always, on the power of the arguments you present in your letter.

44. Sweepstakes

Sweepstakes packages are not just for Publisher's Clearing House and *Reader's Digest.*

Sweepstakes can work very well for charities.

Holding a sweepstakes contest is another attention-getting device. In fact, you say pointblank in your letter that your reason for sponsoring a sweepstakes contest is to get attention for your cause. The psychology you're tapping into is similar to holding a raffle or sponsoring a Bingo game. You're holding out the possibility to your prospective donor of winning something of significant value, perhaps even a lot of money, while at the same time doing something good by sending a donation with your completed sweepstakes entry form.

The odds of winning sweepstakes prizes are the same for those who donate as for those who choose to return their entry form without a donation. And you make that clear in your copy. But many sweepstakes players believe their odds are better if they send a donation, regardless of your assurances to the contrary.

Include two reply envelopes: one labeled "SWEEPSTAKES ENTRY WITH NO DONATION ENCLOSED," the other labeled "SWEEPSTAKES ENTRY WITH DONATION ENCLOSED." Make sure the two reply envelopes are different colors to distinguish them: perhaps red for the "NO DONATION" reply envelope and green for the "DONATION ENCLOSED" envelope. This tactic reinforces the suspicion in the prospective donor's mind that their odds of winning are somehow enhanced by including a donation, even though you've clearly and repeatedly told your reader that's not the case. The odds are exactly equal for donors and nondonors and must be by law.

For prospect mailings, a sweepstakes is a tremendously powerful technique for generating a high response rate, often 8 percent for sweeps packages compared to 2 percent or 3 percent for a conventional prospecting package. But your average donation will only be about $6.

There are millions of people out there who are genetically wired to respond to sweepstakes appeals. These people will enter almost every sweepstakes contest, hoping they'll win the $1 million prize. And many will throw a modest donation in with their sweepstakes entry form.

You don't have to offer a $1 million sweepstakes prize to have a successful sweeps fundraising appeal. A $50,000 or $25,000 prize can work just as well—and, frankly, a less-than extravagant prize is more appropriate for a charity.

Sweepstakes mailings only work in prospect campaigns for noncontroversial causes—causes that anyone would support. Curing cancer, helping hospitalized veterans, feeding and sheltering the homeless, rescuing abandoned pets or abused animals are the kind of general appeal causes that can work well for a sweepstakes contest.

Political issue causes are not strong candidates for a sweepstakes prospecting appeal. Sweepstakes contests should not be used for any cause that is at all controversial. Political issues are always controversial. You don't want to lose half your possible sweeps donors because they disagree with you. Instead, you want to appeal to everyone who is remotely inclined to contribute to a worthy cause. Therefore, you should select causes for your sweeps packages that almost no one will disagree with, such as the need to cure cancer or feed a hungry child.

Once you have sweepstakes donors on your housefile, you'll need to keep mailing them more sweepstakes packages, which will continue to generate a low average donation, but an even higher response rate. You'll now have two housefiles, one for sweeps donors and one for your conventional donors. One housefile is made up of people who like to enter sweeps contests and don't mind supporting your cause once in a while with $5 and $10 donations. The other housefile is made of people who are there because they actively support what you're doing and are not much interested in the sweepstakes contests you're running.

Along the way, you should mail your strongest conventional fundraising appeals to your sweeps donors. Over time, you can persuade about 30 percent of your sweeps file to contribute to your conventional housefile appeals. You can also successfully mail sweeps packages to your regular housefile; although I would not do that more than once a year. For the most part, you should treat your sweepstakes housefile—especially those who have only contributed to sweepstakes appeals—as separate from your conventional housefile. Consider your sweepstakes housefile as a strong prospect list for your conventional housefile.

You might wonder: how can my small charity afford to sponsor a $1 million prize—or even a $50,000 or $25,000 prize? The answer is, you don't come up with the prize yourself. You buy into a sweepstakes contest that has already been set up and may have been going for quite some time. There are companies that do nothing but hold sweepstakes contests. These companies are responsible for the prize money. They then ask advertisers and fundraising mailers to buy into the contest, usually paying a royalty for each letter you mail.

It's not all that expensive to buy into a sweepstakes contest. It might only add a penny or so to the cost of your package. This gives you an idea of how many promotional letters are connected to the typical sweeps contest. A sweepstakes contest can go on for years. Eventually someone will win the $1 million prize, but not before tens of millions of letters are mailed promoting the contest. Needless to say, the odds of winning a sweepstakes prize are infinitesimal.

Because I prefer a less fantastic prize offering for charitable fundraising of $50,000, $25,000, or even just $5,000, often you can handle the prize yourself. You can even sometimes get your vendors to donate the prize money. Not buying into a larger sweeps contest offered by a sweeps company, and, instead, putting up a more modest prize yourself helps greatly simplify your sweepstakes mailings.

Because of past sweepstakes abuse and scandal by advertisers, there are all sorts of laws now governing the conduct of sweepstakes contests. A sweepstakes contest cannot go on beyond a certain time limit. The odds of winning must be stated in the fine print. Sweeps packages are heavily scrutinized by government regulators. And there are other laws and regulations governing sweeps contests—laws that are changing all the time, generally in the direction of getting tougher.

If you're using a sweeps company to sponsor the contest, the company will make sure your package meets all the legal requirements. The company will likely even provide the sweepstakes copy. There are copywriters who specialize in writing only for sweepstakes packages, and they're making a great living. All you'll need to do is supply the fundraising portion of the package and hand it to the sweeps copywriter who will weave it in.

And there are lawyers who specialize in keeping up with all laws governing sweeps contests. You must be scrupulous to follow all laws governing sweepstakes contests, or you could be put out of business, and quickly, with mammoth fines and litigation from some ambitious state attorney general. Because of these legal risks, many charities are abandoning their sweepstakes programs.

The psychology of a sweepstakes fundraising appeal is completely different from conventional direct mail fundraising appeals. Remember, for sweeps fundraising appeals, the cause is mostly a sideshow. It could be almost any cause, as long as it's not controversial. The main event for the sweepstakes player is the sweepstakes contest.

45. Greeting Cards

Enclosing a set of four or five attractive greeting cards or note cards with accompanying envelopes for the cards is a technique that can work well for charitable humanitarian appeals but is not especially effective for political causes.

This also works best for female recipients of your fund appeal. Men are notoriously negligent about writing thank you notes or courtesy letters of any kind. So a set of note cards as a gift won't appeal to most men. But women like them.

The cards should approximate Hallmark quality in appearance. They should have a pleasing design that anyone will find attractive and, most importantly, won't turn anyone off. No offbeat or bizarre designs. An attractive image of a rose or flower on the cover of the cards can work well and is low risk. The same is true for landscapes, which can be attractive and are inoffensive. Famous artwork is also an option, but can often be expensive, requiring stiff royalty fees by owners of the artwork. For charities centered around helping children, artwork from the children you're trying to help can be effective and helps tie the technique to the cause you're writing about. For appeals dealing with Native Americans, consider using their attractive artwork on your greeting cards.

The reply form should be a Receipt Verification Form (or some similar variation), which you ask your readers to fill out and return to acknowledge receipt of the free note cards.

The Receipt Verification Form should be phrased something like this:

Cure Cancer
Gift Receipt Verification

Dear Jim,

Thank you for the lovely gift of Norman Rockwell note cards. The cards arrived in good condition. To help you continue your work to find a cure for cancer, **I am enclosing a gift of:**

[ ]$15 [ ]$20 [ ]$25 [ ]$50 [ ]$100 [ ]Other $_____

Please make your donation check payable to:

Conquer Cancer

[ ] I received my free gift of Norman Rockwell note cards, but I cannot contribute to help find a cure for cancer.

For charitable humanitarian causes, entire housefiles are often built with up-front "premium" or "free gift" packages, which tap into a different psychology from your action-oriented political issue contributors.

The gift is attention-getting. It has perceived value. It creates a suggestion that this gift should be reciprocated with a gift in the form of a donation. After all, that's just basic good manners.

Upfront premium or gift packages tend to generate a low to average contribution. You're hoping for a high response rate of perhaps 4 percent with a lot of $10 and $15 donations.

46. Calendar

This is another form of up-front premium or gift package. If you've built your housefile on gift-enclosed appeals you will

192 ▶ FUND YOUR CAUSE

need to continuously send your housefile up-front premiums or gifts, because that's what triggers your donors to respond.

A calendar is a great gift for a housefile mailing in the fall because your supporters will keep the calendar on their wall all year. Be sure not to send your calendar too late in the year. You want your calendar to be the first calendar they receive, so they'll put yours up on the wall and start filling in dates to remember. Once they've started writing on a calendar, they're not likely to use another one.

Attractive photographs of landscapes for each month work best. As a general rule, don't use photographs of people for your calendar. Landscapes and nature scenes are safest for your photos. Exceptions to this rule might be shots of aircraft carriers, planes, soldiers, and the like for veterans appeals, or firefighters and police officers doing their jobs for firefighter and police charities. The rule is to use images no one will mind having on their wall all year.

A terrific feature of a calendar is that it provides a year-round advertisement for your organization. Use the inside of the front and back cover of your calendar to chronicle the achievements and to state the mission of your organization.

Similar to the greeting card technique previously described, the reply form should be a "Calendar Receipt Verification" that commands a reply from your reader.

47. Bumper Stickers and Window Decals

People love bumper stickers and window decals.

The primary purpose of the sticker is to reinforce the headline message of your package. The target audience for the sticker is not people on the road who will see the sticker on cars, but the reader of the letter.

You want your sticker to make some key point to your reader. Like the headlines in your package, the sticker should, in effect, be another headline aimed at grabbing your reader's attention.

Examples of bumper sticker messages I've used include "Support Term Limits for Congress" for Americans to Limit Congressional Terms; "I Support My Local Police" for a police charity; "I'm a Christian, and I *Always* Vote" for Christian Coalition; "Stop Government Waste"; "Stop Socialized Medicine"; or "Stop Union Political Abuse."

None of these slogans are clever. In fact, avoid clever phrases on bumper stickers. Be absolutely straight forward, clear, and simple. Again, my rule in direct mail marketing is: "If you can't sum up your cause in a single phrase that will fit neatly on a bumper sticker, your mailing is doomed."

So put this rule to the test by actually putting the central message of your appeal on a bumper sticker.

The purpose of your bumper sticker is to announce to your reader what your letter is about. A secondary benefit of a bumper sticker is that it will be seen on cars and help publicize the issue of concern to your supporters. But that's only a distant secondary benefit. The chief purpose of enclosing a bumper sticker or window decal, as with any insert, is to increase donations. If it doesn't increase donations, leave it out and save money.

Since a bumper sticker can add significantly to the cost of a package, perhaps three cents per letter, I will usually test packages with and without the bumper sticker. The wrong sticker, one that is even slightly off message, will often depress returns.

48. Congressional Scorecard

I built the Christian Coalition's housefile of two million members and supporters in the 1990s mostly with a Congressional Scorecard package, which became famous.

I mailed about 80 million copies of this basic package in various updated versions over a five-year period. The package included a Congressional Scorecard, a survey folded in a booklet format, and a six-page letter.

The scorecard was a report in index form on how each member of Congress voted on 10 or 12 issues of concern to the Christian Coalition and its supporters. The letter asked for donations to "help distribute 30,000,000 million CONGRESSIONAL SCORECARDS and VOTER GUIDES to Christian voters in time for the upcoming election."

The letter explained the problem of Christian voters not being as well-informed as they should be concerning how their elected representatives are voting in Washington. The letter proposed wide distribution of the "enclosed CONGRESSIONAL SCORECARD" as the solution to this problem. "These Scorecards will ensure an *informed* Christian vote on Election Day," the letter explained.

To buttress this argument, the letter pointed out that a common practice of liberal politicians in conservative districts and states is to create an impression in their speeches and communications to constituents that they support traditional moral values, but then they turn around and vote against traditional moral values in Congress, because they know their constituents are not paying close attention to votes in Congress.

Figure 7.16

In addition, Congress has mastered the art of concealing controversial votes by making sure the really important vote is a complex procedural vote that only experts who follow Congress closely can understand, and sometimes not even then. The Christian Coalition often included the key procedural votes as litmus test votes in the scorecard.

This drove many liberal members of Congress nuts. They would call the Christian Coalition's offices screaming into the phone. They would point to their vote in favor of, for example, traditional marriage one day and cite that as evidence that they do not support gay marriage. The Coalition would point out that the "sense of Congress resolution" to affirm traditional marriage was really a meaningless gesture. The important vote was concerning the rule that prevented a vote on the promarriage amendment.

The Congressional Scorecard package received enormous media coverage—coverage which also helped fuel the Christian Coalition's rapid growth. The Congressional Scorecard project was very easy for readers to instantly understand. It was clearly effective, as evidenced by all the media coverage and screams of outrage by liberal politicians. And distribution of the scorecard was not only inexpensive to carry out, it was a huge moneymaker for the Christian Coalition.

We could explain to readers that we needed donations to distribute more scorecard packages to Christians. In other words, to mail more of these direct mail packages was to fulfill our promise to contributors. The program and the fund appeal were the same thing. The package was self-fulfilling just by mailing it, which is exactly what you want for a successful prospect appeal.

The Christian Coalition's Congressional Scorecard became a legendary prospect package in the annals of direct mail. It built a housefile, which, in its zenith, generated more than $20 million a year in contributions to the Christian Coalition.

For a more detailed account on the rise and fall of the Christian Coalition, I encourage you to read or re-read Chapter Three in this book, "How to Create a Mass Political Movement and Change History with Direct Mail."

49. Project Budget

When raising money to fund a particular project, include a budget that outlines how much the project will cost and explains line item by line item exactly how you plan to spend the money. Almost without exception, including a budget will strengthen your appeal when launching a new project.

Your budget can be just one sheet of paper, or it can be in the form of a large proposal or prospectus, as described earlier. In the science of persuasion, the more specific you are, the more convincing are your arguments. So, whenever appropriate, include a budget.

I also usually put handwritten notes on the budget to highlight certain key points for the reader. One of these handwritten notes will say something like, "Will you help me fund this budget by sending a contribution today?" or "Your contribution will help me make this budget a reality" or "Please answer my letter by Tuesday, June 21st, so I will know if I'll have the funding needed to put this entire plan in place, or if I'll need to scale back our efforts."

A budget communicates to your readers that their contributions will be used in a specific way to fund a particular project. The money won't just disappear, unaccounted for, into some slush fund.

50. Lawsuit

A strategic lawsuit that will help advance your cause can be a great project for which to raise money. Everyone knows lawsuits are costly. A lawsuit, especially for political issue organizations, also allows your supporters to help deliver a painful blow to the political enemy, because everyone knows lawsuits are painful.

But the lawsuit must also make sense and have a realistic chance of achieving an important objective. My best legal action fundraising appeals were for an organization called Judicial Watch.

This organization's main mission was to use the civil justice system to hold corrupt government officials accountable. Most of Judicial Watch's lawsuits were aimed at uncovering corruption in the Clinton administration, projects that held out enormous appeal to conservatives and those who did not like President Clinton.

A well-aimed lawsuit has all the elements of a successful project for direct mail fundraising. It is specific and easy to understand. It has a beginning and an end—at least theoretically. It has a purpose. It inflicts pain on an enemy. You can demonstrate progress each month, allowing you to report on your latest court appearances and rulings by the judge. You can enclose a copy of your lawsuit complaint, court rulings, and deposition transcripts. You can constantly recount what has taken place so far by including a timeline of events in the legal proceeding. You can raise money to fund specific aspects of your legal proceedings, such as a deposition of a key high-profile enemy witness. My direct mail letters raised millions of dollars each year for Judicial Watch with appeals exactly along these lines.

You can also raise money to file lawsuits designed to achieve a specific policy objective. The American Civil Liberties Union has done this brilliantly with all its lawsuits aimed at getting prayer out of the public schools and references to God out of public places. Lawsuits against tobacco companies and gun manafacturers have had a major impact. Lawsuits by environmental groups against polluters have also been effective.

I happen to believe that our nation is far too litigious. I think trial lawyers seeking enormous jackpots with their class-action lawsuits and the proliferation of public-interest law firms present a serious threat to our free-enterprise system. It's becoming too costly for corporations to take risks, which, in turn, is preventing or slowing down the development of life-saving medicines. The cost of everything is higher because of lawsuit abuse. Nevertheless, from the standpoint of constructing your direct mail program, a strategic lawsuit aimed at a political opponent can be a great project for raising money.

51. Legal Defense Fund

Conversely, if you have the misfortune of becoming a target of one of these lawsuits mentioned in the previous section, you can raise money from your supporters to defend yourself.

This can be an extremely potent appeal.

Earlier in this book I discussed the work I performed for Oliver North's legal defense fund. We raised tens of millions of dollars for Oliver North through the mail.

A legal defense appeal allows you to present yourself as David fighting Goliath. You are under an unjustified assault by your rich and powerful political enemies, and you need help.

I wrote highly successful legal defense fund appeals for the Christian Coalition when it was under assault by the Federal Election Commission and the IRS—an assault we suspected was politically motivated and orchestrated by the Clinton administration. In a legal defense appeal, you can present a bleak picture of how the very survival of your organization is threatened. You can catalogue your legal expenses, and even enclose copies of the legal bills you are receiving every month.

It seemed like almost everyone involved in President Clinton's "sex-gate" scandal had a legal defense fund: Linda Tripp, Paula Jones, and others in this cast of unsavory characters whose names are now mostly forgotten, thank goodness.

President Clinton himself had an enormous legal defense fund for which he raised tens of millions of dollars in contributions. This legal defense fund became a source of scandal in itself. It turned out that the lion's share of contributions came from lobbyists and individuals looking for special favors from President Clinton. But the point remains: Legal defense funds can make great projects for effective fundraising appeals.

52. Short Cover Letter from Luminary or Authority Figure

This is sometimes called a lift note.

If you're unable to find a celebrity or luminary to sign your main fundraising letter, have your luminary sign a short two or three-paragraph note (usually on monarch-sized paper) saying how effective the organization is and urging readers to contribute.

Ideal for political organizations would be to include a letter from the President of the United States, if possible, or a well-known senator or congressman.

Even if the luminary is not well-known, sometimes the luminary's title is impressive and adds credibility to your fundraising appeal. For example, a lift note from a military general for a veterans appeal would be effective.

It's important for your lift note to be signed by a luminary or celebrity who is clearly involved in the issue or cause you are writing about. You would not want Jane Fonda or Alec Baldwin to sign a lift note for a veterans appeal. Notes from these well-known left-wing activists would undermine your veterans appeal.

But a general, even if he's not well-known, clearly can speak with authority on veterans and military matters. In the same way, a congressman can speak with authority on issues before Congress. A congressman can be a great lift note signer if the Congressman is the cosponsor of specific legislation the organization wants passed into law. The paralyzed actor Christopher Reeve signed letters about finding a cure for spinal cord injuries and became a national spokesman for federal funding for stem-cell research.

If you're going to use a celebrity to sign your lift notes and letters, it should not be the hot new box-office star. Remember, direct mail contributors are almost all over the age of 60. Pick a celebrity from their era, a star from yesteryear, someone seasoned citizens will remember and recognize, not a trendy new heartthrob.

A lift note signed by someone who has a dramatic and compelling story to tell about how he or she has been helped by the organization can also be very powerful, often more effective than a celebrity.

I put lift notes on different colored paper from the other components in the package to make the lift note jump out.

53. Testimonials and Endorsements

Testimonials and endorsements are essential features of almost any prospecting letter. Testimonials establish credibility, the organization's or candidate's *bona fides.*

Testimonials from those in a position to know help certify that the organization has a track record of success.

Testimonials and endorsements can take many different forms.

There's the obvious type of testimonial from a well-known luminary that discusses how great the organization is and how effective it is.

But there's also the negative testimonial. This is terrific for political organizations: quote the enemy on how influential, powerful, effective, and even dangerous the organization is.

With the negative testimonial, you achieve many objectives at the same time. You are reminding your readers who their enemy is. "If we have the same enemy, you must be my friend," is the psychology at work here. You raise money most effectively by underscoring the negative. You're doing this by quoting the enemy. Your enemy's quote is telling readers exactly what they want to hear. This is an organization that worries the enemy, so it must be effective. Therefore, by contributing to this organization, I can inflict some pain on my enemy. For these reasons, a negative testimonial from your adversary in political issue appeals can be at least three times more effective than a positive testimonial from an ally.

If possible, for my political appeals, I like to supply my readers a mix of positive and negative testimonials. If you supply only positive testimonials, you'll bore your reader. If you supply only negative testimonials from your adversaries, you'll get your reader's attention, but your reader may begin to wonder if you're some kind of fringe group. Your reader will want to know if there are respected people and organizations who support what you're doing. I also like to include quotes from the media if the quotes demonstrate the achievements and accomplishments of the organization.

A carefully constructed page or two of testimonials will significantly boost results on your prospect mailings. I'll also include them every so often in housefiles, just to remind an organization's supporters that they are backing an organization that is effective, influential, and respected.

The reason direct mail prospect appeals only achieve a 2 percent or 3 percent response rate, instead of a near 100 percent response rate, is credibility. If readers could be certain their donation would achieve what the letter says it will achieve, almost everyone would contribute. If you were to receive a letter from your child asking for money, and if your child gave good solid reasons for why extra money is needed, you would send money because the appeal would be credible.

If you could appear at your reader's door in person and make the case for a contribution, your response rate would be near 100 percent, especially if your prospective donor personally knows you and knows your impressive track record of past success.

In a one-on-one meeting, if you have a track record of past success and if you've delivered on all your past promises, you'll have no trouble persuading your prospective donor that you are credible and that your strategy will continue to work in the future. But you can't meet all your prospective donors in person to make your case.

Providing testimonials from others who are clearly in a position to know of your organization's effectiveness is the next best thing to making your case in person. Testimonials reassure your reader that their donations will not be wasted.

54. Book Packages (Front-End Premium)

Include a small paperback book with your letter.

The book should be directly on message with the direct mail appeal. I usually commission books to be written specifically for a direct mail appeal.

What's great about a book package, used as a front-end premium, is that it gets immediate attention for your letter. Who's not going to pay attention to a letter with a free book enclosed?

At a minimum, your prospective donors will read the first few lines of your letter to find out why you sent them this free book out of the blue. In addition, a nicely produced book will help establish instant credibility for your organization.

The primary purpose of the mailing should be to send out more books. This means your letter must make a strong case that the mere distribution of this book will achieve an important goal. For example, distribution of the book may help get

Figure 7.17

information to voters on a political issue or political opponent that they aren't likely to get from any other source.

Here's how I started a very successful 1993 book package letter for an organization called The Center for American Values:

Dear Friend,

Are you frustrated by the way Bill Clinton was able to sweep the disturbing facts about his past under the rug during the 1992 Presidential election campaign?

My name is Deborah Stone. I am President of the Center for American Values — an organization dedicated to promoting honest government.

If you're like me, you probably watched coverage of the 1992 election in disbelief as the liberal news media ignored one Clinton scandal after another and smeared anyone who dared bring up Bill Clinton's deceptions and long history of corruption.

Would you like the American people to know the full truth about Bill Clinton <u>before</u> the next election?

Because I am well aware of your past support for conservative causes and candidates, I think I know where you stand on this matter . . .

. . . which is why I have taken the liberty to send you a free "special edition" copy of an explosive new book on Bill Clinton that reveals stunning facts on Bill Clinton's long history of corruption.

This book is called:

"SLICK WILLIE:
WHY AMERICA CANNOT TRUST BILL CLINTON."

<u>I need your help to distribute this book to
millions of Americans</u> who, even now, have no
idea what the man who now sits in the White
House is really like.

Before I explain further, please take a few
minutes right now to do three simple things
for me:

1) Please mail me the enclosed "Book Delivery
   Verification Form" so that I will know your
   free book arrived in good condition;

2) Please complete and return the enclosed
   "BALLOT ON THE CLINTON PRESIDENCY"; and

3) Please help me distribute this explosive
   book to 10,000,000 Americans in the next
   90 days by sending your best contribution
   of support.

Wide distribution of this book to voters is
just about the only hope we have of getting
the facts of Bill Clinton's sordid history to
the American people.

Voters won't hear about Bill Clinton's lies,
deceptions and track record of corruption from
the liberal news media. The news media acts
more like Bill Clinton's campaign manager and
cheerleader.

The news media seems to see its role as doing
everything possible to hide and cover-up the
very disturbing truth about Bill Clinton's past.

And when embarrassing facts do manage to leak
out about President Clinton, the media swings

into full "spin" mode to excuse acts of corruption and scandal that would surely have
destroyed any conservative politician by now.

That's why wide distribution of this fact-
filled little book is so important.

It's about the only way we have to bypass the
pro-Clinton liberal news media to put the
facts on Bill Clinton directly in the hands of
voters . . . <u>before the next election</u>.

<u>I am writing to ask for your help</u>.

Specifically, <u>I am writing to ask you to send
a contribution today</u> to support this important
project — a project that has the potential (if
fully funded) to rescue America from one of
the most corrupt politicians ever to rise to
the Presidency.

Notice that the letter makes the case that wide, free distribution of this book is needed to bypass the liberal news
media to get information directly to the voting public—information voters are unlikely to hear anywhere else.

The first page of the letter establishes a need for this project and a unique selling proposition for the organization. The
letter also taps into a deeply held belief by conservatives that
the mainstream news media is hopelessly biased against conservatives and is in favor of liberals.

Most important from an economic perspective, the letter
successfully makes the case that at least part of the solution to
the problem of liberal media bias is distributing more copies
of this book.

We are explicitly saying that contributions will be used to
mail more of these packages. The fundraising letter and the
package are self-fulfilling.

Including a book with your fundraising letter is a guaranteed attention getter. But the book must be directly related to the project for which you're raising money. In fact, it's best if the book "is" the project.

Notice that I've also included a survey with this package, because I include surveys with almost every prospect mailing for a political cause. Including a survey almost always boosts returns. A survey allows me to reinforce the main points of the letter. In this case, the survey is a Ballot on the Clinton Presidency—sure to appeal to conservative readers who will welcome this opportunity to register their disgust with Bill Clinton.

In all, we mailed about two million copies of this book package on roughly a break-even basis to prospect names which added about 50,000 new contributors to the housefile of the Center for American Values.

Of course, book packages are significantly more expensive than a conventional direct mail appeal. Including a book will likely double the printing and production cost of your package, while list and postage costs should remain what they would be for a conventional letter mailed at the nonprofit or bulk rate. You should test a book package against a conventional appeal on the same issue to determine whether the increased returns justify the increased cost of including the book.

For large mass mailings, the book should be no more than 96 pages so that you are not hit with additional postage and your book package can be mailed at the lowest nonprofit letter rate. To be mailed at the lowest rate, nonprofit mail must pass the so-called slot test. Any mail that cannot pass easily through the post office's slot measuring device will be hit with an additional postage surcharge. Pay careful attention to the weight and thickness of the paper you're using to construct your book. And work closely with your post office to make sure your book package does not exceed weight and width requirements for mailing at the lowest nonprofit or bulk-mail postage rate.

Sending a book out of the blue to prospective donors has proven to be a very effective technique for me in many of my prospect campaigns. But it's rare that I can mail more than a million copies of a book package. After crossing that threshold, results usually drop significantly. I think the reason is that people keep their books, and when they see it coming through their mailbox a second and third time, the technique loses its impact. After all, they already have the book. Returns will weaken over time for any prospect appeal, but returns weaken more quickly for a high-impact book package.

55. Special Report

Enclosing a special report works very much like enclosing a paperback book as an upfront premium. But it's less expensive, especially in lower quantities.

When considering a book package, which has substantial initial set-up costs, I'll often test a concept with a Special Report package. This way I can see if there's life in an idea before committing a lot of resources to creating a book.

A Special Report should be mailed flat, not folded, in a 9" x 12" carrier envelope. The psychology of the appeal is very much like the book mailing. At least part of the purpose of the donation will be to help distribute more copies of this explosive and eye-opening Special Report, which will help achieve the specific goal of the organization.

The Special Report mailing is most effective for political-issue organizations, for which educating voters on an issue is at least part of the solution to the problem the organization was set up to address.

56. Book as a Back-End Premium

Offer to send a book in return for a minimum contribution, as a token of appreciation.

This is a back-end premium designed to increase your

average donation. Let's say your average donation for an appeal is $16. Offer to send a book in return for a minimum contribution of $30. This could increase your average contribution from $16 to perhaps $20, a significant jump.

Of course, you also need to calculate the cost of fulfilling your promise. You'll need to pay for books and the cost of mailing the books to your $30 and over donors.

Unlike the book as a front-end premium, this book offer should be a full-length, hardcover, bookstore-quality book. I will include a separate insert, a lift note with a photo of the book, on how great this book is.

Often I find that the increased cost of fulfillment cancels out the increased average gift and often is hardly worth all the hassle. But one key advantage of the back-end premium package is that it can help you quickly identify people who are capable and willing to contribute more than the average amount to your organization or cause. Identifying these better-than-average donors quickly is a significant advantage in increasing immediately the productivity of your subsequent housefile mailings.

Crucial to success is that the book, or other back-end gift, is something your donors will definitely want. This is tricky. I might offer a hot new bestseller that is on-message with the cause the organization is promoting—perhaps even signed by the author to give the book added perceived value. Also, your readers can't buy an autographed copy of the same book at their local bookstore. Anything you can do to make your premium a unique gift your readers can't get anywhere else enhances the value of the gift. Most authors will be pleased to sign as many books as you want them to sign, because any author wants to get as many copies of their book in circulation as possible.

Another key to success is negotiating a good price for the book with the publisher. Most publishers will be glad to sell you 5,000 or 10,000 books for use as a back-end gift to your donors for $5 or $6 each, even though the book might retail for $25 or $30 at a store. I would not want to spend more than $5 or $6 each for a back-end premium for a $30 donor. Another way to cut your cost of fulfillment is to raise the minimum gift required to receive the back-end gift. But if you raise the bar too high, you begin to lose the benefit of offering the back-end gift.

Never assume your back-end gift offer will improve overall returns. Always test a back-end premium gift offer against the same basic package that offers nothing in exchange for a minimum donation.

Often you'll find your back-end gift actually hurts overall results by making your fundraising appeal look too much like a commercial sales pitch. When deciding to make a donation, people use a different part of their brain than they use when deciding to make a purchase. "Should I contribute to this cause I care about?" and "Do I really want this product?" are two completely different questions, requiring different calculations.

If your appeal looks like it's trying to sell a product, this can, and often does, undermine the psychology you're trying to tap into when making your case for a donation.

Offering a back-end premium also violates a key direct mail marketing principle, which is to sell only one thing with your direct mail appeal. You always want to keep your reader's attention focused on one very simple concept. By introducing a back-end premium to your appeal, you are introducing a second concept, a second offer.

So keep these factors in mind when constructing your back-end premium offers. Because of these complications and considerations, I am not generally a fan of back-end premiums, as you probably can tell. But they have their place in your direct mail arsenal and, in some instances, can improve overall results. So when putting together a back-end premium offer, just be sure to test it against the same package without a back-end premium.

57. Newspaper Clips

Including newspaper clips with your letter can significantly strengthen your appeal.

The most potent kind of newspaper clip is an article on the organization, especially an article that is exactly on point with the project for which you're raising money. A newspaper article on the organization, or that mentions the organization, helps establish independent proof that your organization is doing what it says it's doing, and it's doing it effectively in a way that's noticed by the news media.

Be sure to underline or highlight in yellow those parts of the article that specifically mention your organization's name.

Every political issue organization should invest a substantial portion of its operating budget in a media relations department whose sole mission is to garner favorable press coverage of your activities. Even if the media coverage you are receiving is not always favorable, as is often the case for conservative organizations, that's okay, as long as the gist of the coverage is that you are effective.

If conducted skillfully, your media outreach efforts should generate reams of press clippings on your organization to include with your mailings. And media coverage, if it achieves a certain critical-mass level, will begin to do a lot of your marketing work. You want to reach a point where the mail no longer needs to do all the selling, where the claims you are making in your letters are reinforced by substantial media coverage of your activities. People believe your organization is real when they see it covered in the news.

Your ultimate goal is for your organization to become synonymous with the issue itself. The NRA has achieved this status on the gun rights issue and the ACLU on the "all-speech-is-protected-speech" (except for Christians) issue. AARP has achieved this in the seasoned citizens market. The Kleenex brand name is synonymous with tissue paper and is now even a word in the dictionary.

Media coverage of your organization can help you achieve for your issue what Kleenex achieved in the realm of tissue paper.

Once the media starts covering the activities of your organization regularly, your direct mail returns will double and even triple. Soon you won't even need to include all kinds of inserts and testimonials with your mailings because everyone will know you are credible and effective.

But even if the media does not yet cover your organization regularly enough to make your organization's name synonymous with your issue, like Kleenex for tissue paper, you can still significantly increase your direct mail returns by including with your mailing even one newspaper clipping on your organization's activities. One newspaper clipping can easily add 25 percent to your returns.

58. Collage of Headlines and Articles

There's another way you can use newspaper clippings in your mailings. You can include an article or collage of articles and headlines that highlight the problem you are trying to solve.

This is not nearly as effective as including a newspaper article specifically on the organization's activities, but it can help boost returns in the absence of any news clippings on the organization. At best, this is a fallback plan that can help reinforce claims made in your letter concerning the magnitude and seriousness of the problem you are trying to solve with your fundraising appeal. "If the media is covering the problem, it must really be a problem" is the psychology at work here.

The weakness of this approach is that, if your reader is not well aware of the problem already, your appeal will likely crash. You can only raise money to solve problems your reader is already aware of and concerned about. A newspaper clipping that mentions your organization as actually solving the problem your readers care about is at least ten times more effective than news clips about the problem that don't mention your organization.

59. Track Record Insert

Your readers are not going to be persuaded by platitudes and generalizations. They want facts and specifics.

Don't just say, "We are the No. 1 organization" on this issue. Or we are "the most effective" organization in this area. Generalizations and platitudes make no impression on your reader. Instead, back up your claims with specifics on what you've achieved.

An effective way to do this is with an entire separate insert with a phrase in the title of your insert like "track record" or "status report." If it makes sense, I like to include a timeline with specific dates for achievements. This works very well if you're raising money for a lawsuit where you can discuss specific court appearances, depositions and other key dates in the legal proceeding. This can also work well for political campaigns where you might describe with a timeline exactly and precisely what your candidate has been doing for the past month to win the election and what has been achieved so far. The purpose is to demonstrate specific and effective actions you've taken to accomplish the goals your supporters are interested in.

I had an employee once who always provided me with a memo on Friday afternoon describing what he had done that week and what he had achieved for my company. His memos were succinctly written and very specific. It may have taken him 15 minutes to write. I appreciated those memos. I always felt I was getting more than my money's worth with that employee. I never had to check up on his work or wonder what he was doing with his time. Not surprisingly, he has since gone on to start a very successful business.

Treat your donors the same way. After all, your donors are your employers. You're asking your supporters for contributions approximately every month. Let them know, specifically, what you did with their donations last month.

In your prospect mailings, include a track record insert

that outlines your organization's most significant achievements and victories. Be specific. Include numbers. Attach dates to these achievements if appropriate. Don't rely on meaningless general terms like "enormous" or "tremendous." Tell your readers, in detail, what you have actually achieved.

60. Include a Copy of the Ad You Want to Run

Anything you can include in your mailing that clearly shows your reader exactly what you will use their contribution for will significantly strengthen your appeal. Include a copy of a newspaper ad you want to run. List the newspapers in which you want to print the ad, complete with exact costs and circulation numbers. For a radio ad, include a copy of the script. For a TV ad, include the script plus freeze-frame video stills of each scene or, second best, what are called storyboards (scene-by-scene drawings). Be sure to describe precisely what you want to achieve with your ad and the impact your ad will have.

An advantage of the ad package is that your donors understand already that it costs money to run ads. They are also presold on the idea that ads have impact. After all, corporations and political campaigns would not run ads if they were not effective. No business and certainly no political campaign can succeed without a significant advertising budget. The political campaign that spends the most on ads almost always wins.

Raising money to run ads can be very productive for political campaigns and issue-driven organizations.

61. Membership Benefits

People join organizations either because they support the cause or because they want benefits that come with membership. People join the American Automobile Association (AAA) because they want someone to call when they break down on the side of the road. There's no cause associated in the public consciousness with triple-A.

Similarly, people join the AARP because they want discounts on prescriptions, motels, airfares, insurance, financial services, etc. AARP has an extensive lobbying operation defending Social Security and Medicare, but that's not why most seasoned citizens join AARP. They join AARP because of the discounts they receive on all kinds of products.

When setting up an organization, or when determining how to market an organization, you must have a clear understanding of whether the primary purpose is to offer benefits or to advance a cause.

If the purpose is to advance a cause, offering all kinds of unrelated benefits of membership will actually hurt the organization. Your supporters will begin to wonder if you're wasting their money. At a minimum, all your offers of benefits will distract your supporters from understanding your primary mission.

If the purpose of your organization is to find a cure for cancer, don't offer your supporters motel discounts. You'll just confuse your market. You might give your conquer-cancer supporters a newsletter, a membership card, and periodic information on how to minimize the risk of cancer, because these kinds of benefits are at least related to your cause. But don't offer your conquer-cancer supporters mutual funds, discounts on prescription drugs, bargain long-distance phone service, or roadside assistance in case of a breakdown.

I issue this warning because almost every cause-oriented organization I have been associated with wants to become the next AARP with 37 million members.

They say, "Ben, the phone company will give our members a long-distance rate of just seven cents a minute and the organization will receive a 10 percent commission on all these calls. So start promoting this in your mailings."

"Are you nuts?" I'll say. "Not only will this amount to near zero money for your organization, you'll confuse your donors, dilute your brand, and undermine your unique selling proposition."

But my warnings often fall on deaf ears. Many organizations think they can be AARP. The organization's leadership will insist on sending out mailings promoting discount long-distance phone service from a company no one has heard of or offer supporters a prescription drug discount card. The response to such offers is mostly angry letters from the organization's supporters wondering why the organization is wasting money and time on all this silliness.

And consider this: the AARP-style benefits offer asks the reader to make a calculation based purely on self-interest. AARP is really more like a business offering commercial products to its members at a discount—much like Costco or Wal-Mart.

By contrast, the cause-driven offer asks the reader to donate out of a feeling of charity or out of a commitment to some religious or political cause that transcends self-interest.

So be very careful when offering benefits.

You can easily destroy your organization, or do serious harm, by offering an AARP-type benefits package to your cause-driven supporters.

62. Money-Back Guarantee

If you're selling an AARP-style membership benefits organization, include a Money-Back Guarantee. But don't do this for cause-driven organizations or charities.

People expect money-back guarantees when buying a product. A benefits package is a product. People do not expect a money-back guarantee when considering whether to donate to a charity or cause.

I have tested offering money-back guarantees for charitable appeals. The guarantee said something like this: "If you are ever dissatisfied with the work we're doing, or if you ever conclude that we are not using your contribution wisely, we will refund your initial donation—no questions asked."

I discovered that this guarantee actually hurt response rates for charitable and cause-oriented appeals. The reason is:

an appeal to charity is undermined when you suddenly use the jargon of a sales pitch. By using phrases like money-back guarantee in trying to persuade readers to donate to a cause or charity, you are triggering the part of the brain that makes calculations based on self-interest—which is exactly the wrong mindset you want if you are trying to persuade someone to contribute.

Instead, you want your reader to think in terms like, "For the cost of a cup of coffee each day, I can feed a child in Somalia." A concept like money-back guarantee destroys the feeling of generosity and charity you want to create in the mind of your reader.

But a money-back guarantee will strengthen an AARP-type membership benefits offer, which is really a product sale, not an appeal to charity.

63. Hallmark-Style Card for Donor to Sign

This can be great for charities that help hospitalized veterans or hospitalized children. The technique involves sending a card for the donor to sign and return to the charity. The charity then delivers the card to the hospitalized person the charity was set up to help.

I'll sometimes put a handwritten teaser in red ink on the carrier envelope that says something like, "The enclosed Christmas card is not for you" … or "I have enclosed a Christmas card for you to sign."

If the recipient of the charity is a celebrity, birthday cards for the donor to sign and return can also be very effective. For a package I once wrote for hard-core conservatives, I included a birthday card for Senator Jesse Helms for the reader to sign and return.

I'll sometimes take a trip to the Hallmark store to get ideas for cards and occasions to send cards (Valentine's Day, Easter, or an anniversary) and see if I can work the greeting card technique into a direct mail appeal.

Always remember that the purpose of the technique is to draw attention to and underscore the cause you're raising money for. The technique you select must make sense and must strengthen your appeal.

64. Christmas Card

Send a Christmas card to your best supporters.

This will not generate a large immediate return of contributions. Include a return envelope, but don't include a fundraising letter and reply form, or your Christmas card will just look like another fundraising gimmick. In other words, make it a real Christmas card, not a device to generate more contributions. If you receive enough donations to pay for the Christmas card mailing, that's fine.

The purpose of this mailing is simply to thank your supporters and to do something nice for them. Your card tells your friends and supporters that you are thinking of them during the holidays.

This is just a nice thing to do for those who have been answering your letters throughout the year.

Think of your Christmas card mailing as an extra fancy thank you letter. Put some time, effort, and thought into developing a really nice card that your donors would like to receive and display with their other Christmas cards, perhaps even hang on their tree.

For your very best supporters, consider sending a Christmas gift with your Christmas card. The gift should be creative and thoughtful, not costly.

65. Birthday Card

Make an effort to find out the birthdays of your best supporters and send them a birthday card. You can collect this information through surveys and questionnaires you include with some mailings (see the filecard mailing described later).

Birthdays are a great piece of information to collect for your database.

What a shocker it will be for your donors when they receive a birthday card from you. They will be loyal to you for the rest of their lives. Believe me, this will make a lasting impression.

Consider doing this for your $50-plus multigivers. Anyone who has contributed $50 or more to your organization more than once is a loyal supporter. Cement this loyalty by remembering their birthdays. This will likely set your organization apart from all other organizations your donors are also supporting.

Remembering the birthdays of your supporters is yet another creative and memorable way to thank your contributors. You should always be thinking of creative, high-impact ways to thank those who are supporting you and your cause.

66. Interoffice Memo Carrier

This is an envelope your readers are sure to open.

And, since getting your reader to open your envelope is the first battle in the war for the contribution, this carrier envelope should certainly be in the arsenal of every direct mail copywriter.

An interoffice memo envelope like this should include material that is privileged and internal, such as a draft of a proposal you would like feedback on from your readers.

With this technique you are treating your supporters as if they are part of your inner-circle—a member of your decision-making group.

The envelope lists the handwritten names of people inside the organization who have received the envelope and examined its contents. The last name listed is the reader's name.

Combine this interoffice memo envelope with a yellow Post-it note on a component inside the mailing to which you want to draw the reader's attention.

This package should be highly personalized. For those receiving the package first class, use actual stamps. And use multiple stamps (four, five, or six stamps are best). If you are sending the package bulk or nonprofit rate, use a meter on a label. This will make the envelope appear to have been run through a postage meter.

Avoid using Bulk Rate stamps, Nonprofit Org stamps, or preprinted indicias on carrier envelopes because they telegraph to the reader that this is mass-produced junk mail.

Since you want feedback from your readers with the Interoffice memo envelope, a survey should be part of this mailing. The survey questions should be about the draft proposal you are sending them. Leave plenty of space on the survey for your readers to write their own comments.

The survey should be for Internal Use Only, designed to improve the draft proposal, which you will submit to your supporters in final form later.

67. Year-End Letter

This is a recap of what we did with your contributions, the results we achieved, and our goals for the following year. This letter is different from an Annual Report mailing in that it's

Figure 7.18

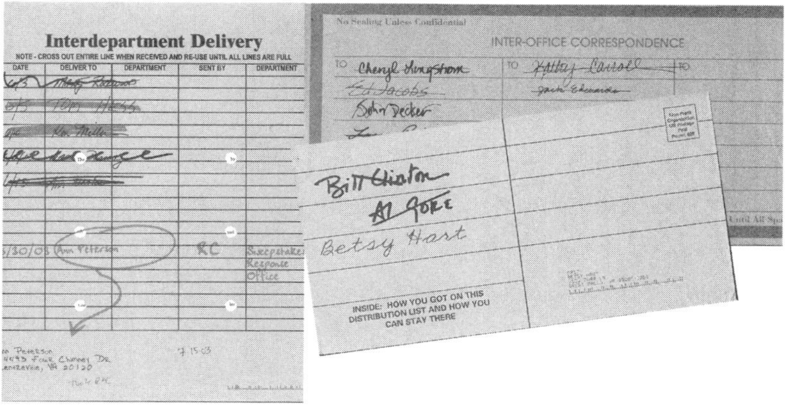

very conversational in tone, in contrast to the more formal appearance of an Annual Report.

A year-end letter should be mailed in December, whereas an Annual Report (which takes more time to compile and prepare) can be mailed as late as February.

The year-end letter has no special involvement device. It should be very personal and chatty. Personalize every page for the top 20 percent of your housefile. This could be an eight-page letter, or longer. After all, you're discussing your achievements for an entire year and outlining your goals for the following year, so this could require a lot of space. In fact, if this isn't a long letter, your organization is doing something wrong.

I'm a strong believer in year-end letters. Every nonprofit organization that relies on voluntary donations to survive should send a year-end letter every December. And don't forget to reference the holidays.

68. Yellow Post-it Note

Put a yellow Post-it note on the first page of your letter, on your reply form, or on your reply envelope. The yellow Post-it note serves much the same purpose as the P.S. It gives the reader the bottom line for why you're writing.

Your Post-it note message should mention the project, a deadline, a request for a donation, and any other action item.

The Post-it note technique is strongest when it's personalized. Tests also indicate that the Post-it note works best if it's yellow, not some other color. Who knows why? That's why we test. I guess yellow works best because that's what people are used to seeing with Post-it notes.

These are Post-it notes you and your vendors manufacture yourselves. They're just little squares of yellow paper with glue on the back top edge. Be sure the glue your vendor uses to affix your little yellow squares of paper is not too strong. You want your reader to be able to easily peel your Post-it note off your letter, or wherever you're affixing it. Don't make the glue too weak either. You don't want your Post-it note falling off the paper and ruining the effect. I've experienced both these unpleasant problems with much wailing and gnashing of teeth. So pay close attention to the glue issue.

The Post-it note seems always to boost results, but it also adds cost. You'll need to do your calculations to determine if the increased returns justify the increased cost.

Also, just because a technique increases returns does not mean you should use it for every mailing. It would get old and lose its impact over time. Other techniques work just as well.

You should strive to vary the look and feel of your packages to maintain donor interest. A baseball pitcher might have a great fastball, but if that's his only pitch, hitters will soon get a read on it and start smashing it out of the park.

A great fastball pitcher also needs a good change-up and curve ball. The same principle holds true for direct mail. No matter how strong a technique appears to be, you can't use it all the time. You need a vast array of strong pitches. Don't be a one-trick pony. The yellow Post-it note is another weapon in your direct mail arsenal to boost returns.

69. Event Invitation

If your organization is holding a major event—perhaps an anniversary gala, a major news conference or some big occasion, featuring an impressive list of luminaries and celebrities—invite all your best contributors, including those who live a long distance away. Your invitation should look something like a wedding invitation or an invitation to some important event. Use calligraphy or a script font (printed by machine) to address the square invitation-style carrier envelope. Make sure your R.S.V.P. reply and invitation are consistent with the look of a properly constructed invitation.

Along with an impressive looking invitation printed on card stock, include a letter explaining the significance of the event. The letter can be four pages or more, like your other direct mail appeal letters. Perhaps there will be a charge associated with the event, perhaps there won't. It depends on how much the event itself will cost and the economics of your organization. What's important is to invite all your best donors to attend.

Along with the invitation, suggest to your invitees that they send a contribution even if they cannot attend. Be sure to request an R.S.V.P. from your invitees, even those who will not attend. This is your involvement technique and ensures a high response rate to your mailing.

In your cover letter explaining the event, remind your invitees of all the great achievements of your organization, the important project your organization is working on now, and, as always, never forget to make a compelling case for a donation.

Only a very small fraction of your contributors will travel any significant distance to attend your event. But they will be flattered to have been invited. About 10 percent of your invitees will likely send a contribution along with their R.S.V.P. telling you they won't be attending. This mailing can be enormously profitable for your organization. But don't be shocked if a few of your supporters do travel substantial distances to attend your event.

This is an effective mailing for candidates.

Candidates hold fundraising events and press conferences all the time. The candidate is missing a great fundraising opportunity if he fails to take advantage of the invitation technique in connection with at least one or two major campaign events.

70. Invitation to Join an Exclusive Club

Another way to use the invitation format described above is to ask your best donors to join a special club. The club should have a prestigious sounding name like President's Club, Chairman's Council, or Inner-Circle.

You can use the invitation format to ask your readers to become monthly givers, or $1,000-a-year givers. You'll need to set some required giving level for membership in this exclusive club, whatever you decide to call it.

Most long-established organizations have several clubs, all with different contribution requirements. For the majority of organizations, the most productive, exclusive giving clubs will be your monthly giving club and your $1,000-a-year club. As your organization matures, you might even develop a $10,000-a-year club and even a $100,000-a-year club.

The key to success with the giving club strategy is to promote the club as exclusive and prestigious. The desire for honor, recognition, prestige, and exclusivity are always strong motivators for people to increase their giving commitment. Tap into all these desires in promoting your giving clubs. Be sure to attach a separate list of impressive benefits your reader will receive by joining your exclusive giving club.

The Republican and Democratic National Committees use this strategy very effectively. Appeals based on prestige and exclusivity work well for organizations like the RNC or the DNC because essentially, they are selling their supporters access to powerful and influential people. They are telling their supporters, join us, join this prestigious club for this amount and you will meet and rub shoulders with key lawmakers in the nation's capital. You will be noticed by those who run our country. This strategy is also effective for candidates, especially incumbents and those who have a good chance to win, for the same reason: contributors want to join a winner. They want to buy access, which they feel they can perhaps tap into after an election.

The Heritage Foundation, a conservative think-tank located on Capitol Hill near the U.S. Senate, executes this strategy brilliantly. The Heritage Foundation raises about $30 million a year by selling two basic ideas:

1. It is strategically positioned in the nation's capital to promote conservative values and free-market economic principles to America's lawmakers and policymakers.

2. Heritage's $1,000-a-year and over givers (its President's Club members) are invited to exclusive briefings to meet with and hear from congressional leaders, White House senior staff, and even, on occasion, the President of the United States.

Heritage, an astoundingly successful fundraising machine under the skillful direction of my old boss Ed Feulner, has many different giving clubs targeted at different giving levels. Heritage's $1,000,000 givers are sometimes awarded seats on the foundation's Board of Trustees. But that's another topic.

The invitation package is a great way to promote giving clubs up to the $1,000 level. Cultivating donors above the $1,000 level requires a personal one-on-one relationship and an entirely different strategy.

71. Monthly Givers Club

Create a monthly givers club.

This is most effective for Christian or religious organizations, whose supporters are used to tithing and contributing each week to their church or synagogue.

Choose a name for your monthly givers club, something like Patriot Club or Eagle Club. Ask club members to pledge to give $20 per month. Encourage club members to permit their monthly gift to be automatically charged to their credit card, which ensures near 100 percent pledge fulfillment from your monthly credit card givers.

As with your other giving clubs (your $1,000, $5,000, and $10,000 clubs) offer some benefits to becoming a monthly giver, such as a lapel pin with the organization's logo, or perhaps a different logo developed specially for club members.

Other benefits might include a free subscription to a special publication, "available only for Eagle Club members," a special "Eagle Club Membership Card," a "free video" on the central issue your supporters are concerned about, an "Eagle

Club baseball cap," access to the toll-free "Eagle Club 800-number hotline," invitations to strategy meetings and legislative briefings in Washington, D.C, and periodic email alerts on breaking news.

Your letter should state that you are thankful for every contribution people send, but then make it clear that your organization relies on regular contributions, especially the faithful monthly givers, to fund its projects.

Explain how your monthly givers allow you to budget and plan your organization's finances more accurately and effectively. Instead of wondering if donations will arrive to fund your projects, you will know for certain how much will arrive from your faithful and reliable monthly givers.

Everyone will understand this because everyone knows that they need predictable, reliable cash flow to fund their household or cover their business's fixed operating costs.

Your monthly giving appeal should be mailed on December 20th, so it lands in homes between Christmas and New Year's. Be sure to ask your readers to send their first monthly gift for the month of January in response to this letter.

Also, make sure your letter and reply form include an option for the donor to just send a one-time gift and decline a monthly giving commitment. About 60 percent of your contributions that arrive in response to this appeal will be from those who choose the one-time gift option. This will ensure that your mailing does not lose money, and may even net some money out of the gate.

Include 12 reply envelopes, each marked for a particular month throughout the year. Encourage your supporters to keep these envelopes in a safe and convenient place where an envelope can easily be pulled out each month to mail in their monthly gift. The 12 reply envelopes command your reader's attention and help reinforce what you are asking your supporters to commit to.

In addition, those who pledge to send $20 a month should receive a statement in the mail each month (with a reply envelope) reminding your monthly givers to send their donation for the month. Send your statement (which looks like a bill) on the 20th of each month so it will arrive just before the first of the month when most people pay their monthly bills. If your monthly giving statement goes out late, you will see a significant drop (as much as 15 percent or more) in your pledge-fulfillment rate.

Use telephones in combination with the mail to promote your monthly giving club. This is also an excellent appeal to combine with a 30-second taped precall and postcall telephone message I described earlier. Over time, you should be able to persuade about 8 percent of your housefile to become monthly givers. Your monthly giving club, as it matures, can provide as much as 40 percent of an organization's net operating budget. But you must be committed to promoting monthly giving.

Only spend serious resources promoting monthly giving to your multigivers, those who have given at least twice to your organization. For those who have only given once, devote your efforts toward trying to get a second contribution before you attempt to convince them to become monthly givers.

Promote your monthly giving club in your newsletter and other institutional publications, but don't send your one-time givers your monthly giving package. Send these folks a package just asking for another one-time donation. Until people have contributed at least twice to an organization, they cannot yet be considered truly loyal supporters and are not yet ready to consider a monthly giving commitment.

The reason most organizations don't have a monthly giving club is that your initial mailings promoting monthly giving likely will only break even or net very little money out of the gate. The profit for the organization comes later. Most organizations are too impatient or too strapped for cash to spend the necessary time, effort, and resources to make monthly giving work.

72. Quarterly Giving

Use this option when promoting your $1,000-a-year giving club. Some of those who you persuade to join your $1,000-a-year club will be in a strong enough financial position that they can just mail in a $1,000 check once a year when it's time to renew.

But there will be a significant portion of your $1,000 givers who will much prefer to pay in quarterly installments. This is not true for your $5,000-, $10,000-, and $100,000-a-year contributors. Anyone who can give at that level each year is not concerned about installment payment plans.

But your $1,000-a-year contributors are not necessarily wealthy. Many of these folks will be people of regular means who are just very committed to your cause and are willing to stretch themselves to become members of your $1,000 giving club. So be sure to offer the quarterly payment option to your $1,000 givers.

73. Lifetime Membership

Selling Lifetime Memberships can be an effective method of increasing a donor's financial commitment to an organization.

The NRA does this very well. There is a certain core group of NRA supporters who love to display their Lifetime Member card, which they carry proudly in their wallets. Lifetime Member indicates true commitment to a cause.

In addition, Lifetime Membership in an organization should carry with it a host of impressive benefits available to no one else. One important benefit is that members won't need to renew every year and will save money over the long run with their Lifetime Memberships.

You'll need to give careful thought to the amount required to be a Lifetime Member. Five times the amount of the annual dues is usually a good number. I think ten times is too much. Waiting five years to break-even on your Lifetime Membership is long enough. But every housefile is different, so you'll need to test offers to see what's most effective. But don't go below three times the amount of the annual dues, because you'll cheapen the value of being a Lifetime Member.

In addition, you'll need to consider the fact that you won't be able to ask your Lifetime Members for annual dues each year. But that's all right. One $250 check for a Lifetime Membership means you've identified a truly loyal supporter who loves what you're doing. You'll be able to go back to these folks with other appeals, such as your President's Club and Inner- Circle major donor membership invitations and other high-end mailings—far better than a $15, $20, or $25 annual membership appeal.

The Lifetime Member offer is a great donor upgrade strategy for the right organization. It must be the kind of organization that was primarily built on membership appeals—or which, at a minimum, has a strong membership component to its housefile.

74. The Index or File Card Mailing

Mail an index card with all the information you have on the donor, including giving history, with your letter.

Explain that you are trying to make sure all the information you have on your supporter is correct. If the mailing is for a political-issue organization, explain that you must be sure that all your information on the supporter is accurate so that you can contact them at a moment's notice as Election Day approaches or before a key vote in Congress takes place on a matter of great importance to your supporters.

Ask your readers to verify that all information on the index card is correct or to correct any errors and add missing information.

Include an Information Verification Questionnaire as part of the reply form. Each question on the questionnaire asks the reader to simply mark "Yes" or "No" as to whether each piece of information is correct. Be sure to leave space with each question for the reader to write the correct information if the information you have is in error.

Construct the package so the blue- or red-lined index card

shows through the window of the carrier. Use the index card as the name and address piece to fly the package. To do this, you'll need to use a weak glue to affix the index card to the reply device, not such a strong glue that will prevent your reader from detaching the index card so they can fill out the reply device and questionnaire. For your best donors, use a paper clip instead of glue to attach the index card to the reply.

The file card is admittedly hokey and a little implausible. Everyone knows that data is kept in computers and no longer on index cards, like in the old days before we had computers.

But, amazingly enough, the visual impact of the index card can be a very productive mailing for an organization.

This is also a great way to in fact make sure the information you have on your donors is accurate. Just correcting all the errors that always and inevitably creep into a housefile database will significantly improve the performance of your housefile program. You'll also be able to gain additional information, such as email addresses and birthdays of many of your supporters so you can send birthday cards to your best donors.

75. Greenbar Mailing

This is a combination status report and budget shortfall package.

The reply form is printed on computer greenbar colored paper with pin feeds down the sides, like the old computer paper that came off pin-feed dot-matrix printers. The green bars or stripes are printed in light green ink. The stripes are green and white, about an inch or so tall, and alternate down the entire page. Though I've never tried it, I think you could also print this reply on graph paper and perhaps achieve the same effect.

The reply form includes a graph showing the status of a fund drive that's underway. The graph charts the progress of the fund drive over a period of time, and also shows a revenue shortfall, which must be closed if the project is to be fully funded. It's a variation on the thermometer concept you've seen on TV telethons.

The reply form asks the reader for a specific contribution amount, based on the reader's previous giving history, to help close the budget shortfall and ensure full funding for the project. I often circle the contribution request in red and draw attention to the amount with a handwritten note, also in red. The greenbar reply form should show through the window and should be the name and address piece that flies that package.

This mailing is only effective for a housefile.

76. Self-Mailers

A self-mailer is produced on a special kind of machine where the entire appeal is printed on one piece of paper, is sliced up in various ways, and is then folded together and mailed with no separate carrier envelope.

The self-mailer violates many important principles of direct mail fundraising. It completely wrecks any notion that this is a personal letter from one person to another. The format screams that this is a mailing that is being shot out to hundreds of thousands if not millions of people. It screams junk mail.

But don't completely write off the self-mailer yet, because this format can offer some key advantages.

For one thing, most prospect letters in conventional No. 10 window envelopes are not personalized anyway. The salutation is "Dear Friend" or some other generic term, because containing cost is so vitally important in prospecting where you are trying to get $10, $15, and $20 donations. That level of donor is not expecting an expensive highly personal letter. So you've already destroyed the idea that your mass-market prospect letter is a personal appeal. It's very clearly a one-size-fits-all appeal.

Remember, direct mail fundraising is a science of trade-offs and compromises. You want to personalize, but you can't afford to personalize much in your conventional No. 10 window envelope prospect appeals—at least not if your average donation is $14 and you're doing well if you receive a 2.5 percent response rate.

By contrast, your junk-mailish-looking self-mailer can offer far greater opportunities for extensive personalization, because the mailer is all printed on one big sheet of paper before it's sliced up, folded, glued, and mailed.

In addition, a big-format self-mailer can really jump out in a mailbox because it looks so different from all the other conventional envelopes.

Almost all my successful self-mailer appeals have been survey packages, I think, because the self-mailer format enhances the official-looking quality of the survey. The format can help the survey package look serious. For this reason, I usually make self-mailers resemble government documents, like something my reader might be getting from the Census Bureau or other official agency or research institute.

Self-mailers can also be constructed to include petitions, postcards, and address labels. But I have not had much success

Figure 7.19

with these techniques in self-mailers. However, we have had success with sweepstakes packages in the self-mailer format.

Another advantage of the self-mailer is that it can be produced inexpensively in very large quantities. One drawback of the self-mailer is that you'll be hit with a postage surcharge because of its unconventional shape. The biggest drawback is that the format is very expensive in quantities under 500,000. And cost is not especially low until you hit mail volumes on a package of one million pieces or more.

For this reason, almost all my self-mailers are modifications of packages that have proven to be successful in a conventional envelope and which I believe have the potential to mail two million copies or more. A self-mailer can also give new life to a conventional envelope package that donors on prospect lists have already seen several times before.

Self-mailers seem to attract a different kind of donor than a conventional envelope package, certainly a lower-dollar donor for the most part. You'll receive a lot more $5 and $10 contributions in response to the self-mailer. You will receive very few donations over $100 and almost none over $1,000.

I use two companies principally for my self-mailers: Veritas and Moore Response. These companies specialize in self-mailers and have developed many different formats. There are many other companies that produce self-mailers as well.

One reason I'm not a big fan of self-mailers is my belief that, as a general rule, you should not write your copy and create your package to fit a rigid, inflexible format. Instead, you should select a format that will accommodate your copy. Another way to say it: don't let the format dictate what you put in your fundraising package. If the format is too restrictive, I don't like to shoehorn my copy into the format.

Conventional envelopes allow the copywriter great flexibility. You can have as many pages and inserts as you like. And envelopes come in all different shapes and sizes. Also, people are used to receiving letters in conventional envelopes. You will never receive a letter from mom or a friend in a self-mailer.

Still, there is a place for self-mailers. A self-mailer is another arrow a fundraising agency should have in its quiver.

77. The "Kitchen Sink" Package

I regularly combine techniques and strategies in my packages. I'll use a survey and a petition in the same package, and combine this with a yellow Post-it note, a $1.75 check, postcards to Congress, one of my specially designed gaudy-looking reply envelopes, a short additional lift letter from a celebrity, testimonials, a budget proposal, newspaper clippings on the organization's effectiveness, and perhaps even a bumper sticker.

I might even send such a package out in a box. Who wouldn't open a box?

Of course, this is an extreme example to illustrate my point that I like "kitchen sink" packages. That's what I call packages that include just about everything but a kitchen sink.

If I could, I would club the reader on the head with a kitchen sink to get his attention. That, in essence, is what I'm doing with the kitchen sink approach.

A big consideration here is cost.

You must ask the question: Will adding this extra item and extra cost to the package generate more money coming back in reply envelopes?

When writing my first prospect appeal for a new client, I like to load up the package with techniques and inserts, often including an eight-page letter.

I do this because I know that each item and each technique I include in the package will almost certainly increase returns. I want to find out with this first-launch prospect package if the issue or organization I'm writing for has a chance for success. So I mail a loaded package to the best names I can find to see if there's life.

Assuming it works well, I will then start stripping items from the package to lower the cost without reducing returns significantly. I'll turn my eight-page letter into a four-page letter. I'll eliminate techniques and combine inserts. I'll tinker with and refine every aspect of the package with a view toward dramatically reducing cost without sacrificing results, perhaps even improving results with a more focused laser-like message. I'll strive to distill the package to its essence.

I'll do this because I know I can't mail millions of copies of this package if the cost is too high. I won't be able to mail profitably to marginal lists or low-dollar givers with a costly package. Eventually I'll figure out through trial and error and constant testing what makes this particular cause or issue sing.

But until I figure all this out through extensive testing, I will often use the "kitchen sink" approach in writing my first prospect appeal for a new client. And I'll send this package to my best lists. That's because I don't want the organization's mail program to fail because I selected the wrong technique or chose the wrong line of argument. Instead I'll use all techniques and arguments that hold out the prospect of persuading people to contribute.

I'll leave no stone unturned. If I leave out an argument or technique or a compelling insert in order to save space and paper, I'll always be concerned that this was the argument, this was the technique, this was the enclosure that might have lifted my response rate a quarter of a percent, which could mean the difference between success and failure.

I want to use all my best weapons in my first prospect appeal for a new client. I want to give the package the best possible chance to achieve success. I want to appeal both to petition signers and survey responders. I want to bring all my best arguments to the reader for sending a donation. I want to get the reader's attention. I want to dazzle the reader and involve the reader in the issue. I want a bulging envelope full of stuff that my prospective donor can't ignore and will surely open. Once I see that the mail program has achieved liftoff with my kitchen sink package, I'll then work on refining and cutting the cost of my prospect appeal.

I've never liked the cliche "less is really more." For the most part in direct mail, as in life, I believe "more is actually more." That is, the more you include in your package, the more money will come in, assuming of course that every item and every word in the package is on point, provokes interest, and contributes to closing the sale.

CHAPTER **8**

Lists Are Your Lifeblood

Not enough attention is paid to lists by direct mail fundraisers. In fact, I know of no one in my profession who spends enough time on lists—including me.

The list, or list segment, you select for your mailing is more important than the letter itself.

It's possible for a lousy letter to work to a good list. But it's impossible for any letter to work to the wrong list.

A mailing list is not just a way to reach your market. It is your market.

I'll discuss lists for your prospecting program first, then your housefile program.

Lists for Prospecting

The mailing list business is an enormous industry. There are approximately 30,000 lists available for rental. There are about one billion names on these lists.

If you wonder why you receive so much mail every day from businesses, charities, political causes, and candidates— all wanting you to send money for something—it's because your name and address is being rented by list owners, list managers, and list brokers.

Your name is being rented or sold, most likely because

you bought something through the mail or you contributed to some cause in response to a letter.

Once you're on a mailing list, it's very difficult to get off, because your name and address is being sold and rented to dozens of organizations and businesses. You would have to not answer a piece of junk mail for about three years before you started to see a noticeable decline in the amount of commercial and fundraising mail in your mailbox.

You would also have to not buy anything over the Internet, not use your credit card, not subscribe to any magazines, and not fill out any forms that ask for all your contact information at stores. In addition, you would need to move to a poor neighborhood. If you live in a wealthy neighborhood, you'll receive a lot of direct mail just because direct mail marketers know you have money to spend.

For direct mail fundraising, you are looking for specific kinds of lists to build your housefile.

You would start out by trying to rent lists of donors to similar organizations. If you're raising money to cure cancer, for example, you would want to compile a list of all other organizations trying to cure cancer. And you would find out which of these cancer organizations rent their donor lists.

In the direct mail business you typically do not buy a mailing list. You rent a list for a one-time use. If you want to mail to the list again, you must rent it again. But then anyone who answers your letter becomes part of your housefile. In other words, the name is now yours and you are free to continue to send letters to that person without renting that name again. But you are not permitted to continue to mail letters to those who do not respond to your prospect appeal unless you rent the list again.

Names and addresses of donors who have contributed $5 or more in the past 18 months typically rent for 10 to 12 cents per name for a one-time use. This is usually the kind of list I order.

To be safer, sometimes I'll order names who have contributed $10 or more in the last 12 months. I might need to pay a higher price for these names because these names are considered better names. The more recent the contribution, the better the donor.

This is an important point, worth underscoring, because it's counter-intuitive. People who have contributed most recently and most often are the most likely to contribute to your appeal. You might think these would be the weakest prospects, on the assumption that these donors must be tapped out since they contribute so often. But these recent hotline frequent contributors are, by far, the most likely to answer your letter with a contribution. Those who have not contributed in a long time are weak prospects for a donation.

A list of $10-plus donors is stronger than a list that includes $5 donors. And a list of multiple donors is far better than a list of donors who have contributed only once.

If you're raising money to cure cancer, your lists of donors who have contributed to this issue in the past will be your "A" group of lists—the lists most likely to work for you.

But many cancer organizations will not cooperate with you, because many won't rent their list to a competing organization.

You'll then need to put Plan B into effect.

Plan B is to make a list of organizations that fight other diseases and to find out if these organizations rent their lists. The idea here is that those who contribute to fight Alzheimer's, arthritis, and heart disease might also want to cure cancer.

Once you build a sizeable housefile from these Plan B lists, you'll then have some clout to start negotiating with other cancer organizations to mail their lists, because they're going to want to mail their letters to your list.

For example, you can work out name-exchange agreements with other cancer organizations. A name exchange is when you allow one organization to mail to your list of, say, $5+ last 18-month donors in exchange for that organization letting you mail its list of $5+ last 18-month donors.

The best prospect lists for your organization are lists of donors who have contributed through the mail to similar organizations, dedicated to similar causes. But if you're mailing a prospect package that is extraordinarily successful, you can often go beyond this group of "usual suspects."

For example, you should test your mailing to people who have contributed to a similar cause in response to a telephone solicitation, over the Internet or in response to a TV, radio, or newspaper ad. Direct mail compiled lists will always be stronger than lists compiled in some other way. But if your prospecting package is strong enough to break out beyond the "usual suspect" lists, you've got a gold mine on your hands, because you are adding donors to your housefile who are not on the lists of competing organizations.

You are developing a one-of-a-kind housefile list.

By the way, writing a breakout package for a copywriter is like a major league baseball player hitting a grand slam in the World Series. Writing breakout packages is what copywriters dream about.

Now back again to lists.

A great living can be made by just learning lists.

Learn everything about lists. Attend seminars on lists. Learn all the list jargon and terms, so you don't sound like an amateur when ordering lists.

Think about lists all the time. Ask about lists. Subscribe to every direct mail marketing publication, such as *DM News, Contributions, Nonprofit Times,* and *Direct Marketing* magazine where you will find countless ads from list companies advertising their lists. Become a member of the Direct Marketing Association. And make a special point to attend direct mail marketing seminars, which are offered all the time by the Direct Marketing Association.

Many mailing lists can be found through the Standard Rate and Data Service, which publishes the *SRDS Direct Marketing List Source.* This service will tell you what lists are available on the open market, describe the list, and tell you who to contact to rent a list. SRDS breaks down lists into many different categories for direct mail business offers and fundraising solicitations. The Marketing Information Network (MIN) offers more than 20,000 lists online. Dun & Bradstreet compiles lists of businesses and the executives of these businesses. D&B also compiles lists of individuals by profession.

There are many list services and list brokers. You should find a reputable list broker to help you who specializes in the market you are trying to reach.

Be open to hand-compiling your own lists, especially for highly targeted appeals that hold out promise of a big return on investment and not just relying on renting lists that are on the open market. Become a list maniac.

Here are some crucial points to keep in mind when conducting your list work for your prospecting program.

1. Be crystal clear in your list orders

A mistake in the way you order names can be catastrophic.

It's very easy to fall into direct mail jargon, and then discover later that different people attach different meanings to the jargon. When ordering a list from a list broker or an organization, write your order very clearly, precisely, and in plain English. Find out what terms they use and exactly what each term means. Get on the phone with the list broker and go over your written list order verbally, line by line, word by word. Assume nothing. Make sure you understand exactly what kind of names you are getting for your mailing. Get everything in writing. If you're not sure what their terms mean, get clarification IN WRITING.

2. Learn how to read a list data card

Even if you use a list broker, you will still be making the decisions as to what kinds of names you want to order from particular lists for your mailing.

Learn how to read a list data card. This is jargon that means a sheet of paper that describes a particular list and which segments are available for rent. Each data card includes a paragraph or two about the background of the list and how the list was compiled. You will want to know what percentage of the list is direct mail generated. You will want to know the precise issue, set of issues, and product offers the list was built around.

Understand the terms and the selects available for rent. In general, the more name selection options available the better. You may be able to select not only according to contribution history, but also by gender, age, geographic region, and issue interest.

Pay careful attention to what kinds of organizations have rented a list you are considering, and especially what organizations have rolled out or mailed a continuation with this list. Are the organizations who have mailed continuations similar to yours?

If so, this is probably a good list to test. If you see a lot of tests but few continuations, this is likely a weak list.

Question every list's hygiene. Ask how often the list is updated and corrected. Many list suppliers will guarantee the cleanliness of their lists and refund postage costs on letters returned (called pixies or nixies) in excess of some reasonable percentage. About 15 percent of the population moves every

Figure 8.1

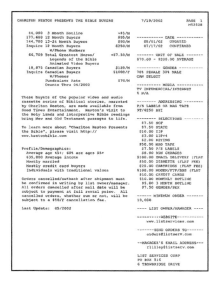

year, so lists go out of date very quickly. So ask tough questions about the hygiene of lists you're renting. Try hard to get guarantees of list cleanliness in writing.

Another important factor to consider is the direct mail techniques used to build the list you're considering renting. For example, some lists are built mainly on sweepstakes appeals, and are therefore not likely to be strong prospect lists for a conventional fundraising appeal. Others are built mostly on front-end premiums. Still others are built mostly with survey or petition packages. Ask the list supplier about the kinds of packages that built the list.

And always test before you roll out, especially on a list that you have not used recently. Often lists can appear very similar from their data card descriptions but will yield radically different results. The data card descriptions will guide your initial decision to test a list, but only your test results can dictate whether you continue or roll out on a list.

3. Find a good list broker

List brokers are a great resource. List brokers are paid on commission. Usually they take a 20 percent commission on names they find and supply for you. This commission is paid by the list owner, not you. You would typically pay the same for a list whether or not you use a list broker—though, as in real estate transactions, this can also be negotiated.

You want to make sure your list broker is paid well, and that your relationship is a profitable one. Good list brokers are worth their weight in gold. Be sure you select a list broker who specializes in the market you're trying to reach. If you're raising money for a political cause, don't use a list broker who specializes in product catalogues.

But don't rely on your list broker to make decisions. Your list broker only makes recommendations. You and only you will make your final list decisions. So even if you have a list broker, you should still make a habit of collecting and studying List Data Cards.

4. Try to negotiate "net-net" payment terms on prospect lists

When you rent lists of similar prospects, say, lists of people who have donated to cure cancer, you will find many duplicate names between lists. As your organization grows, you will also find it more and more difficult to rent lists that don't have a high rate of duplication with your own housefile list.

In a net-net name arrangement, you only pay for the name once and only pay for names that are not on your list. And you agree to mail only to unique names. Some list owners won't agree to a pure net-net arrangement.

In the alternative, ask for a modified net-net deal. For example, you might ask for a net-net deal up to a maximum of 40 percent off the price of the list. Be creative in how you negotiate for renting lists. Use your imagination to get the best possible deal on prospect names.

5. Ask to exchange lists for a one-time use

This is a great way to dramatically cut the cost of your prospect mailing.

The idea here is that you want to be able to mail to the housefile lists of other organizations, and they want to mail to your housefile list. Negotiate a list exchange.

Be sure though that you are exchanging the same kind of names. If you are allowing an organization to mail to your $10+, 0- to 18-month contributors, be sure you are getting names that fit this exact description. Make sure you're trading apples for apples, not apples for apple skins.

Some lists are available for exchange only and not at all for rent. These are sometimes the best lists, because they aren't getting hit with so much direct mail.

6. Don't rely on your memory to select your lists

Before selecting lists for your donor acquisition mailing, be sure to have a complete list of lists in front of you with results history for every donor-acquisition mail program you've conducted over the last 36 months or so. It's easy to forget good lists you've mailed in the past.

In addition, have your list broker send over a complete set of data cards—especially data cards of new lists on the market.

Pay careful attention to each new list that comes on the market. Keep all your data cards on file. Have a separate file for new lists.

7. Pay special attention to lists that are growing quickly

The best prospects are those that have contributed or bought something recently. A rapidly growing list will contain a large portion of brand new donors who have not been hit hard yet with repeat housefile mailings.

8. Appeals should be tailored to lists you're mailing

Most direct mailers mail one-size-fits-all prospect packages.

This is especially so when one has found a control package. The "control" package is direct mail jargon for an organization's most successful prospect package. A prospect package is a control package if it's successful and is beating all other prospect packages. When another package proves more successful, it becomes the new control.

But once you have a successful prospect package, make adjustments in the copy to appeal to specific lists and audiences. When you acquire a list, you are gaining access to a market. Each list has its own unique characteristics. People on a list are united by a particular interest. Your letter should be written to take that interest into account.

For example, you might be writing a letter to people who have supported finding a cure for diabetes. But you're trying to raise money to cure cancer. Mention the fact that you know of their interest in finding a cure for diabetes and how important that is. And then get into your cancer appeal.

The fact that you know of their interest in finding a cure for diabetes, even though you are raising money to fight cancer, makes your letter more personal. You know something about the reader. This gets your reader's attention, and makes the reader more likely to read your letter.

You should also tailor your letter to match the average contribution of donors on the list you are writing to.

If you're mailing to people who customarily contribute $50, don't ask for $15. If you're mailing to people who have shown they can contribute $1,000, don't ask for $50. Someone who typically contributes $1,000 will not be impressed by any mailing asking him for $15, $25, or $50 and might even be insulted.

If you're writing to magazine subscribers, reference the magazine in the first few lines of your letter to show you know something about the person to whom you are writing. You'll need to get the list owner's permission to do this. Try to get a separate lift note from the editor-in-chief of the magazine list you are mailing to.

If you're raising funds for a political campaign and you are writing to registered Republican voters who own Jaguars, again, you should ask for more than $15. You should ask for $100, $500, or $1,000. The same holds true if you're writing to subscribers of *Forbes* magazine or the *Wall Street Journal*. You should figure these people are capable of giving more than $15 or $25. You should ask for at least $50 or $100.

On the other hand, if you are writing to people who typically give only $10, it would be disastrous to ask these folks for $25, $50, or $100. They will throw your letter in the trash, thinking "this organization expects too much from me. Too rich for my blood. I'll send my $10 to an organization that will appreciate my donation."

As with every other part of your direct mail program, you must design your strategy to meet people where they are comfortable. Never try to take donors out of their comfort zone. Making subtle changes, even in your breakout control package, to take into account the list you are mailing will improve your returns dramatically.

Of course, you'll want to test your list-specific tailored

package against the one-size-fits-all control package to see if the changes you chose to make to target particular lists were the right changes and to see if it's worth the effort and extra cost to write your package for a particular list or set of lists.

In most cases, tailoring your letters specifically to the lists you are writing to will be well worth the effort and extra cost.

9. Test various segments of a list

Often I hear direct mailers say that a list they tested did not work. I then find out that they only conducted one 5,000-name test of $5+ 0- to 18-month donors from the list.

Maybe this select from this list won't work for you. But $10+ last 12-month donors might work just fine. Or maybe the list owner will let you mail to multidonors only, which are at least three times stronger than one-time givers.

You should also conduct gender tests. Women and men respond differently. Some causes appeal more to women, others more to men. There are many more men than women on the NRA's housefile. But Traditional Values Coalition's housefile is about 60 percent women. Women seem to be more interested in moral issues, men more interested in economic issues.

A list that might not work well if you mail both to men and women may very well work if you mail your appeal to just women or just men, depending on the cause.

Geography can also make a difference. You're more likely to find supporters of a Christian conservative organization in the South than in Massachusetts. If your organization is concerned about stopping illegal immigration, you'll likely have more success finding supporters in border states than in Iowa.

You should also test by age. The great majority of direct mail donors are over the age of 60. The reality is people do not start contributing until their kids are out of the house and out of college and most not until their retirement years.

Lists of direct mail contributors you rent are already pre-screened for age, almost by definition. No real need to conduct age select tests of these lists. But what about other lists you might rent, such as compiled lists or lists of magazine sub-scribers or book buyers? You will certainly want to start by ordering a test select of names over the age of 60, and then test younger age groups later if your over-60 select proves suc-cessful.

The point is to not assume a list is no good for you just because your test of one broad select failed. Be surgical in your testing. Find out every select the list owner will let you test. Choose a series of intelligent tests. You'll likely have to pay more for detailed and narrow selects, but the bigger return may well be worth the extra cost. Instead of ten cents a name for the standard select of $5+ 0- to 18-month donors, it may be worth spending fifty cents or even $1 per name to rent only $50+ 0- to 12-month donors. Remember, 1,000 $50+ donors will be far more valuable to your organization than 10,000 $10, $15, and $20 donors.

And don't just accept what's printed on the data card as the only selects available. Negotiate the selects you want with the list owner. Be a strategist. Come at the prospect list you're renting from many different angles.

10. Repackage successful appeals and remail them to the same lists

Successful packages can often be repackaged with different techniques, carriers, formats, graphics, etc., and remailed through prospect lists that have worked well.

People remember how packages look, not so much the specific words that are in a package. By putting otherwise iden-tical packages in different clothes, such as different looking envelopes, different colors, different paper stock, different graphic layout, most of your readers will assume it's a differ-ent letter.

As always, however, be sure to test your different look packages. A change in the way a package looks can dramati-cally affect returns, up or down.

For example, I was using a yellow Post-it note very

successfully for a prospect appeal I had been mailing for months. I then tried using a light blue Post-it note instead, just to change the look and to see if color was important. My returns dropped 25 percent. In this case, keeping the Post-it note yellow was important, I guess because it looked more like a standard yellow Post-it note people are used to seeing.

So make changes to the look and feel of your successful prospect packages. Constantly experiment. And always test your changes.

11. Beware of list owners who load your test with good names and give you garbage for your rollout

You will occasionally run into the dishonest list owner who gives you gold-plated names (for example, 60-day hotline or multigivers) for your 5,000-letter prospect test. This produces dishonestly tremendous results on your test. You then order the rest of the names in the select you think you tested. Your 100,000-letter rollout then crashes because the broker sent you weaker names than you tested, perhaps threw in all the nondonors and people who may not have contributed in years. This can be a financial catastrophe. It's an old scam.

What can you do about this?

Answer: Not much, except make sure you're using a great list broker who knows the lists they're recommending and knows who the charlatans are. Very few list owners will pull this scam on you, because they want a good reputation so that organizations will continue to rent their lists in the future. If you're in the business of renting lists, nothing will kill your business faster then getting a reputation for loading up tests. It would be like a casino cheating people. It wouldn't be long before no one showed up to play at that casino any more.

Still, there are a few steps you can take that will minimize your risk. One is to roll out in stages. Never take for your roll-out more than five times the number of names you tested.

Another strategy I used with a list owner who I knew was loading up tests was only to order tests, never rollouts. That way

I knew I was only getting the very best names, often getting 15 percent response rates on the supplied test names.

I always look at test results very carefully. If I notice something out of the ordinary, such as a very high response rate, or a higher-than-expected average contribution, I'll order another 5,000 or 10,000 names in the same select and test again.

12. Beware of the incorrectly run select

A related problem is ordering one select and getting something else, not because the list owner was dishonest but was just sloppy and made a mistake. This happens sometimes, and errors are not easy to prove. Again, there's not a whole lot you can do, except ask your list broker to raise holy heck with the list owner.

Over time, as you gain experience with the lists you use most often, you will learn to spot out-of-the-ordinary results. Mostly, you'll just have to be guided by your experience.

You'll learn the characteristics of many of the lists you'll be mailing. And you'll know in your gut that something just isn't right.

13. If the list owner rents you a test, be sure your purchase order includes a written agreement to let you roll out to the balance of the list

One nasty trick some list owners pull is to make a little extra money by letting you test a list, but then deny your order to roll out to the list later. Often this happens when list owners notice your letter is too competitive with something they're doing. List owners will then sometimes steal your idea for their mail program.

The way to prevent this from happening is to state in writing on your purchase order that granting permission to test a list includes an agreement to allow a rollout to the list within 60 days of the test if the test is successful.

14. If you,re prospecting with a non-sweepstakes appeal, require the list owner to remove all "sweeps-only" donors

Some organizations have built a large portion of their housefile with sweepstakes appeals. An appeal that uses a sweepstakes contest to draw the reader into the letter is a powerful marketing technique. But responders to sweepstakes appeals tend to answer only appeals built around a sweepstakes contest and are weak prospects for conventional fundraising packages. It's fine if a donor has contributed to both sweepstakes and conventional fundraising appeals. What you don't want are sweeps-only or unique-sweeps donors if you're mailing a conventional package.

Political-issue causes do not usually use sweepstakes appeals. Sweepstakes contests are most effective for causes that are not controversial, which anyone would support, such as curing a disease or feeding hungry children. So don't worry about this rule if you're renting political issue lists.

But when mailing a conventional prospect fundraising appeal to a list that belongs to a large national charity, be sure to stipulate in your order that you do not want any unique-sweeps or sweeps-only donors. This little instruction can make an enormous difference in the performance of your prospect campaign.

Remember, smart direct mailers spend a lot of time weeding out people who are least likely to respond. Sweeps-only donors are not likely to answer your conventional appeal. Weed them out.

Managing Your Housefile List

The housefile is the lifeblood of every nonprofit charity and political campaign. The housefile is the result of all your prospecting. The housefile is your moneymaker.

It's the equivalent in business of your customer list.

These people have shown with their donations that they like what you're doing. They support you. And they aren't just casual supporters. They agree so strongly with what you are trying to do that they have taken the time and trouble to take out their checkbooks and mail you a donation.

Here are some crucial rules and procedures for managing your housefile list.

1. Set up a computerized database

Some organizations do this themselves. Others maintain their database (housefile) at a professional database maintenance company. If you decide to do this yourself, there are some off-the-shelf computer programs designed specifically to help you set up your own fundraising database. But most organizations should not do this themselves, just as most organizations should not own their own printing presses and mailshops. You should contract out these sorts of specialized services.

Setting up and maintaining a large database of donors is an enormous, highly-technical task that requires software, a data-entry system, and skilled computer technicians. I've seen many organizations nearly destroyed when they've attempted to bring their database operation in house, only to have it run by amateurs. Almost always these organizations go back to using a professional database maintenance company. Your housefile is too valuable an asset to have it maintained by amateurs who are not trained in fundraising.

It may make sense for some of the very largest organizations to maintain their own database because they may have developed some highly specialized needs and can afford the elaborate systems and all the staff required to support a large database maintenance operation. And very small organizations of a few thousand donors can maintain their own database with off-the-shelf computer programs.

But if your housefile database contains more than 10,000 donors and fewer than 200,000 donors, you should almost certainly use an outside professional computer database management company that has many nonprofit organizations as clients.

2. Set up your caging operation

Reply envelopes must be picked up at the post office, opened, contribution checks deposited, and information entered into your database. This is called batching and caging in direct mail jargon.

This is another big job you should almost certainly contract out if your fundraising program is of any substantial size; that is if you have more than 10,000 donors on your housefile. There are large companies that specialize in this labor-intensive task.

3. Data entry

Sometimes the data entry is handled by the caging company, sometimes by the database maintenance company. In some cases, the caging company and database maintenance company are the same organization. You will need to have a clear understanding of how all the necessary information (names, addresses, contribution amounts, etc.) gets from reply envelopes and into your computer database. Making sure this information is entered accurately into your database is absolutely critical to the success of your organization.

Think of it this way: I might spend $10 (in prospect losses) to find a new $10+ donor. If the name of the donor is incorrectly spelled by the data entry person at the caging or database maintenance company, my investment in finding this new donor is essentially lost. Data-entry errors are very costly to your organization.

One way I guard against this is to have the name and address entered in the computer twice. If the information is entered exactly the same way both times, we assume it's correct. This is called double data-entry verification. This procedure might double the cost of your data entry but will be well worth the added cost. It's certainly worth it for those who contribute $15 or more to your organization, though perhaps not for your $5 donors. As an alternative, you might also consider partial double data-entry verification for your under-$10 donors, in which just the name of the donor is entered twice. It's most important to get the name exactly right. The post office can usually deliver the mail even if the address is slightly off.

Other steps to cut down on data-entry errors include "finder number" and barcode scanning systems, which I won't get into here. These systems also have their shortcomings.

I'm always looking for ways to cut down on these costly mistakes. Data-entry errors are one of the biggest problems in fundraising. This is more of a problem for fundraisers than for commercial mailers, because successful fundraising depends so much on building a sense of personal relationship with your donors. An effective fundraising letter must be a personal communication from one person to another. This effect is completely sabotaged when the name of your supporter is spelled incorrectly. And, of course, if the address is wrong, the letter might be undeliverable.

4. Collect as much useable information on your donors as you can

The most important information you'll need to collect is the amount and date of contributions and what appeals your donors answered. This will allow you to know how much to ask for in the future and will enable you to tailor your house-file appeals to issues and projects that are of most interest to your donors.

You will find that some of your supporters will give to some projects and not others. Some respond best when there is a survey, others when you ask them to sign a petition, others to sweepstakes appeals, others to annual membership renewals, while some respond best when you enclose a $1 bill.

You need a coding system to keep track of what appeals your donors answered. The codes for each mailing go on the reply form.

How will this help?

Well, you might find that a significant portion of your

donor base who have not contributed in a long time originally came on to your housefile by answering a membership appeal.

You should send these people membership appeals instead of the usual "hope you'll come back" letter to your expirees.

Some of your donors will only respond to survey appeals. You should send these folks surveys. Others respond best to appeals that include an up-front premium ("free gift"), such as address labels, a set of note cards, or a wall calendar. Others only answer appeals that come in the form of a sweepstakes contest. So don't expect your sweepstakes givers to answer membership appeals.

You may need to break your housefile down into sub-housefiles, and treat each subhousefile differently to get the most from your housefile mail program.

There's no point in sending survey packages to folks who have never responded to a survey package and likely never will.

If your organization is a multi-issue organization, such as the American Conservative Union, which deals with a range of political issues, you'll need to break your housefile down according to issue. Someone who answers a prospecting appeal calling for tax cuts should not then be sent housefile appeals calling for prayer in school.

This problem is why direct mail is far more effective for single-issue organizations, such as the National Rifle Association or the Sierra Club, than for multi-issue organizations. The most productive housefiles are those that are all united by one cause or issue. For multi-issue organizations, such as the American Conservative Union, I build what are in effect separate housefiles for each issue or cause we want to address.

You will of course have overlap. Some people will support a number of different causes. And this creates a management problem. Which appeal should these people receive in any given month?

One way to decide is to have people who have given more than once to a particular cause receive the appeal for that cause, but not the cause to which they have given only once. Another way to handle the problem is to have different mail dates for different causes (perhaps two weeks between mailings), and those who have given to more than one cause would receive the mailings on all the causes they've given to. Handling the problem this way will generate more income for your organization but also means some of your donors will receive a lot of mail.

You should also strive to collect as much personal information as you can on your donors, especially on your best donors. Ask for birthdays and names of their family members as part of a survey. You'll be able to write far more personal appeals if you have this information. You'll dazzle your reader if you're able to ask how members of their family are doing and reference their actual names. Your donors will be amazed if you remember their birthdays and send a birthday card.

Obviously, you can't afford this level of personal treatment for a $10 donor. But you can for a $100 donor, and it will be well worth the investment.

You'll also want to ask for phone numbers, fax numbers, and email addresses so you can contact your donors at a moment's notice with an appeal that is especially urgent or with breaking news that will be of special interest to your supporters.

Be sure you know the gender of each donor and his or her proper title (Mr., Mrs., Ms., Miss, Dr., Father, Reverend, etc.).

Gender is important because women and men respond differently to different types of appeals. And getting the title right is as important as getting the rest of the name right.

Try to find out what name they use in casual conversation. The name might be Benjamin, but the person might go by Ben. You should know the person's familiar name to make your appeal more personal.

Each bit of information should be contained in its own separate field on your database so that you can retrieve it piecemeal and as needed. A copywriter must be familiar with all information available on a database to write an effective, highly personal letter that will sound like you know the person.

The more information you have on your donors, the more personal you can make your letters. This will dramatically improve the performance of your housefile mailings.

But make sure the information you're collecting for your database is useable in your letters, for segmenting your list, and for the overall management of your fundraising efforts. Have a specific, well-thought out purpose for every piece of information you are collecting. I've seen organizations go over-board in collecting data on donors they will never use. This is just a waste of money and makes your database unmanageable.

5. Make sure there aren't duplicate names on your database

There are few things more annoying to your supporters than receiving multiple copies of the same mailing on the same day.

Talk about destroying your attempt to make your appeal as personal as possible!

Computer programs can identify likely duplicates, but they aren't perfect. For example, a computer program can identify two records where the name is spelled differently but is at the same address as a likely duplicate.

For your best donors, perhaps the best 10 percent or 20 percent of your file, a human eye should examine the records, printed out in alphabetical order, to identify not just possible duplicate records, but other potential problems with the data that only a human eye and brain with the capacity to make judgments will notice.

You should not rely exclusively on a computer program to keep your housefile list clean, especially your top 10 percent or 20 percent of your donors. It's well worth the effort and cost to examine the records of your best donors with human eyes.

6. Steps to keep your housefile list clean and accurate

Be a fanatic about the hygiene of your housefile list. And I mean a nut case. There are few things more important to the success of your direct mail fundraising program.

Running your list through a National Change of Address (NCOA) program at least every six months will help. NCOA is a constantly updated database generated by the U.S. Postal Service. About 20 percent of Americans change their address every year, and any list loses about 50 percent of its value every year if it's not "NCOAed."

Your reply forms should always include an instruction to your reader in red to "Please make any necessary corrections to your name and address on this reply form." Be sure any corrections your supporters write on reply forms are entered into your database.

Verify names and addresses during telemarketing calls, and make sure the changes are made in your database. Undeliverable first class mail will be returned to you by the post office. These are called nixies or pixies in direct mail jargon. Remove the bad addresses after making every effort to correct the bad addresses. You can also print "Address Correction Requested" on your outer envelopes and, for a fee, the post office will correct a high percentage of wrong addresses. This service can be costly, so do this perhaps only twice a year.

Send out questionnaires periodically to your supporters asking them to verify and correct the information you have on them. Questionnaires provide a great opportunity to update and correct errors on your database. Consider offering some incentive to your supporters, such as a gift or special report, for every questionnaire completed and returned.

Standardizing formats, merging multiple files, eliminating duplicates, and updating and verifying addresses also are all essential to keeping your housefile productive. Failure to keep your list clean and accurate will bankrupt you quickly.

7. Establish your "unduping" policy

I do not want my best housefile donors to receive prospecting letters. I undupe these names against all prospect lists because I want to treat these people as special. I want to treat these folks like I know them, as friends. I also want to ask these supporters for larger contributions than I ask for in prospect mailings. But this rule only applies to the top 20 percent or 30 percent of the best donors on my housefile.

The rest of your housefile (the bottom 70 percent) can and should continue to receive prospecting letters—that is, don't undupe these names against prospecting lists.

"Housefile" is a somewhat elastic term.

For the purpose of this discussion, I define it as those who have contributed at least $10 or more to an organization within the last 18 months.

The reasons for not unduping the bottom 70 or even 80 percent of your housefile donors are many. But here are three key reasons for making sure these weaker donors are not omitted (unduped) from your prospect mailings:

▶ You want to identify your multiple givers as quickly as possible because your multigivers are at least three times more likely to contribute again than donors who have yet to send a second contribution. Many on your house-file will give more than once to a prospect package. Some will give three and four times to the same prospect package. Donors are not very valuable to an organization until they become repeat or multidonors.

▶ Donors who have contributed only once to your organization are more likely to contribute again to the prospect package they have already contributed to than to a housefile package. You know only one thing for certain about donors who have contributed just once to your organization: They liked the prospect package, so keep sending it to them until it stops working.

▶ Repeat, repeat, repeat your message is a key marketing principle. Nike, McDonalds, Crest, Tide, and the most successful consumer brands show the same ads over and over again because they know it will take many impressions on your brain before their message sinks in. The same is true in direct mail, which is just another form of advertising. Your message must be simple, focused, and repeated over and over again to your target market. Just because they answered your letter once does not mean they remember answering it. Nor does it mean they could explain to their friends what your organization does.

Most people contribute to a direct mail letter out of impulse.

They liked what they read at that moment, sent back a donation, and then went on to something else. A few days later, they've forgotten your letter and your organization completely.

The big advertisers know this fact of life. They know they can't stop repeating their message to their target audience. They know the battle for market share is really a battle for a share of people's attention, a battle for minds. That's why you should continue mailing a successful prospect package until it stops working. It's also why you should not undupe your housefile against prospect lists, except for the best 20 percent or 30 percent of your donors who clearly do know about your organization and should be treated with extra care.

When prospecting, I undupe all $25+ multiple contributors on an organization's housefile who have contributed at least once in the past 12 months.

I would say there are very few good reasons to undupe the bottom 70 percent or even 80 percent of your housefile from receiving prospecting letters. In fact, not keeping these names in your prospect mailings can be catastrophic to both your housefile and prospecting mail programs.

Unduping your entire housefile list against prospect lists can cut your prospect results in half, if you have a large housefile of 100,000 donors or more. Someone must pay for prospect losses (the continued building of your housefile). It might as well be the weaker names on your housefile who help pay for your donor-acquisition program.

Unduping your entire housefile against prospect lists will also hurt your housefile by failing to deliver more prospect mail to your one-time givers, which, in turn, will give them fewer opportunities to become multigivers. Your prospect letters are usually your least expensive packages, because they're produced in large quantities. Making sure your weaker donors receive prospect mail is a great way to keep your organization's name in front of your less-committed donors. And you're achieving this goal with low-cost packages that have proven to be successful.

8. Protect your list

Your housefile list is your most valuable asset. Protect it by salting your list with about fifty decoy or seed names.

These are names and addresses scattered throughout your housefile of people who are not real donors but are monitoring all mailings to your list. You'll want to include these decoy names whenever you rent or exchange your list and whenever you mail a letter to your list. Your decoy names should have addresses representing every geographic region of the country or area to which you are mailing.

The best decoy names are friends and relatives you have scattered across the country. Ask your decoys to be diligent about sending you every letter they receive as part of your own housefile program or others mailing to your housefile as part of a name-exchange or list rental arrangement. Your decoy names should use fictitious first names or fictitious middle initials to distinguish mailings to your housefile from their other mail. And your decoy helpers should write the date on the outer envelopes they receive showing when the letter arrived before mailing your "seed" letters back to you.

In addition, there are companies that specialize in list security and can provide unique decoy names for salting your list.

One company is called U.S. Monitor. There are others as well. Your decoys should send in contributions and develop a giving history so they will be treated as real donors.

There are many reasons for why you should take such elaborate measures with your system of decoy names to track all mailings to your housefile:

▶ You'll know immediately if your housefile has been stolen and is being used for unauthorized mailings. Your list is protected under trade and copyright laws as private property. But the law requires you to show that you have taken reasonable steps to protect your list. And you must be able to demonstrate with your decoys that your list has been stolen and is being used for unauthorized mailings. Courts recognize a decoy system as strong evidence of illegal use of your mailing list.

▶ You'll want to track when your own mailings arrive in people's homes. If all your decoys receive your mailing on schedule, you'll know there was no production problem with your mailing. Unfortunately, mailshops sometimes mess up and fail to get mailings out on time. Your decoy system will alert you to any problems with your mailing.

▶ If you're renting your list to others for a one-time use, your decoy system will let you know your renters are mailing your list only once, are mailing on schedule, and are mailing the letter you approved.

Think of your housefile list like a safe full of money. Don't leave your safe open for anyone to walk in and take what they please. If your list is of any significant size, anyone with even a modest knowledge of direct marketing could easily take your list if it's not protected and make hundreds of thousands or even millions of dollars with it. Even if they never mailed to it themselves, they could make an enormous sum of money just renting your list under a different name, perhaps as part of a compilation list along with other lists they might have. Most people I have run into in this business are very honest. But there are professional list thieves out there who understand very well the value of a mailing list. Theft of your list could severely damage or even destroy your organization. You have invested a lot of money to build your housefile. Take every step to protect it. Guard it like Fort Knox.

9. Keep an updated copy of your housefile in a safe deposit box
Once a week or so, put a complete and updated copy of your housefile list in a safe deposit box. Fires and other accidents happen. Computers crash. Sometimes sabotage occurs. You always want to keep an updated copy of your housefile in a safe deposit box at a bank. This is your back-up plan that can protect you from disaster.

CHAPTER **9**

A Checklist of Crucial Direct Mail Basics

1. Be sure to say who to write the donation check to on the reply form
I know this seems so simple and obvious, but I've seen direct mail packages that fail to say prominently to whom to write out the donation check.

2. Put the organization name and address on all components, except perhaps the outer envelope
About 8 percent of donations come from people using their own envelope which is called "white mail." So it's very important to put the name and address of the organization on every component in the package. As a general rule, I don't put the organization's name on the carrier envelope, because it tells the reader that this is probably a fundraising appeal. I usually like to create mystery on the carrier. But you should include the address of the organization on all other items in the package.

3. Put footers in the bottom right corner of each page directing your reader to keep reading
Footers on letters should say (Please continue letter), (Over, please), (Next page, please) or some phrase to let the reader know there is more to read.

4. Number the pages

Though there's no need to number the first page. I like to spell out page numbers—Page Two, Page Three, etc. This makes the letter look a bit more personal and high end.

5. Try not to end a page with a period

Have the sentence break in the middle and continue on to the next page, if at all possible. Strive to have this be an especially interesting sentence that will compel your reader to turn to the next page.

6. Use an old-fashioned typewriter font for your letter

Courier and Prestige are fonts you should use for your letter. Avoid using a desktop publishing font like Helvetica or Times Roman.

You may use desktop publishing fonts with your enclosures and inserts, anything that's not the letter, which should look like it's been typed (even though everyone will know you used a computer). I've gone so far as to make the Courier characters in my letter a little crooked and off center in places in an attempt to make it appear as if the letter may have been typed on an old manual typewriter. This is going a little far. But you get the point.

Among the Courier fonts, pica (10 characters per inch) is easier to read than elite (12 characters per inch). Over time this rule may change as people get even more used to seeing letters lasered with Times Roman. You should periodically conduct a font test to see if more donations continue to come in with Courier than with a desktop publishing font like Times Roman. Courier is still winning the tests I've conducted lately, I think because those who contribute to direct mail appeals are mostly over the age of 60. They are still more comfortable with the old typewriter look.

7. Indent the first lines in paragraphs of letters five spaces

Indents are a device to catch the eye of your reader and keep your reader moving through your letter.

8. Paragraphs should not be more than six lines

Big blocks of undifferentiated text are intimidating to readers. They're also ugly. Long paragraphs and large blocks of text just look like too much work to wade through. Your letters must be scannable, eye catching, and easy to read.

Don't make every paragraph the same length.

Some paragraphs can be just a few words, or even just one word. Others can be one line, two lines, or three lines. Mix it up, but no paragraphs more than six lines.

9. The signature should be in blue ink

The signature should look as real as possible and should stand out. Black signatures blend in too much with the rest of the black letter copy.

People expect signatures to be blue, not green, red, orange, pink, or some other color. Also, be sure the signature is legible, not one of those doctor's signatures you can't read.

For high-dollar givers, consider actually hand-signing each letter. It's obvious to readers when a signature is real, not printed. So it may well be worth actually hand signing letters to your best supporters. It doesn't take long to hand sign a thousand letters.

I've also found inks that will smudge a bit after they are printed, further enhancing the personal look of printed signatures. The signature and how it looks is important.

10. To draw special attention to a particular paragraph, indent every line in the paragraph ten spaces (one inch) on both sides

This is just another way to enhance the scannability of your letter. For these special block-style extra-indented paragraphs, you can bend the *no paragraphs longer than six lines rule* a bit.

11. Lines in letters should be single spaced with one additional space separating paragraphs

Again, readability, ease on the eyes, and scannability are what you are striving for with your layout. This is just how letters should look.

12. Do not justify the right margin of letters

The right margin of your letter should be ragged. Not only does a justified right margin make for more difficult reading, it destroys the personal look of your letter.

I once had a printer present me with the final printed copy of my letter, boasting with a smile that he had "fixed it" by justifying the right margin. He thought I would be pleased with his diligence. More than 500,000 copies had been printed.

Aaarrrrrgh!

13. Shorten the name of the writer to sound more familiar and friendly

Instead of "Louis" use "Lou." Instead of "Benjamin" use "Ben." Instead of "Katherine" use "Kathy." The exception to this rule is if the letter is signed by a general, a judge, or some other very high government official, such as the President of the United States. In these cases, using a shortened first name or nick name could weaken the power of the official title. "General Robert E. Lee" is far stronger and more appropriate than "General Bob Lee."

But for the typical head of an organization, it's better to use the more familiar sounding shortened first name. Congressmen and senators should also use the shortened version of their names in their letters. "Congressman Tom Delay" is far better than "Congressman Thomas Delay."

14. Put in place a proofreading system

Each page should be initialed by two people who have read every word of the package carefully. This will minimize mistakes. The reality is that a typo will not usually depress the results of a mailing, but it can be embarrassing.

I once had a very bad typo in the very first line of my letter that mailed something like a million copies. It was too late; the package had been mailed by the time I caught it.

The client was outraged. I sat on pins and needles waiting for returns to start coming in. The end result was that the mailing did just fine, exactly as well as I expected it would without the bad typo in the first line.

I know a copywriter who likes to put a typo intentionally and prominently on the first page of every letter. He thinks this helps give a letter a more homemade genuine look and actually helps catch the reader's attention.

I'm skeptical of this claim, though it has a certain plausibility. Even so, it's certainly not worth the cost in terms of a negative client reaction, especially since it's usually the president of the organization's name on the letter.

Best just to have a proofreading system.

15. "First Class" should be stamped in red twice on reply envelopes (if they are not BREs)

This helps draw the reader's attention to the reply envelope, emphasizes urgency, and suggests that a reply is expected.

16. "First Class" should be stamped in red on carriers of first class mail

The exception to this rule is if you are using a large commercial first class envelope with a green diamond border.

17. First class mail should look first class

Don't use ink jets or crummy-looking cheshire labels on your reply forms for first class mail. You're spending a lot of money to mail your letter first class. Make everything in your letter look personal. Your first class letter should look like a letter from a close friend.

18. Put more than one stamp on first class mail

This helps emphasize that this is first class mail and also helps make the letter look more personal. If you're paying for first class mail, make sure the donor will notice it.

I like putting eight stamps on envelopes. This helps create interest. It's like a neon sign telling the recipient of the letter, "Look at me, this is a first class letter."

19. Carriers that are the least bit questionable should be cleared by the post office before you print them

There are strict regulations governing the appearance of carriers for mail going out at the lower nonprofit rate. These regulations are changing and getting stricter all the time. Nonprofit-rate mail is about nine cents per letter less than commercial bulk-rate mail.

The post office loves to disqualify nonprofit-rate mail and charge the full commercial rate. On a million pieces of mail, that's $90,000 more you'd be paying for failing to preclear your nonprofit carrier envelope with the post office.

Yikes!

And each post office has its own way of interpreting postal regulations. So just because one local post office told you your carrier is fine, doesn't mean another will.

20. Don't put mail codes, I.D. numbers, or other ugly numbers near the donor's name or other personalized message

This completely destroys the personal effect your packages are attempting to achieve. No one wants to be treated like a number.

21. Is the contribution tax-deductible?

Be sure to say so on the reply. Not only is this important information some of your donors will want to know, but you are required by law to tell the donor whether or not contributions are, or might be, tax deductible.

22. Make sure to establish minimum and maximum contribution requests at the start of each job

For example, if someone has contributed $50,000 before, you may not want to ask for that amount. Instead, you might want to ask for $10,000 or $5,000.

Or if someone has contributed $5 as their highest previous contribution, don't ask for that amount. Ask for $15 or

$20. Whatever the criteria, be sure to make conscious decisions at the start of each job. Don't simply let the computer program make all your decisions for you.

23. Are you rounding up your contribution requests?

When asking for highest previous contribution (HPC) or most recent contribution (MRC), make sure a decision is made as to whether to round up to the nearest $5 or $10. For example, you may not want to ask for $27.53 cents, if that's a contributor's HPC. On the other hand, you might want to ask for such an odd amount.

Again, a decision must be made at the start of each job. It's a question that must be answered. Again, don't let the computer program make your decisions.

24. Determine your defaults for personalization

The defaults might be different for the address and salutation parts of the letter than for the body of the letter (and probably will be). In general, your first choice in your salutation should be: "Dear [Title/Last Name]." If you don't have your reader's title in the title field of your database, then just use [First Name only]. If no name is available, use [Dear Friend] or nothing if personalization is asked for in the body of the letter.

The unfortunate reality is that no database is perfect. Every database is missing information. Your default strategy must account for missing information.

So think through all the personalization defaults for each part of the letter where personalization is called for. You're paying a lot for personalization. Make sure it's done right and that you make the most of it. Wrong personalization can do more harm than no personalization.

25. Look for opportunities to personalize

I see a lot of money spent on personalization, and then opportunities are missed for personalization. Refer in your letter to the donor's town and state, past contribution amounts, and other information collected as part of the donor's record in your computer database.

26. Take every step to make your personal letter look and feel personal

Laser the reader's name and address above the salutation on the letter. Put a specific date on the letter, as you would if writing a personal letter to a business associate.

If you are personalizing every page of the letter, as you might in an appeal to high-dollar givers, put the person's title and full name stacked over the page number in the upper right corner of each page.

However, don't overuse the reader's name in the body of the letter. This can look phony and insincere. When writing to a friend, you would never use your friend's name throughout the body of the letter. This is fake personalization and destroys the genuine personal effect you are striving for.

27. Get on every mailing list you can

Make contributions to many organizations. If you see the same package coming through your mailbox over and over again, you know it's a winner. Rip off the idea (obviously not word for word).

28. Put list "source codes" on reply forms

Be sure to include codes on reply forms identifying the list or housefile list segment the donation or response came in from. You'll need this information to track the results of your mailings.

I might break a housefile mailing into 10, 20, or more segments, each with its own code. This will allow me to track how each segment is performing and whether I should drop or add some segments to future housefile mailings.

Similarly, each prospect list will also require its own code on the reply form so you can track how each list is performing.

You can't produce reports on mailings or track the results

without source-coding your replies. Putting list *source codes* on all reply forms is fundamental to managing every aspect of your direct mail program.

29. Make list "source codes" a permanent part of a donor,s giving history

Every donation should be linked to a source code. This information will allow you not only to track how particular lists and list segments are performing, but will allow you to tailor future appeals to what your supporters have contributed to in the past.

Over time, you may find that there are segments of your housefile that only contribute to survey packages, others that only contribute to sweepstakes appeals, and still others that only contribute to up-front premium offers. Source codes allow you to dissect your housefile and target segments of your housefile with the kinds of appeals to which these donors will be most responsive. Source codes (sometimes called "motivation codes") allow you to target donors and groups of donors with laser-like precision and maximize income.

30. Bid out all jobs

Don't use the same printer and mailshop all the time. You'll find they will start becoming complacent about the work and your prices will start slowly creeping up. Bid out every job.

And once the lowest bid comes back, offer additional incentives to get the price lower. One incentive I use a lot is the likelihood of future big rollouts if this is a prospect package.

The cost of the package is often the difference between a success and failure for a mailing.

31. Cut costs by projecting your needs into the future

Take advantage of downtimes (bad mail times) for your vendors to get lower costs and then mail later. Also, if you know you are going to mail 300,000 copies of the same prospect package each month, consider printing 600,000 and hold half in inventory until the next mail date.

32. Use low-grade paper and consider reducing paper weight

You buy paper by the pound. So ask your printer if it's cheaper to print on 50-pound instead of the more typical 60-pound paper. You'll want to test this to see if the more flimsy paper hurts your results. I have not seen any difference for my prospect and low-dollar housefile appeals.

However, you may want to use heavier paper for the high-end of your housefile, the best 10 percent or 15 percent of your donors.

33. Become familiar with how your printers and mailshops work most efficiently

Ask your printer and mailshop for suggestions on how to cut the cost of your package without compromising the look and feel of your appeal. For example, your vendor's ability to laser letters on continuous forms will help you economize. Some printers can personalize all four pages on one big sheet of paper and have a machine slice and fold the paper all at once, thus avoiding the problem and cost of a four-way letter match.

The point here is for copywriters and creative people to thoroughly understand the capabilities of the vendors you're using. Ask your vendors for copies of all the formats they offer. Treat your vendors like the partners they are. Describe what you are trying to do and the impact you want to achieve. Ask for samples of the largest volume mailings they've produced over the last six months. Your printers and mailshops will be happy to give you all kinds of ideas if you ask and bring them into the creative process early.

34. Don't use bleeds in your artwork if you Don't have to

A bleed is running the color to the edge of the paper. This is expensive. It's hard to imagine an instance when this extra cost is really necessary for a fundraising appeal. Fancy, slick-looking graphic art usually depresses returns.

35. Don't use graphic art that makes your printer's job more difficult than necessary

Avoid creating a graphic design that requires a lot of careful, detailed work by the printer. You'll just run up your cost without improving returns. Ugly almost always works better than pretty in fundraising.

36. Don't print deadline dates

Deadline dates should be handled by lasers and inkjets, not a printing press. You'll want the freedom to adjust any deadline dates you have in the package. Mail dates are missed all the time for all kinds of reasons. You don't want your mailing to go out after the deadline or "due back by" date in the letter or on the reply form. And if you have inventory, you'll want the freedom to change the deadline date so you can use the inventory later.

37. Plan in advance

Few things are more costly than rushing a job and making last-minute changes. Sometimes rush jobs can't be avoided, especially in political campaign and issue fundraising. But 98 percent of rush jobs I see are the result of poor planning.

Do a mock-up or dummy of your package to make sure it all fits together, especially if your package uses odd-size envelopes. For example, make sure your reply form fits neatly and easily in the reply envelope. Have your package checked in advance by the post office (before you print and insert) to make sure you're in compliance with postal regulations and get all the bulk mail discounts you're expecting.

38. Check all bills carefully

A surprisingly high percentage of bills that come in from your direct mail program will be incorrect. And very few of these incorrect bills will be lower than you expect. They will be higher. Be sure to compare your bills to all your signed purchase orders. In fact, make sure all orders are done with a written purchase order. Order nothing verbally.

39. Decide the insertion order of components

The insertion order makes a difference in results of the package. Typically you'll want your letter to be the first item your reader sees. But sometimes you'll use a special attention-getting device (such as a $1 bill, free gift, or USPS priority mail reply envelope). In this case, you'll want the attention-getting device to show first, since the purpose of the attention-getting device is to get the reader's attention.

Whatever the insertion order of your package, make sure it's a conscious decision. Determining the insertion order of components is part of your marketing strategy. Nothing should be left up to the mailshop to decide. Nothing should be left to chance.

40. Make sure legally required disclaimers are on all fundraising reply forms

Most states require some type of disclaimer on contribution reply devices describing whether contributions are tax deductible or not, where financial statements on the organization can be obtained, and a host of other information on the organization. Many states require charities to be registered with the state in order to conduct fundraising solicitations in the state.

I believe most of these requirements are an unconstitutional abridgement of free speech and freedom of association. Courts have disagreed with me about this so far. But you risk being fined severely if you are not in compliance with each state's laws and regulations governing fundraising.

Read the disclaimers and state registration language on the reply forms of the large charities and you'll see what I'm talking about. Your disclaimers should look something like theirs, assuming your organization is similar in type. Is your organization a 501(c)(3), a 501(c)(4) or something else? These are IRS designations. The various legal requirements are different for different kinds of charitable organizations.

Sweepstakes appeals have all kinds of legal requirements and disclaimers of their own.

Interestingly, there are no such onerous state registration requirements for pure political fundraising, such as for election campaigns or political action committees. Apparently, it would be a constitutional violation to prevent candidates from writing to voters. There are, however, important federal and state election law requirements you'll need to be familiar with if you're raising money for a political campaign.

The best advice here is to consult a nonprofit or election law attorney (depending on what kind of organization or cause you are raising money for) to make sure you are in compliance with all federal, state, and sometimes even local laws governing fundraising solicitations.

CHAPTER 10

More Strategies to Boost Results

Should you find a "Big Name" to sign your letter?

This is a key question, the answer not always obvious. A big name letter signer can significantly increase returns on your prospect mailing. But it must be the right signer.

The wrong big name signer can distract attention from your appeal. For example, if you're raising money to cure cancer, you probably would not want your letter signer to be Oliver North, Jesse Helms, or Rush Limbaugh. Nor should your letter signer be Jesse Jackson or Ted Kennedy. You would turn off too many of your possible cure-cancer supporters by using a controversial politically charged signer for such a cause.

Instead, try to find a well-known celebrity who has had to overcome cancer. A great letter signer would be someone like cyclist Lance Armstrong, five-time winner of the Tour de France.

Richard Viguerie wrote a letter for our "Conquer Cancer Now" client signed by golfing great Arnold Palmer. This was a powerful letter signer because Arnold Palmer is well-liked by everyone, is of the same generation as most direct mail contributors, and had a well-known fight with prostate cancer.

Arnold Palmer is also a beloved noncontroversial figure almost everyone would trust.

Former actor Christopher Reeve was signing letters to raise money to find a cure for spinal cord injuries. This was an excellent choice for a letter signer because Reeve was paralyzed from the neck down, the result of a tragic and freak accident falling off a horse.

It would not be nearly as compelling to have a celebrity sign your letter who has no known association or connection with the cause for which you are raising money.

If you're raising money for Republicans, you could have no better letter signer than George W. Bush or, even better, Ronald Reagan in his day. If raising money for Democrats, former President Bill Clinton might be a good choice—though Clinton's record of scandal and reputation for slick doubletalk might cause even die-hard Democrats to think twice about his claims. Democrats should test Clinton's signature before rolling out with any large prospect mailing. Jimmy Carter might be a better choice.

If your cause is protecting the environment, perhaps Ralph Nader or Al Gore would be a good letter signer for you. Of course, you should conduct tests of many different letter signers. It could be that Ralph Nader and Al Gore would turn off many Republicans and conservatives who also want to protect the environment without shutting down American industry. Much will depend on the kind of environmental protection organization you are trying to build.

Is the organization going to be consciously left wing, or is it trying to appeal to a broader audience? The answer to this question will help determine what type of big name you ask to sign your letter.

You would use different letter signers for different markets. General Norman Schwarzkopf would probably be a great letter signer when writing to veterans on issues of importance to veterans and people in the military.

Whoever your letter signer, it should be someone who

creates a good feeling in your audience. Mike Tyson, the former heavyweight boxing champ, would not be a good letter signer because of his prison record and generally thuggish behavior.

Entertainer Michael Jackson would not be an effective letter signer. He's too odd for most people. So fame alone is no criteria for being an effective letter signer.

The purpose of the letter signer is to help establish credibility for your letter. The best letter signer is someone with a sterling reputation who has a clear connection with the cause you're raising money for.

Consider using a celebrity from yesteryear as a letter signer—not a current celebrity. Remember, almost all your direct mail donors are over the age of 60. So you'll want to select a celebrity who is famous to those over 60, not an icon to the under 30 crowd, not today's new sex symbol.

The most powerful letter signer can be someone who's not famous at all. It could be someone with a riveting story to tell in connection with the cause or organization.

If you are raising money to help the families of victims of the 9/11 attack on the World Trade Center and Pentagon, you might ask a member of one of these families to help you tell their story in a letter they would sign.

If you are raising money to pass legislation, consider asking the member of Congress who is sponsoring the legislation to sign your letter. The congressman won't be well-known nationally. But his title and role in sponsoring the legislation helps to substantiate claims in your letter.

Retired generals, admirals, judges, congressmen, and senators can be effective letter signers because these are clearly people of stature and, presumably, credibility.

But there's a downside of using the big name letter signer for your prospect appeals.

Your housefile may not respond well to receiving subsequent letters from the actual head of the organization who may not be well known. Your donors were happy to answer a letter from General Schwarzkopf, Arnold Palmer, or former President Jimmy Carter, but "Who is this Harvey Smith fellow who's now sending me letters?"

This is a problem if you build your housefile with a big name letter signer, a problem which can be handled in several ways:

▶ Try to get a commitment from your big name letter signer to also sign housefile letters. This solves the problem.

▶ Failing that, ask your big name, prospect letter signer for a short "lift letter" testifying to the effectiveness of your organization, which you can use repeatedly and in various ways for your housefile appeals.

▶ Failing that, "Plan C" is to be prepared to accept lower returns from your housefile for a time until you find those donors on your housefile who indeed do care about your cause, with or without the big name letter signer.

There is another downside of the big name letter signer, especially those who hold current official positions in government or who are current celebrities still in the midst of their careers.

These people are likely to be very picky about the letters they sign and can be nearly impossible to work with. Most likely you'll be dealing with their staffers who have nothing to gain and everything to lose from letting their boss sign your letter. There will be delays and much hemming and hawing. The end result will be a letter that has no emotional energy.

In most cases, I would much prefer to have the little-known head of the organization sign my prospect appeal than a big name who significantly alters the copy in my letter. I would make an exception to this rule if the signer of my letter were the President of the United States.

But short of that, it's generally not worth having a big name signer if part of the price is to take the emotional energy out of the letter.

That's another reason to use big names who are retired from their careers to sign direct mail letters. Not only are these older celebrities more likely to be known and trusted by your over-60 seasoned citizen direct mail audience, they will be far less finicky about the letters they sign.

Most of my successful prospect letters have not been signed by celebrities or big names. They have been signed by the head of the organization. I like the idea of helping the head of the organization become a big name by mailing tens of millions of prospecting letters under his signature.

There's no doubt that the right big name celebrity signer can significantly boost response to a prospect appeal. But I also want to be sure that I am building a true housefile with my prospect letters, that is, a housefile that is truly committed to the cause I'm writing about. I want to find donors who will continue to answer letters from the head of the organization. As a general rule, I only want to have a big name celebrity sign my prospect letters if this person will have an ongoing relationship with and commitment to the organization.

A great example of an organization's proper use of a celebrity signer was the NRA's use of the great actor Charlton Heston.

Heston has been a well-known Second Amendment activist for as long as anyone can remember. He always proudly proclaimed his support for the NRA, even before he had any formal position with the NRA.

It was a stroke of brilliance when the NRA asked Charlton Heston to be president of the organization.

Wayne LaPierre, as executive vice president, continued to be the operational head of the NRA and signs most of the housefile appeals. But Heston became the public face of the NRA in the 1990s. He toured the country and gave speeches on why the Second Amendment is important to keeping America free. He attended and spoke at NRA meetings. He appeared on TV to argue the NRA's case and defend the NRA's stance on Second Amendment issues.

Heston actively promoted no political cause besides the Second Amendment. Yes, he was a conservative on other issues as well. But the issue he spoke out on publicly and almost exclusively was the importance of the Second Amendment. That was his issue.

Heston was also ideal as a letter signer for the NRA because of the kind of actor he was. He wasn't a comic actor like Steve Martin or Eddie Murphy. Heston played serious epic characters like Moses and Ben Hur. Who wouldn't believe Moses? Who can forget Heston as Moses in the classic movie standing on Mount Sinai handing down the Ten Commandments from God?

So when searching to find a big name letter signer for your prospect appeals, strive to find someone who suits your cause as Charlton Heston suited the NRA. Someone your readers will instantly recognize. Someone who is serious. Someone your readers will trust. Someone clearly identified with the cause you are writing about. And someone who will have an ongoing relationship with and commitment to your organization. This won't be easy, but will be well worth the effort if you're successful.

Prospect Lists that Work

So often clients ask me, "Why do we keep mailing the same lists over and over again?"

"We keep mailing them because they continue to work," I answer. "When they stop working, we'll stop mailing them."

Think of it this way.

If you mail a prospect appeal to a list, it may return 3 percent. This leaves 97 percent of the people on that list who did not respond. The notion that you should not mail successful lists over and over again as long as they work defies logic, or certainly seems to lack business sense.

The Phoenix Syndrome

Sometimes I have a prospect package that's a blockbuster for many months, but then it suddenly crashes. It's not out of date.

It just suddenly starts doing horribly. What happened?

Even the most successful packages need a rest. The best direct mail contributors are on many different lists, supporting various causes. If these donors keep seeing your letter arrive in their mailbox every few weeks or, in some cases, every few days, your package will begin to lose its impact.

But if you rest your control package for 90 days or so, you will likely see the package bounce back to its old form. This is sometimes called the Phoenix Syndrome. A seemingly dead package can rise back up out of the ashes, simply by giving it a 90-day rest.

For this reason, many large charities prospect quarterly with their control package. By always putting 60 to 90 days between prospect campaigns, this virtually assures your control package never crashes—assuming your control package does not go out of date.

I think this strategy is too cautious.

I will constantly test various formats and different looks for my control package, making the control look like completely different packages, at least at first glance. People don't remember the text of your package nearly as much as they remember what a package looks like. So make what is essentially the same package look different.

If you have three or four different variations of a control, you may never need to give your prospect program a break. You can simply rotate your various different-look versions through your lists. If the packages look different enough, you may even be able to mail essentially the same letter through the same lists every few weeks or so.

Timing Your Appeal

Very often, packages rise and fall because of timing. The package might be fine, but the timing bad.

For example, your prospect campaign might be doing very well, and then suddenly war breaks out or the President is shot.

Major national disasters—such as the 9/11 terrorist attack on America—tend to paralyze our prospective donors. The direct mail fundraising climate is suddenly changed dramatically by such events.

There is nothing you can do about these unexpected national disasters, except to make sure you never have so much mail out there that an unforeseen catastrophe will put your organization out of business.

But there are other timing issues you can account for.

For example, six weeks before a national election, which is the first Tuesday in November, I rein in my mail programs for all our clients, even for my political appeals. I do this because there is so much competition in the mail. Every political campaign is mailing their voter contact letters. All the major national and state political parties are mailing heavily in the fall of national election years.

In addition, fall is the time when commercial mailers, such as catalogues, are starting to flood mailboxes in preparation for Christmas.

Conventional wisdom says the fall is one of the best times of year to mail. I think fall is one of the worst times of year to mail for many charities and nonprofits because there is so much competition in the mail, so many letters and appeals flooding mailboxes.

In recent years, I have had far more success mailing in July and August, which conventional wisdom says is the worst time of year to mail. Since most of the major mailers don't mail much in July and August, there is not nearly as much competition in the mailbox for my mailings. Though I have started to see Christmas catalogues arriving in my mailbox in August in recent years—no doubt because these commercial mailers are noticing that the ferocious fall competition in the mailbox has hurt their mailings.

Before embarking on a major prospect campaign, I always check with mailshops to see what the volume of mail looks like. If their work is very light, I'm excited because I know the competition in the mailbox will not be so intense. If mailshops are jammed with business, I ease up on my prospect mailings. I don't want my appeal to be drowned out by 30 other commercial and fundraising appeals arriving at my reader's home on the same day.

Another factor in timing is the kind of appeal you are mailing. If your mission is to deliver toys to poor children in time for Christmas, your fall mailings will be stronger than at other times of the year. So if you are mailing a Christmas appeal, you have no choice but to mail during the heaviest mail season of the year.

What's in the newspaper headlines will often dictate the timing and subject matter for political issue appeals. If America is at war, your campaign to pass tax cuts is not likely to succeed. Timing is critically important for almost all political cause appeals.

Another timing issue is when your readers are most likely to have money to contribute. Since most people have more cash in the bank at the beginning of the month than at the end of the month, you should time your fundraising appeal to arrive on or about the first of the month. A mailing that arrives in the first few days of the month will usually perform 15 percent to 25 percent better than the same mailing that arrives on the 20th of the month. At the end of the month, many people are pinching pennies in an effort to make it to the first of the next month when they will have a new paycheck or new Social Security check in hand.

Creating Synergy by Combining Direct Mail With Other Direct Response Media

When sending fundraising appeals to magazine subscribers, consider buying a prominent direct response ad in the same magazine. This can significantly improve results for your prospect mailing by reinforcing your message with your target audience. Make sure your magazine ad is also a direct response ad. Include a coupon/contribution form readers can clip and mail in with a contribution. Your magazine ad should be on the same issue as your mailing.

If your magazine ad is powerful and constructed properly, often you can come close to breaking even on your cost. Better yet, try to negotiate an arrangement where you agree to pay the magazine a portion or even all the money that comes in from the ad. This makes the ad no risk to you. You still get the names that come in from the ad, while the magazine may get all the money that comes in. But there will be no out-of-pocket costs to you for running the ad. Your profit will be the names that come in from the ad. As importantly, you've reinforced the message of your mailing, improving response there. Most magazines won't want to be paid only on money generated by the ad, but some will, especially in weak economic times when ad revenue is down.

Combining telemarketing with your mailing is another effective way to drive up response rates. It's possible now to call donors with a 30-second prerecorded message for 10 cents, even as low as 6 cents per long-distance call. The prerecorded message should be from the letter signer and simply alerts your target audience to watch for your very important letter that will be arriving in the next few days. For your housefile, be sure your prerecorded phone message also thanks your donors for all their past support. Your 30-second prerecorded phone call can improve the results of your mailing by 15 to 20 percent.

I like this approach so much better than traditional telemarketing, where you try to make the entire sale on the phone. Not only is traditional telemarketing very costly, typically $2.50 to $5 per completed call, but this kind of invasive telemarketing can be a big turnoff to your house-file donors. I much prefer the 30-second prerecorded phone message that can be left on voice mail or an answering machine that simply announces that an important letter will soon arrive and urges the listener to watch for it.

Let Your Readers Contribute by Credit Card

On the reply form, give the donor the option of using a credit card.

I did not think this was a good idea until recently. A few years ago, when I included the credit card option on reply forms, only about 2 percent of the contributions that came in were from credit cards—hardly worth the paper to include the credit card option. More importantly, I thought the credit card option detracted from the personal letter look I was trying to achieve with my fundraising letters. But recently I've noticed that about 8 percent of donations will be from credit cards if you include a credit card option.

And donations from credit cards will tend to be substantially larger, as much as 100 percent larger than those that come by check. The average donation by check might be $17, while the average donation by credit card might be $33. I now believe you will almost always bring in more money if you include a credit card option on your reply forms. But this is a relatively new development.

A few years ago, people were worried about the security of their credit card numbers. But that concern has dissipated. Everyone now uses credit cards to buy virtually everything, including their groceries. Including a credit card option on your reply form makes contributing easier for many people. You should do everything you can to make contributing as easy as possible.

CHAPTER 11

Raising Funds for Small, Local, and Specialized Causes

The roof of your local public library is leaking and books are being destroyed every time it rains.

Why not launch a direct mail campaign to patrons of the library asking for donations to fix the leaky roof?

Developers are trying to buy and tear down an historic tavern once frequented by George Washington and are planning to build townhomes in its place.

What a great project for a Protest Petition mailing to the city council, and perhaps also to the governor and state legislature, to block this project!

Of course, this mailing will also include a request for contributions to fund the grassroots campaign you are waging to stop this development. Another mailing might invite citizens to gather and protest in front of City Hall, gaining front-page local media coverage, thus adding more fuel to your campaign.

Every letter you mail, of course, should remind readers of the need for contributions to your "Ad Hoc Citizens Committee to Save the George Washington Tavern," so you can organize a grassroots public rebellion that will get the focused attention of local politicians and force action to save the historic landmark.

Perhaps you and your neighbors want to build a public park for your children so they have a safe place to play.

Use direct mail to raise money from the local community to buy the land and build the park.

Build a children's museum. Expand your church or synagogue. Sustain your local performing arts center. Raise funds for your child's Cub Scouts pack. Support your school, your college, your fraternity or sorority, or your local Lions Club. Help a homeless family in your community. Save a Civil War battlefield from being ruined by strip malls. Stop the new property tax increase the city council has just proposed. Build a new recreation center for your town.

All these causes and projects, along with many others you'll surely think of, are candidates for robust direct mail fundraising campaigns.

In fact, direct mail can work even better for local and specialized causes and projects than it does for large, impersonal national charities and nonprofits.

The more local the cause or project, the more passionately people will feel about it. The local project is something supporters will benefit from personally, or at least they will see the benefits firsthand. Supporters of a national charity must rely on secondhand reports of success, and generally never know for sure if their contribution had an impact, or even if the charity is accomplishing much good at all. Donors to national charities and causes, at best, hope their donations are accomplishing some good.

But supporters of local causes and projects can see for themselves if progress is being made and if the money is being properly handled.

You won't be able to build a million-supporter housefile like Mothers Against Drunk Driving. But you can build a far more loyal housefile for a local or small specialized cause. And each letter you mail will be far more profitable than letters mailed by any national organization.

Instead of netting 50 cents or 75 cents on average for each letter you mail to your housefile, you may be able to net $10,

$25, $50, $100, or more for each letter you mail, depending on the cause.

So each letter you mail for a local cause can be 10, 20, or even a 100 times more profitable than a letter for a large national charity.

A variation of the local cause or project is the specialized cause that has a built-in constituency and a high degree of affinity. Good examples are a college, a fraternity, or a school.

Alumni of these institutions may not be locally situated, but they feel part of a defined community with a shared experience. Many alumni feel loyal to their college or fraternity. Some remember those days as some of the best times of their lives.

I have great memories of Burke Mountain Academy where I went to high school and of Dartmouth where I went to college. I feel part of these communities. In a way, they are like an extended family. When I meet another Burke Mountain Academy alum or another fellow Dartmouth alum, we always have something in common to talk about. I'm interested to hear news about these institutions. I'm especially interested to hear from classmates.

This is great for fundraising. It's almost the equivalent of raising money for a local cause in terms of tapping into an intense emotional feeling.

When raising money for the *Dartmouth Review,* a conservative student newspaper I helped launch at Dartmouth in 1980, I raised hundreds of thousands of dollars with carefully targeted mailings to about 1,500 Dartmouth alumni. My letters to this highly select, very loyal group would usually receive a 40 percent response rate and a $75 average contribution, thus generating about $45,000 for each mailing at a cost of only about $3,000.

We would conduct about five of these mailings a year. We could have conducted more mailings and brought in more money if we had needed to. But we had enough money to publish and distribute the student newspaper by just conducting five or six mailings a year. No point in raising more money than we needed to do the job.

Fundraising letters for these kinds of causes should not look like the mass-market variety that you would mail to $15 donors for a national charity. There should be none of the typical direct mail gimmicks you'd use to get attention for your million-piece prospecting mailers for a national charity. No gold foil address labels. No upfront premiums. No $1.50 checks. And no window envelopes that you'd see in national mass-market appeals.

Instead, you'll want to make each letter as personal as possible. Each page should probably be personalized, with the reader's full name spelled out, flush right, in the upper right hand corner of each page, starting with the second page.

Include handwritten personal notes, handwritten addresses on carriers, reply envelopes with stamps already affixed, paper-clipped to the reply form—in short, all the steps you would take when writing to a high-end $100+ contributor to a national organization. Send your letter first class with stamps, not a meter, on the carrier.

Lists for these kinds of local and small specialized causes will almost certainly need to be compiled by hand. Though, if your cause is local, the post office will supply you addresses of every resident in a given area. But for local causes, consider hand-delivering your fundraising package door to door in a big envelope.

Then follow up with personal phone calls and perhaps even a personal visit. It's not easy to say "No" to a request for a contribution when you're asked in person. Have you ever said "No" to a Girl Scout who asks you to buy cookies?

Invite people to become members of the steering committee for your project, followed by a request for financial support.

An important goal of your local project campaign is to get people actively involved. You want people attending meetings and doing other things for your cause besides just giving money.

The community's active participation in your campaign will greatly enhance your fundraising effort and will help cement supporter loyalty for what you are trying to achieve.

Recruit volunteers to do much of the leg work for your local project campaign, such as stuff envelopes, make phone calls, deliver your fundraising packages door to door and even make personal visits to community residents to enlist support for your project. Such local campaigns can also serve to strengthen a community by bringing people together for a common cause and create lasting friendships for those involved in these community action crusades—in addition to actually winning the battle, funding the urgently needed project, or addressing the crisis.

For local causes, you will likely need to hand-stuff your own mailings. It just isn't worth hiring a professional lettershop for mailings of under 3,000 letters. Most lettershops charge minimum set-up fees of $1,000 or $1,500 before inserting and assembling the first letter. But assembling and inserting your own mail packages can actually be a benefit by allowing you additional opportunities to personalize with handwritten notes, and the like. You'll also have more quality control over your mailing if you, your friends, relatives, and volunteers assemble and stuff your mailing yourselves.

A key advantage that the local cause or issue has over the large national charity is that you can spend a lot more money and effort finding and cultivating donors because the return per donor is so much larger.

The usual response rate in prospecting for a national charity is 2 percent or 3 percent with an average contribution of $12 to $18. But for popular local projects and causes, you might get a 20 percent response rate and an average contribution of $50. And instead of the 5 percent to 10 percent response rates and $21 average contributions large national charities receive for their housefile appeals, your local cause may be able to garner a 40 percent response rate and an average gift of $75.

You can see how this changes the economic equation in

terms of the money and effort you can invest to find and cultivate a donor for your local cause. You can even go so far as to visit people personally a few days after your mailing goes out to answer questions and raise the level of participation in your local cause. Instead of a follow-up phone call that you might do for your national mass-market appeal, you can actually do a follow-up personal visit for your local cause. Or, better still, have your grassroots army of citizen volunteers knocking on doors a few days after your letter goes out. You can also have meetings of your supporters and potential supporters to whip up enthusiasm for the project.

You can't do that for a large national organization, except for those who are contributing $500 or a $1,000 or more. And notice how you do not need nearly as many contributors to create a viable, powerful local organization fighting for a local issue—an organization still capable of raising hundreds of thousands, perhaps even millions of dollars a year in some cases.

Churches, Synagogues, and Local Religious Institutions

I am amazed that churches rarely send out mail to their members. Most churches rely entirely on weekly collections at Sunday services to cover their monthly operating costs.

These mailings need not include direct requests for contributions every time, or even most of the time. Most should not include reply forms, except perhaps a survey or space inviting comments.

Let's say you want to build a new facility to accommodate your expanding membership. Your mailings might present budgets for what it will cost to complete construction of this new facility and perhaps blueprints or drawings for what this new facility will look like. The mailings can include calculations of what each family will need to contribute on average if the new facility is to be built on schedule.

Another great opportunity for churches to stress the need for strong financial support is to involve the entire congregation in planning the following year's budget.

Hold two congregational meetings concerning next year's budget. One should be in November to propose and discuss the budget. This meeting should include a talk by the pastor and others outlining the church vision and goals for the following year. The second meeting should be in December, when the congregation would vote on and, hopefully, approve the proposed budget. Between the two meetings, personalized pledge cards are mailed and sometimes hand delivered to homes. Members of the congregation are asked for the total amount they plan to give the church for the entire following year.

The church I attend suggests an annual average "fair share" pledge of about $3,000 a year for an individual and $6,000 per year for a family. We make it clear that it's perfectly okay for those who can't afford this to pledge less, but we then encourage those who can afford more to contribute more. The "fair share" contribution idea is presented as a guideline. Of course, if the suggested "fair share" average amount is not achieved, the proposed church budget must be scaled back. All this is made clear in the two congregational budget planning meetings, in at least one Sunday sermon on the subject, as well as in letters to the congregation during the month-long budget-planning period.

The idea is to get the congregation fully involved in the budget planning, to require the congregation to vote on and approve the budget, and, in this way, to drive home the point that funding the proposed budget will require a significant financial commitment from every member, not just a few dollars or some loose change tossed in the collection plate on Sunday.

Similar to other kinds of local project campaigns, raising money for a church, synagogue, or other local religious institution should combine mail, meetings of all involved, and personal visits by church leaders to homes aimed at inspiring enthusiasm, answering questions, presenting the vision, and getting people personally involved in what the institution is seeking to achieve.

Your mailings throughout the year can then chart the progress of your church. Are the contributions coming in enough to fund your budget? Do you need to inspire the congregation to give a little more this month if possible to close any budget shortfall? Perhaps a sermon on the subject of tithing is called for. Or perhaps your budget is too ambitious and needs to be scaled back.

Or if there's no budget shortfall, your monthly letter can thank God for blessing the congregation with such abundance and of course thank church members for their generosity. And your letter can report on the great progress of your church's many projects, including the impact of the new radio ad campaign your church has launched on the "light rock" station to find new members.

Your mailings to your church membership should not be heavy-handed. As with all direct mail, your letters must be appropriate to the organization and community to which you are writing. Knowing your audience is essential to all direct mail fundraising success.

Your letters to the congregation should be informative. Unlike in direct mail for national organizations, this is a case where you need not hit your reader over the head with constant requests for support. The message will get through because your reader already is intensely interested in the success of the church to which she belongs. No hype is needed here. Your letters to this audience should serve mostly as reinforcement and encouragement to your congregation. People will love getting a monthly letter from their pastor reflecting on matters of concern and interest to the congregation.

After all, isn't that exactly what the Apostle Paul did with his epistles? In letter form, he addressed matters of concern to Christians of his time in various cities, which turned out to be exactly the same issues Christians are wrestling with today.

Amazing!

Pastors can and should follow in this tradition, issuing monthly epistles on matters of concern to their congregations. If the letters are good, relevant, insightful, informative, and interesting, you are sure to see increased loyalty and enthusiasm in your congregation, a growing membership, and a substantial rise in contributions.

This may sound a bit mercenary. But every pastor I know monitors contributions in the collection plate on Sunday. He wants to make sure he can cover the church's overhead, just like any other business. And every pastor I know is thrilled to see new people come through the door on Sunday. The successful churches make every effort to get the names of all new visitors, along with their addresses and phone numbers, in order to make follow-up phone calls and mailings, and encourage these visitors to come again next Sunday.

The fact is, churches are commercial enterprises selling a product, just with a nonprofit tax-exempt status. And churches, like all other nonprofits that rely on public support, must use modern marketing techniques to succeed. And why not? After all, an important goal of a church is to get the Gospel out to as many people as possible.

The same principles apply to synagogues or any other religious institution. Use modern marketing techniques, including the mail, to get your message out, raise the funds you need to operate, and maximize impact on your community.

Visitors Lists: Raise Funds for Any Place that People Visit

Let's say you want to raise money for a museum, a war memorial, an historical site, a performing arts center, an art gallery, an exhibit, a zoo, a scenic park, or some other attraction where people visit.

This is similar in some respects to raising money for a church or for a local community project, because you will be raising money from people who share a common experience. You will be raising money from your visitors.

Set up a system to capture the names, addresses, phone numbers, and email addresses of all your patrons. You should be fanatical about this. Let them know you plan to mail them a free book, a fine art print, a photograph of the spectacular waterfall, or something else of value relating to the attraction as an inducement for your visitors to give you this information.

This list then becomes a powerful direct mail fundraising list. The Holocaust Museum in Washington, D.C., attracts about 1.2 million visitors a year. This is a direct mail fundraiser's dream because most of the work has already been done for the direct mail fundraiser. We don't need to explain to our readers what the Holocaust Museum is or why it's needed, because its power and importance have already been presold to your readers. They've been there. They've seen it. They've experienced it for themselves. And many of these visitors will gladly contribute to sustain this powerful and moving exhibit.

Other well-known attractions I visit that I now receive fundraising mailings from include Colonial Williamsburg, Mount Vernon, and the Vietnam War Memorial. But I don't receive nearly as much fundraising mail as I should from these historic places. And I visit many other wonderful attractions and then never receive any follow-up mailings at all. I scratch my head in amazement at this.

Why don't I receive mailings from the Smithsonian Institution, the Grand Canyon, Yellowstone National Park, or the zoo, which I visit with my kids at least three times a year?

What a missed opportunity for the managers of these attractions to get contributions from me and millions of other people who visit these wonderful places.

It's so much easier to raise money through the mail for something your reader has already experienced. There's really nothing the fundraising copywriter needs to prove to the reader. Just ask for contributions to help sustain, preserve, and improve the museum, exhibit, or attraction, so that others can share in the experience.

Remember, 80 percent of successful direct mail fundraising is having the right list. A poorly written, poorly executed direct mail letter will still work to the right list, at least at some level. But the best direct mail package in the world won't work to the wrong list.

In conventional direct mail fundraising, where you must rent lists for your prospecting campaigns, most of the cost and much of the work must go toward building your list of contributors.

Not so with attractions that people visit. This is your list. You don't need to rent names of prospects. You have, in essence, a captive audience for your mailings.

Your list of visitors to your exhibit or attraction is like a gold mine. It's similar in many respects to a college or school's list of alumni. Your fundraising letters really don't need to be much good to succeed to this group. Just ask and money will pour in from your list of visitors, assuming, of course, the experience of your attraction is a good one for your visitors.

So instead of the letter having to do the selling, the attraction has already done the selling for you. The job of the letter is little more than to pick up the money.

You won't have nearly as much success raising money from people who have never seen your attraction—people who never actually experienced what you are writing about. This would be a lot like trying to raise money to build a local recreation facility from people in another town who will never benefit from the project. This would be a fruitless exercise.

So be doggedly diligent about compiling and maintaining your list of visitors. And then just follow the principles and precepts described throughout this book to write winning direct mail packages.

But here's one hint about writing to your list of visitors.

Use a lot of upfront premiums related to the attraction. Send an impressive frameable photograph if your attraction is a zoo or scenic park. Send a fine art print if your attraction is an art gallery or museum. Books and wall calendars with photographs of the attraction are also great to send. Membership appeals can also be effective, as are giving clubs where prestige and exclusivity is attached to large gifts of $1,000 and more. Perhaps have a Wall of Honor for your super givers.

Review the list of techniques and strategies in Chapter Seven to increase response. Simple, straight-out asks for contributions are also fine if you have a specific project you need money for. Perhaps you want to expand your museum, repair a war memorial, or fix the hiking trail in the scenic park. There's no end to projects for which you can raise money with your list of visitors.

As with every list, those who don't answer your letters will eventually go by the wayside. You'll stop mailing to them. But you will find your core of diehard supporters. That will become your housefile, which you can write to over and over again to ask for contributions.

As with all fundraising, the 80/20 rule will apply. That is, 80 percent of your net income will come from 20 percent of your best givers. So you will send more highly personalized, elaborate, and impressive fundraising packages to this elite group, just like with every other direct mail fundraising campaign described in this book.

All the regular marketing principles apply. But you have this one big advantage, your ace in the hole. And that's your list of visitors, a list that grows every day, year in and year out, a list of potential donors that never stops growing as long as the attraction stays open for business. This is paradise for the direct mail fundraiser.

Raise Money for Your Specialty Publication

Certain magazines can lend themselves to generating intense reader loyalty. Usually these are opinion magazines with small circulations, not general interest commercial magazines like *Time, Newsweek,* or *People.*

Direct mail fundraising will work for *National Review,* the best known conservative opinion magazine, and its more liberal counterpart *The New Republic.* Direct mail will be even more effective the more hardcore the ideological tilt of the magazine. Hard-left publications like the *Nation* or *Mother Jones* should have especially robust direct mail fundraising programs to their subscribers.

Bill Buckley sends out several fundraising letters a year to his *National Review* subscribers. These letters are highly profitable for the magazine. *National Review* relies on these fundraising letters to supplement revenue from subscriptions. *National Review* would have a difficult time continuing to publish without its relatively modest direct mail fundraising program to its subscribers.

National Review operates at a loss, as do most opinion magazines. They need contributions to survive. In fact, most of these ideological opinion magazines are organized as nonprofits.

Some opinion magazines have a few benefactors that make up the revenue shortfall with large contributions every year. Marty Peretz does this for the *New Republic.* He essentially owns the magazine and funds much of it himself. But all good opinion magazines, even those like the *New Republic* who have a large benefactor, are missing a great opportunity if they don't have a direct mail fundraising program.

Subscribers to these ideologically-oriented publications will be happy to send occasional contributions to keep their favorite magazine going. Subscribers to these opinion magazines are a community, united by a shared ideology or set of philosophical beliefs. These subscribers want to make sure their point of view, as expressed in the opinion magazine, isn't lost to bankruptcy.

CHAPTER 12

Internet Fundraising

This is a book about direct mail fundraising.

The big money for nonprofits is still raised with direct mail. A tiny fraction is raised through the Internet. Still, it's worth touching on the subject of the Internet so far as it relates to enhancing your direct mail fundraising and in thinking about your direct mail fundraising.

There are two main categories of fundraising over the Internet:

▶ There is fundraising for stand-alone Web sites that are not connected to a traditional nonprofit organization.

▶ And there's using the Internet to fundraise for your nonprofit organization.

Raising Money for Stand-Alone Web Sites, or Virtual Communities

As with fundraising for opinion magazines described in the previous chapter, you can also raise contribution money for opinion or ideologically driven Web sites.

These Web sites are essentially electronic magazines. Most have an interactive component, chat rooms, bulletin boards, and the like. The great feature of a Web site is that it can post new articles every day, even every half hour.

For example, *National Review* has an excellent Web site called **NationalReviewOnline.com.** It's a completely separate operation from the magazine, has its own editor, and many different writers than the ones who usually appear in the printed version. The Web version, in my view, is superior to the printed version because new articles are posted throughout the day, every day. The writers are often young kids in their twenties. So there's an edgy, far more provocative quality to the writing you'll see on National Review Online than what you'll find in the more stodgy printed version.

Another great Web site along these lines is **Jewishworldreview.com.** In addition to covering issues of concern mostly to religious Jews and people concerned about Israel, the site is also conservative and carries virtually every conservative opinion columnist.

Others on the Right include **FreeRepublic.com, Townhall.com, DrudgeReport.com, Newsmax.com, WorldNetDaily. com,** and **Lucianne.com** (a site named for the former book agent who found herself in the middle of Bill Clinton's Monica Lewinsky zippergate scandal). **Lucianne.com** is an especially entertaining Web site, quirky and funny as you'd expect, reflecting Lucianne Goldberg's personality, but with a lot of good information and gossip on it every day for conservative political junkies.

By the way, the Right has taken over the Internet with a proliferation of conservative, news-oriented, opinion Web sites. The Left is far behind in this area.

For a Web site to be successful, it must be absolutely fascinating. It must be updated with new articles and new information every day—preferably throughout the day. And it should have an edgy quality to it. These kinds of sites, on both the Right and Left, are excellent candidates for raising contributions from their readers or visitors.

The first goal of your "opinion Web site" is to capture

email and postal addresses of your online visitors. The second step is to send your readers occasional fundraising email, as well as other email communications, including news alerts, polls, petitions, and the like. Those who contribute in response to email will then become hot prospects for traditional postal mail fundraising appeals.

There are many effective ways to induce your online visitors to give you their email and postal mail addresses.

You can mail them a free special report on a subject you know will be of interest to your visitors. You can ask your visitors to sign a petition to their congressman or participate in a survey, which requires them to fill out an online form that asks for your reader's email and postal addresses.

Another strategy is to require visitors to register in order to access the most desirable areas of your Web site. I'm not a fan of this strategy because most people don't like to register. It's too steep a requirement for most net surfers. They'll just skip it and move on to the next site.

Far better to offer something free, like an "Explosive Special Report" to induce your visitors to give you their email and postal addresses. Or ask your visitors to sign a petition to their congressman, where it's clear there's a need for this information so petitions can be sorted and delivered to the correct members of Congress.

In this first effort to capture information on my online visitors, I'm careful not to ask for too much information, such as home phone numbers. This can be a turnoff. I just want enough information so that I'll be able to reach my online visitors again, at least by email, and hopefully also by postal mail.

As with all other forms of direct marketing, the goal is to make it as easy as possible for your reader or visitor to give you the contact information you're looking for, and you must give them a reason to give you what you want from them. The first goal is to capture the email address and, at most, the postal address. Then the email and postal appeals and product offers can flow later.

A great feature of fundraising with email on the Internet is that, unlike with postal mail, it costs almost nothing to send an email fundraising appeal. You can send out an email to hundreds of thousands of people for a few hundred dollars, or less.

The cost in terms of money, effort, and brainpower is capturing the information you need on your visitors so you can compile the list you need for your fundraising solicitations and product sales. Remember, in all direct response marketing, 80 percent of the job is compiling your list, building your housefile that you can go back to over and over again with fundraising appeals and product offers.

Reply forms or contribution forms for your email or Internet fundraising appeals are called *landing pages* in Internet jargon.

Almost all your contributions in response to an email appeal will be by credit card. The landing page is where your contributor enters all the relevant information, such as credit card number, expiration date, amount of the donation, and the name and address of the contributor.

Figure 12.1

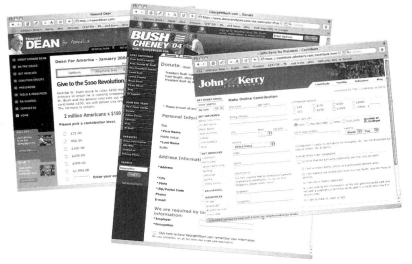

The landing page should also include your organization's postal address in case the contributor wants to send the contribution through the mail. Very few contributions will arrive by postal mail. Some will. More importantly, including a physical address for the Web site gives your visitor a sense that the Web site is also an actual place, has a physical location somewhere. The contribution isn't just going off into cyberspace.

Throughout your fundraising email copy, you'll need to include links to the landing page. Each link should say something like "Please click here to contribute," underlined and in bright blue type.

This link appears everywhere you ask for a contribution.

You may also have links that say "Please click here to sign your petition" or "Please click here to fill out your survey," also underlined in bright blue type, which is an Internet signal that this is a link that will take you somewhere else.

In addition, your Web site should include an opportunity on every page of your site for your readers to make an online contribution. As with all nonprofits, charities, and causes, you must constantly and continuously remind your supporters of the need for contributions to sustain the organization and advance your cause. The same is true for your cause-driven Web site.

Your contribution button, as with your links in your email appeals, should say "Please click here to contribute" or "Please click here to donate." And near each contribution button (which appears on every page), you should include some accompanying text that reads something like: "**FreeRepublic.com** relies on voluntary contributions from our visitors and members to sustain operations and keep building our online community of profreedom activists. Any contribution you can send will allow us to continue to improve and expand the reach of **FreeRepublic.com.**"

By the way, most of the sites I've mentioned here don't do a very good job of fundraising or of bringing in contributions. They sustain their Web sites mostly with product sales and advertising. Or they're just financing their Web sites on their own, out of their back pocket. A number of excellent Web sites are just one person in a basement office with a personal computer. So they can keep going with almost no money. These ideologically driven Web sites are missing a big opportunity by not seeing their regular visitors as a community of people who will gladly support their Web sites with contributions if asked. But people will not contribute unless they are asked. And they should be asked often.

What if Matt Drudge were to send out an appeal to his readers announcing that he needs contributions to keep his Drudge Report Web site going? Otherwise he might have to shut down the site and go get a real job. Contributions would pour in.

So continue to sell products (books and the like) that will be of interest to your Web site visitors. Continue to sell ads, if you can, though you need to be able to show a lot of "traffic" through your Web site to attract significant advertising. But the biggest revenue source for your cause-oriented ideologically driven Web site can be voluntary contributions from those who like your site and want to see it continue.

But how do you actually bring visitors to your site? How do you let your people on the Web know you exist? How do you drive traffic to your site?

In my view, these questions are putting the cart before the horse.

The first question is, do you have a Web site worth visiting? Is it good? Actually, a successful site can't just be good, it must be great. When people arrive, will they stay? Will they become loyal faithful visitors? Will coming to your site become part of the daily, even hourly, routine of a certain group of people?

The best sites are those that reflect the quirks and personalities of the person running it. **The Drudge Report** and **Lucianne.com** are excellent examples. Not only is the information good, gossipy, and fun to read, they are constantly updated. And they reflect the unique personalities of the pioneers behind them. And people go to these sites because they are good. Word gets out about these sites over the Internet. People will always find the good sites.

In the Kevin Costner movie, "Field of Dreams," the mysterious voice tells Costner, "If you build it, they will come."

That's not quite right. A lot of companies launched Internet businesses in the late 1990s. But very few people came. These companies, like "Dr. Koop dot com," spent billions of dollars on advertising to drive people to their sites. But the sites were no good. They stunk. Were in fact nearly useless. So when people arrived at the site, they went away as fast as they could.

Yuck.

But if the site is great, people will come and stay.

That's not to say you should not work hard on letting people know about your Web site. Far from it. But first make sure you have a great Web site that people are visiting over and over again, every day. And by great, I don't mean lots of fancy graphics. People want news and information on subjects and issues of interest to them, daily news and information they can't get anywhere else. Once you have this, there are many ways to get the word out about your Web site. Here are a few:

▶ Ask your loyal visitors to email and tell their friends about your Web site. They will anyway if you're running a great site.

▶ If you're launching a petition campaign concerning some breaking issue of urgent importance to your readers, ask your readers to email your petition appeal to their friends. Just like with any cause-driven organization, your Internet Petition Campaign should be directly connected to the mission and purpose of your Web site.

▶ The same if you're conducting a poll on an issue. Ask your readers to email the poll to their friends, thus bringing new people to your site.

This is called viral marketing in Internet jargon.

But again, if the site is no good, or just so-so, these strategies will be to no avail. Your Web site must be really good to succeed. In fact, it must be great, absolutely fascinating, and one of a kind, which is why there are so few economically viable Web sites.

Using the Internet to Raise Money for a Traditional Brick and Mortar Nonprofit

Can you do it? The answer is "Yes" and "No"—mostly "No," at least so far.

Sure, contributions can trickle in through your nonprofit's Web site. But the big money for traditional nonprofit organizations is still raised with direct mail. There is not one substantial nonprofit organization that is sustained in any significant way by contributions over the Internet. But there are many that are sustained entirely with contributions from direct mail.

I still do not think it's a good idea to send donors to your Web site to contribute with your direct mail appeals. If you send readers to your Web site, they can easily get lost wandering around the Web. Their computers can freeze up and then they'd have to reboot. Servers jam up and go down all the time. I often find ordering over the Internet a frustrating experience. Half the time I give up and go onto something else.

This may change in the future, as servers and Internet connections get faster and more reliable and as more and more people have instant access to the Internet with easy-to-use hand-held devices, and the like. But we're a long way from that. The Internet is still in the Model-T phase of development as a marketing medium.

In today's environment, sending your direct mail letter reader to your Web site is a distraction. It takes your reader away from your letter, your reply form, and your return envelope—a recipe for disaster for your mailing.

Including a "contribute by credit card" option on the reply form now works for most organizations because everyone is used to using credit cards for their everyday transactions, but even this is a relatively recent development.

We're many years away from being able to profitably direct readers of our fundraising letters to Web sites to contribute. The most you should do is include the Web site address somewhere on the letterhead.

Web sites are important for other reasons. They help establish an organization's credibility. But they are not yet reliable tools for capturing a significant percentage of contributions for a traditional nonprofit organization. Most people would still much prefer to put their donation check and reply form in a return envelope and drop it in a mailbox the old-fashioned way.

A key reason the Internet has been such a failure for fundraising purposes for traditional nonprofit organizations is that their Web sites are no good. They aren't worth visiting on a daily basis.

Their Web sites aren't any good because, unlike Matt Drudge, the traditional nonprofit organization is not in the Web site business. The Web site for these organizations is an afterthought. They have a Web site because they think they need one. Some consultant told them they needed a Web site and offered to design it for a fee. So every significant nonprofit organization now has a Web site. And none of them are worth visiting. At least none that I've run across. I call them brochure Web sites, because that's all they are.

The only reason I would visit Web sites of nonprofit organizations is to find out how to reach them, or to find out what they do. But my visit will likely be a one-time event. I will not visit these sites every day like I do with **DrudgeReport.com, NationalReviewOnline.com, Newsmax.com, Lucianne.com** or **FreeRepublic.com.**

So when I'm talking in this chapter about raising money for your Web site, I'm not talking about the kinds of afterthought brochure-style Web sites set up by traditional brick-and-mortar nonprofits. These Web sites are costs, probably necessary costs to establish credibility for the organization.

But these Web sites are not big profit centers, and almost all are money losers.

The successful ideological and issue-driven Web sites are Web sites only. They are stand-alone operations. Their entire business is the Web site itself. These sites are packed with news and they're updated every day. They have a particular ideological perspective. The Web site is what they do. The Web site is their entire focus. The Web site is not an offshoot of some other organization.

Now that I've thoroughly trashed the Internet as a fundraising medium for traditional nonprofits, let me backpedal a bit with this caveat.

There have been and will continue to be great Internet fundraising success stories.

One such story was Senator John McCain's presidential run in 2000. McCain upset George W. Bush in the New Hampshire primary. His defeat of Bush in New Hampshire received enormous media coverage. He was on the cover of all the news magazines. He was the man of the hour. The McCain for President campaign received millions of dollars in online credit card contributions through his campaign Web site.

But these contributions were generated by all the free media coverage he received. Many people wanted to jump on the McCain bandwagon. They wanted to contribute to his campaign. These people did not have a direct mail appeal in their hands, no reply form, no reply envelope, no way to contribute except to go online, surf the net and find McCain's Web site, which many people did.

Nearly every political and issue-advocacy organization then spent a lot of money on consultants setting up their Web sites and credit card contribution pages (landing pages). But very few contributions ever came through these sites.

The huge fundraising success of the McCain Web site was entirely driven by a one-time event, his upset victory of Bush in the New Hampshire primary, and the tidal wave of free media coverage he received. Once Bush bounced back and trounced McCain just about everywhere else, contributions stopped coming in through the McCain Web site. The same holds true for the campaign of Howard Dean for President. He collected millions of dollars in contributions because of all the free media he received driving supporters to his Web site. Dean also ran a campaign geared toward a hard-core segment of liberal activists, which helped his Internet fundraising.

But there's no way for most organizations to rely on this kind of free media coverage to drive people to their Web sites as occurred with the McCain and Dean campaigns. These were somewhat freakish occurrences, created by special situations, not a fundraising strategy. There's no way to plan for that. No way for most organizations and causes to systematize this as an ongoing fundraising program.

But there is an exception.

A disaster relief organization like the Red Cross can bring in substantial contributions through its Web site. When a huge disaster occurs, like the September 11th attack, a hurricane, mass starvation in Ethiopia or some other well-publicized catastrophe, many people will surf the net to find the Red Cross Web site and make an online contribution.

The Red Cross will then, over time, develop a housefile of people who will send contributions over the Internet, and who will also become hot prospects for traditional Red Cross direct mail fundraising appeals.

But even here, it's the free media generated by the catastrophe that drives people to the Red Cross Web site. And people go to the Red Cross Web site because the Red Cross is so well-known. The Red Cross has such a well-developed name that when people want to help disaster victims they instantly think of the Red Cross over all other charities. So the Internet can work well for the No. 1 disaster relief organization like the Red Cross that can depend on free media to bring people to its Web site in the event of a megadisaster.

Most organizations are not situated like the Red Cross. Still, every nonprofit organization should have a Web site.

Not only is a Web site expected of any serious organization, but some people who learn about your work will want to support you, and some will find you on the Internet. Contributions will trickle in, even if your Web site is not especially elaborate or interesting. Your Web site acts like an electronic brochure for your organization. It's not a place people will visit on a regular basis, but your organization should have a Web site anyway.

CHAPTER 13

Summing Up

I have given you hundreds of rules, principles, tips and strategies to ensure the success of your direct mail fundraising campaigns. But if you forget everything else you've read in this book, please remember the following three points:

- ▶ Write your letters as if you are writing to one person, not a million people.
- ▶ Be very specific about how you plan to use the contribution you are asking for.
- ▶ Keep the promises you make in your letters.

Your letter must strive to capture a sense of one person standing in someone's kitchen making a one-on-one personal appeal.

That's not an easy assignment for a direct mail copywriter, especially when you are writing to a million people you don't know and who don't know you. But that's what you must do if your letters are to be successful.

As important, you must show precisely how you intend to use the contribution you're asking for.

Why don't we receive a near 100 percent response to our fundraising appeals? Why doesn't everyone who receives my letter in the mail send back $10, $15, or $20 to help feed a hungry child?

Are people really so cold-hearted that they don't care about the child? Do people not want to cure cancer? Do people not want to help the hospitalized soldier? Do people not care about the hurricane victims?

Of course people care about these things. And people want to help. So why do only two or three percent of people answer a successful prospect appeal? Why do the other 97 percent or 98 percent pitch the letter in the trash?

They pitch our letters in the trash because they fundamentally don't believe them. They don't trust the promises made in the letter.

If every reader really believed that her $15 would go to help a hungry child, you would receive a near 100 percent response to your letter. But most readers don't believe the letter.

They believe most of their contribution will go to the charity's administration and overhead and that little, if any, of their contribution will actually go toward feeding the hungry child.

This puts a burden on both the charity and the fundraising letter writer. The burden on the charity is to actually do what the letter says it will do with the contribution. This is a moral obligation, but it's also a sound business practice: deliver on your promises and you will have loyal customers, or in this case loyal donors. Your donors will never leave you if you carry through with all your promises.

The burden on the copywriter is to be more persuasive.

The most persuasive arguments a writer can use are facts.

Don't write to your reader with generalizations, platitudes, cliches. Talk about your actual results. Show photos of what you are achieving, testimonials from those you have helped, a budget that will show line item by line item how you will use the donations you receive from your readers. Describe specifically what will be accomplished with her $10, $15, $20, or $100 contribution.

Once your supporters see how you are using their contributions, that you are keeping your promises, that their donations are clearly making a difference (even if only a small difference) your organization, your charity will be swamped with contributions.

Go back again to the idea I mentioned earlier of a friend coming to your home in person and reporting to you that a neighbor had lost his job and can't pay his heating bill. His heat has just been cut off. It's January in Vermont, and it's 10 degrees below zero. He and his wife have four young children. Would you contribute $20 to help turn this family's heat back on?

Of course you would.

You would contribute a whole lot more. You might even offer to have the family move into your home until the heat was back on. You would go to extraordinary lengths to help this family, because you would know for certain that your contribution was needed and would actually help. Almost anyone would do whatever they could to help this family.

Americans are the most generous people on earth. They want to contribute to worthy causes, and they do. Americans love to help. Americans send tens of billions of dollars in voluntary contributions to churches, charities, nonprofits, and political campaigns every year. But Americans are also intelligent. They can sense a snow job. They can tell if you are sincere.

Unfortunately, there are a few charlatan fundraisers and charities out there who give charitable fundraising a very bad name. And the media loves to cover any fundraising scandal they can find.

But the truth is the charlatans and flimflam men out there don't last very long. They are not successful in the long run. Most aren't successful in the short run.

The point I always try to keep at the forefront of my mind when I write my direct mail fundraising letters is that all these names and addresses in our computer database are not just bits of information. They are real people who have dreams, concerns, and aspirations, just like you and I have. They share many of our goals. They worry about our nation. They want

ass on an even greater nation to their children and grandchildren. That's why they contribute.

I always make a point to read the letters that come back
from donors in response to my letters. This helps remind me
how real these people are. I strive to write my letters as though
I am writing to my mom or best friend.

It's very easy for those of us in the direct mail fundraising
business to lose sight of the fact that we are writing to real
people. We get caught up in the science of direct mail and the
techniques we use. Do I send a survey with my letter or a sweepstakes offer?

Science is certainly important in direct mail, as is technique in boosting response. You must understand how to struc-
ture your arguments and marshal your facts. You must
understand the components of how to make an effective pres-
entation of your case, just like a skilled attorney knows how
to present a persuasive case to a jury in a court of law.

But all these skills are secondary in importance to understanding that you are writing a letter to an individual—a real
person. And you are asking this person to trust what you say.

You must guard that trust. You must keep the promises
you make in your letters. You must believe what you are writing. You must speak the truth. If you will do that, you can
make many blunders in science and technique, and still write
very successful direct mail fundraising letters.